THE

UN

C000137042

Editor - Charles Heyman

ISBN 0 85052 804 6

Price £5.95 (Mail Order inc. Post and Pack £6.50)

Pen & Sword Books Ltd
47 Church Street
Barnsley S70 2AS

Telephone : 01226 734222   Fax : 01226 734438

www.pen-and-sword.co.uk

The Information in this publication has been gathered from
unclassified sources.

Front Cover: HMS Gloucester at sea.
Rear Cover: Soldiers from 16 Air Assault Brigade
deploy from an RAF Chinook.

(Photographs by permission of UK MoD).

CONTENTS LIST

CHAPTER 1 - THE MANAGEMENT OF DEFENCE

General Information

Populations - European Union - Top Five Nations

Germany	82.1 million
United Kingdom	58.8 million (2000 estimate)
France	59.4 million
Italy	57.9 million
Spain	39.2 million

Finance - European Union - Top Five Nations
(1999 Figures)

	GDP		Per Capita Income
Germany	DM3,700 bn	(US$1,900 bn)	US$23,142
United Kingdom	£890 bn	(US$1,400 bn)	US$23,809
France	FFr8,800 bn	(US$1,400 bn)	US$23,569
Italy	Lit2,1251 tr	(US$1,100 bn)	US$18,998
Spain	Pta93 tr	(US$569 bn)	US$14,515

UK Population - 55,729,349
(1991 census)

England	46,382,050	Wales	2,811,865
Scotland	4,998,567	Northern Ireland	1,573,282

The population split in Northern Ireland is approximately 56% Protestant and 41% Roman Catholic with the remaining 3% not falling into either classification.

UK Population Breakdown - Military Service Groups
(2000 estimate)

Age Group:	13-17	18-22	23-32
Men	1,905,000	1,795,000	4,096,000
Women	1,818,000	1,711,000	3,962,000

UK Area (in square kilometres)

England	130,423
Wales	20,766
Scotland	78,133
Northern Ireland	14,160
Total	**243,482**

Government
The executive government of the United Kingdom is vested nominally in the Crown, but for practical purposes in a committee of Ministers that is known as the Cabinet. The head of the ministry and leader of the Cabinet is the Prime Minister and for the implementation of policy, the Cabinet is dependent upon the support of a majority of the Members of Parliament in the House of

Commons. Within the Cabinet, defence matters are the responsibility of the Secretary of State for Defence. The Secretary of State for Defence has three principal deputies; the Minister of State (Armed Forces); the Minister of State (Defence Procurement) and the Parliamentary Under Secretary of State for Defence.

The Missions of the Armed Forces

The MoD mission statement for the armed forces reads as follows "Defence policy requires the provision of forces with a high degree of military effectiveness, at sufficient readiness and with a clear sense of purpose, for conflict prevention, crisis management and combat operations. Their demonstrable capability, conventional and nuclear, is intended to act as an effective deterrent to a potential aggressor, both in peacetime and during a crisis. They must be able to undertake a range of Military Tasks to fulfil the missions set out below, matched to changing strategic circumstances." These missions are not listed in any order of priority:

A: Peacetime Security: To provide forces needed in peacetime to ensure the protection and security of the United Kingdom, to assist as required with the evacuation of British nationals overseas, to afford Military Aid to the Civil Authorities in the United Kingdom, including Military Aid to the Civil Power, Military Aid to Other Government Departments and Military Aid to the Civil Community.

B: Security of the Overseas Territories: To provide forces to meet any challenges to the external security of a British Overseas Territory (including overseas possession and the Sovereign Base Areas) or to assist the civil authorities in meeting a challenge to internal security. (An amendment to legislation in due course will formalise the change of title from "Department Territories" to "Overseas Territories").

C: Defence Diplomacy: To provide forces to meet the varied activities undertaken by the Ministry of Defence to dispel hostility, build and maintain trust, and assist in the development of democratically accountable armed forces (thereby making a significant contribution to conflict prevention and resolution).

D: Support to Wider British Interests: To provide forces to conduct activities to promote British interests, influence and standing abroad.

E: Peace Support and Humanitarian Operations: To contribute forces to operations other than war in support of British interests and international order and humanitarian principles, the latter most likely under UN auspices.

F: Regional Conflict Outside the NATO Area: To contribute forces for a regional conflict (but not on an attack on NATO or one of its members) which, if unchecked, could adversely affect European security, or which could pose a serious threat to British interests elsewhere, or to international security. Operations are usually under UN or Organisation for Security Co-operation in Europe auspices.

G: Regional Conflict Inside the NATO Area: To provide forces needed to respond to a regional crisis or conflict involving a NATO ally who calls for assistance under Article 5 of the Washington Treaty.

H: Strategic Attack on NATO: To provide, within the expected warning and readiness preparation times, the forces required to counter a strategic attack against NATO.

This mission statement is further sub-divided into a number of Military Tasks (MT) which accurately define the way in which the missions are actually accomplished.

Total British Armed Forces - Overview (as at 1 October 2000)

Regular: 211,700; Locally Entered 4,100; Regular Reserves 241,300; Volunteer Reserves 50,700; Cadet Forces 131,900; MoD Civilians 115,100 (includes 14,700 locally entered civilians).

Regular Army 110,100; Royal Navy 42,800; Royal Air Force 54,700; (figures include all trained and untrained personnel). Royal Naval figure includes some 5,900 Royal Marines. Planned redundancies will bring the RAF figure down to 52,500 - probably by the end of 2001.

Strategic Forces
4 x Vanguard Class submarines each with 16 x Trident (D5) Submarine-Launched Ballistic Missiles (SLBM) deploying with 48 x warheads per submarine. If necessary a D5 missile could deploy with 12 MIRV (multiple independently targetable re-entry vehicles). Future plans appear to be for a stockpile of 200 operationally available warheads and 58 missile bodies. Strategic Forces are provided by the Royal Navy.

Royal Navy
42,800: 12 x Tactical Submarines; 3 x Aircraft Carriers; 32 x Destroyers and Frigates; 21 x Mine Counter Measures Vessels; 3 x Assault Ships; 23 x Patrol Craft; 3 x Harrier Squadrons; 10 x Helicopter Squadrons; 3 x Commando Groups and 1 x Logistic Unit (Royal Marines). Royal Fleet Auxiliary - 7 x Tankers; 4 x Fleet Replenishment Ships; 1 x Aviation Training Ship; 5 x Landing Ships; 1 x Forward Repair Ship; 1 x Ice Patrol Ship; 6 x Survey Ships.

Merchant Naval Vessels Registered in the UK, Crown Dependencies and Overseas Territories: 101 x Tankers; 80 x General Cargo Ships; 44 x Refrigerated Cargo Ships; 78 x Cellular Container Ships; 45 x Ro-Ro Ships; 7 x Passenger (Cruise) Ships; 12 x Large Tugs.

Royal Air Force
54,700; 5 x Strike/Attack Squadrons; 5 x Offensive Support Squadrons; 5 x Air Defence Squadrons; 3 x Maritime Patrol Squadrons; 5 x Reconnaissance Squadrons; 2 x Airborne Early Warning Squadrons; 14 x Transport, Tankers and Helicopter Squadrons (including 6 x Helicopter Squadrons now part of the Joint Helicopter Command); 2 x Search and Rescue Squadrons; 4 x Surface to Air Missile Squadrons; 5 x Ground (Field) Defence Squadrons.

Army
110,100 (excluding some 3,669 Gurkhas); 1 x Corps Headquarters in Germany (ARRC); 1 x Armoured Divisional HQ in Germany; 1 x Operational Divisional HQ in UK ; 3 x Brigade Headquarters in Germany; 14 x Brigade Headquarters in UK; 1 x Air Assault Brigade in UK.

National Police Forces: England and Wales 125,000 Scotland 14,000, Northern Ireland 11,000.

Ministry of Defence (MoD)

In 1963, the three independent service ministries were merged to form the present Ministry of Defence (MoD). This large organisation which directly affects the lives of about half a million servicemen, reservists and MoD employed civilians, is controlled by The Secretary of State for Defence and his two deputies.

The Secretary of State for Defence chairs The Defence Council. This Defence Council is the body making the policy decisions that ensure the three services are run efficiently, and in accordance with the wishes of the government of the day.

Defence Council

The composition of The Defence Council is as follows:

The Secretary of State for Defence
Minister of State (Armed Forces)
Minister of State (Defence Procurement)
Parliamentary Under-Secretary of State for Defence
Chief of the Defence Staff
Vice-Chief of the Defence Staff
Chief of the Naval Staff and First Sea Lord
Chief of the Air Staff
Chief of the General Staff
Permanent Under-Secretary of State
Chief of Defence Procurement
Chief Scientific Adviser
Second Permanent Under-Secretary of State

Chief of The Defence Staff

The Chief of the Defence Staff (CDS) is the officer responsible to the Secretary of State for Defence for the co-ordinated effort of all three fighting services. He has his own Central Staff Organisation and a Vice Chief of the Defence Staff who ranks as number four in the services hierarchy, following the three single service commanders. The current Chief of the Defence Staff is:

Admiral Sir Michael Boyce KCB OBE ADC

Admiral Sir Michael Boyce joined the Royal Navy in 1962. After completion of basic training he qualified as a Submariner in 1965 and in the next 7 years he served in HM Submarines ANCHORITE, VALIANT and CONQUEROR, also qualifying in this time as a torpedo and anti-submarines specialist. He then completed the Submarine Commanding Officer's Qualifying Course in 1973 and subsequently commanded HM Submarines OBERON and OPOSSUM before serving as Staff Warfare Officer to Captain (SM) Submarine Sea Training.

After promotion to Commander in 1976 he attended the Royal Naval Staff Course and from there he joined Flag Officer Submarines' Staff as a Staff Warfare Officer. He then commanded HM Submarine SUPERB after which he spent just under a year in the Ministry of Defence (Directorate of Naval Plans) where he was promoted to Captain in 1982. This was followed by command of HMS BRILLIANT and then appointment as Captain (SM) Submarine Sea Training.

Admiral Boyce

In 1986 he returned to the Ministry of Defence to the Directorate of Navy Plans and Programme as assistant Director (Warfare) and in 1988 he attended the Royal College of Defence Studies. He then served as Senior Naval Officer Middle East in the rank of Commodore before becoming Director of Naval Staff Duties (DNSD) from August 1989 to June 1991.

From DNSD he was promoted Rear Admiral and in July 1991 took up the duties of Flag Officer Sea Training and Naval Base Commander Portland. In November 1992, he assumed the duties of Flag Officer Surface Flotilla which until January 1994 included the NATO appointment of Commander Anti-Submarine Warfare Striking Force.

He was promoted to Vice Admiral in February 1994 and was Knighted in the 1995 New Year's Honours List. Promoted to Admiral on 25 May 1995 he simultaneously took up the appointment of Second Sea Lord and Commander-in-Chief Naval Home Command.

In September 1997, Admiral Boyce became Commander-in-Chief Fleet with the accompanying NATO appointments of Commander-in-Chief Eastern Atlantic and Commander Allied Naval Forces Northwestern Europe. During October 1998 he assumed the appointment of First Sea Lord and Chief of Naval Staff and became principal ADC.

In February 2000 Admiral Boyce was appointed as Chief of the Defence Staff replacing General Sir Charles Guthrie who had been Chief of the Defence Staff since May 1997.

Chain of Command
The Chief of the Defence Staff (CDS) commands and co-ordinates the activities of the three services through the following chain of command:

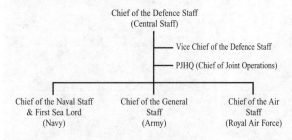

The three single service commanders exercise command of their services through their respective headquarters. However, the complex inter-service nature of the majority of modern military operations, where military, air and naval support must be co-ordinated, has led to the establishment of a permanent Tri-Service Joint Headquarters (PJHQ).

Permanent Joint Headquarters (PJHQ)

The UK MoD established a Permanent Joint Headquarters (PJHQ) at Northwood in Middlesex for joint military operations on 1 April 1996. This headquarters brought together on a permanent basis, intelligence, planning, operational and logistics staffs. It contains elements of a rapidly deployable in-theatre Joint Force Headquarters that has the capability of commanding rapid deployment front line forces.

The UK MoD Defence Costs Study of January 1994 identified a number of shortcomings with the command and control of UK military operations overseas. The establishment of PJHQ was an attempt to provide a truly joint force headquarters that would remedy the problems of disruption, duplication and the somewhat "ad hoc" way in which previous operations had been organised

MOD officials have described the primary role of PJHQ as "Working proactively to anticipate crises and monitoring developments in areas of interest to the UK. The establishment of PJHQ has set in place a proper, clear and unambiguous connection between policy and the strategic direction and conduct of operations. Because it exists on a permanent basis rather than being established for a particular operation, PJHQ is involved from the very start of planning for a possible operation. It will then take responsibility for the subsequent execution of those plans if necessary."

PJHQ, commanded by the Chief of Joint Operations (CJO), (currently a 3 star officer) occupies existing accommodation above and below ground at Northwood in Middlesex. PJHQ is responsible for planning all UK-led joint, potentially joint, combined and multinational operations and will work in close partnership with MoD Head Office in the planning of operations and policy formulation, thus ensuring PJHQ is well placed to implement policy. Having planned the operation, and contributed advice to Ministers, PJHQ will then conduct such operations. The most recent example of an operation planned by PJHQ is the UK involvement in Sierra Leone and the September 2000 rescue of the UK hostages.

When another nation is in the lead, PJHQ will exercise operational command of UK forces deployed on the operation.

Being a permanent joint Headquarters, PJHQ provides continuity of experience from the planning phase to the execution of the operation, and on to post-operation evaluation and learning of lessons.

Principal additional tasks include:

Monitoring designated areas of operational interest
Preparing contingency plans
Contributions to the UK MoD's decision making process
Exercise of operational control of overseas commands (Falklands, Cyprus and Gibraltar)
Managing its own budget
Formulation of joint warfare doctrine at operational and tactical levels
Conducting joint force exercises
Focus for Joint Rapid Reaction Force planning and exercising

Overview Of International Operations.
From 1 August 1996 PJHQ assumed responsibility for current operations in the Middle East and the Former Yugoslavia. Non-core functions, such as the day-to-day management of the Overseas Commands in Cyprus, Falkland Islands, and Gibraltar, are also delegated by MoD Head Office to the PJHQ. This allows MoD Head Office to concentrate in particular on policy formulation and

strategic direction. As of December 2000 PJHQ has been involved with UK commitments in the following areas:

Albania, Algeria, Angola, Bosnia, Burundi, East Timor, Eritrea, Honduras, Iraq, Kosovo Montserrat, Mozambique, Sierra Leone, East Zaire, West Zaire.

Headquarters Structure

PJHQ brings together at Northwood some 420 civilian, specialist and tri-Service military staff from across the MoD. The headquarters structure resembles the normal Divisional organisation, but staff operate within multidisciplinary groups which draw from across the HQ. The headquarters must have the capability of supporting a number of operations simultaneously on behalf of the UK MoD.

PJHQ in the MoD Chain of Command

PJHQ Headquarters Structure

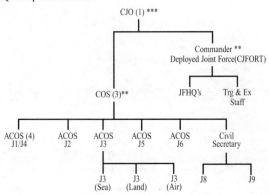

Notes:
(1) CJO - Chief of Joint Operations; (2) *** Denotes the rank of the incumbent (3) COS - Chief of Staff; (4) ACOS - Assistant Chief of Staff.

Joint Rapid Reaction Force (JRRF)
The JRRF is essentially the fighting force that PJHQ has immediately available. The JRRF provides a force for rapid deployment operations using a core operational group of the Army's 16th Air Assault Brigade and the Royal Navy's 3rd Commando Brigade, supported by a wide range of air force and maritime assets. The force uses what the MoD has described as a "golfbag" approach with a wide range of units available for specific operations. For example, if the operational situation demands assets such as heavy armour, long range artillery and attack helicopters, these assets can easily be assigned to the force. This approach means that the JRRF can be tailored for specific operations ranging from support for a humanitarian crisis to operations including high intensity operations.

The "reach" of the JRRF will be enhanced by the Royal Navy's new amphibious vessels HMS Albion and HMS Bulwark, due to enter service in 2001. Both of these ships will be able to carry 650 troops plus a range of armoured vehicles including main battle tanks. A flight deck will allow ship-to-shore helicopter operations.

Responsibility for providing units to the JRRF remains with the single service commands which ensure that units assigned are at an extremely high state of readiness. JRRF units remain committed to NATO and a JRRF-assigned battalion group provides the UK commitment to the Allied Command Europe Mobile Force (Land).

The force commander is the CJRRFO (Chief of the Joint Rapid Reaction Force) who is responsible to the Chief of Joint Operations (CJO) at PJHQ. CJRRFO is supported by the Joint Force Operations Staff at PJHQ which would provide the deployable staff element of the JRRF when the force is deployed on operations.

The overall 2000 PJHQ budget is £335 million (US$502 million). The annual running costs of the Headquarters is estimated at £33 million (US$49 million).

Included in the overall PJHQ budget are the costs of the UK forces in the Falkland Islands, Cyprus and Gibraltar. Major operations such as the 1999 Kosovo commitment are funded separately by way of a supplementary budget and, in almost all cases this requires government level approval. Small operations and the cost of reconnaissance parties are funded from the standard PJHQ budget.

Joint Force Logistics Component
The Joint Force Logistics Component (JFLogC) provides a joint logistic headquarters with force logistics under the command of PJHQ. It delivers co-ordinated logistic support to the deployed Joint Force in accordance with the commander's priorities. The composition of the JFLogC will be determined by PJHQ during the mission planning stage. Two logistic brigades have been assigned to JFLogC, one of these brigade will be ready from March 2001 and the second available from March 2003.

Staff Branches
The Staff Branches that you would expect to find at every level in a headquarters from the

Ministry of Defence down to garrison/station/port level are as follows:

Commander - The senior officer of the formation who, in a large headquarters could be an Admiral, General or Air Marshal. The Army often refers to the commander as the GOC (General Officer Commanding), the Royal Air Force to the AOC (Air Officer Commanding) while the Royal Navy uses the term Flag Officer.

Chief of Staff - The officer who runs the headquarters on a day-to-day basis and who often acts as a second-in-command.

Gl Branch - Responsible for personnel matters including manning, discipline and personal services.
G2 Branch - Responsible for intelligence and security
G3 Branch - Responsible for operations including staff duties, exercise planning, training requirements, combat development & tactical doctrine.
G4 Branch - Logistics and quartering.
G5 Branch - Civil and military co-operation.

An operational headquarters in the field will almost certainly be a tri-service organisation with branches from the Army, Navy and Air Force represented. The Staff Branches are the same for all three services.

Defence Logistics Organisation (DLO)
In 1999 the post of Chief of Defence Logistics (CDL) was created to reorganise the single service logistic support chain into a tri-service logistic organisation, designed to deliver more cost effective support by rationalisation of common functions and processes on a defence-wide basis.

For the first year CDL managed the single service organisation of Chief of Fleet Support, Quartermaster General and Air Member for Logistics. The DLO became a unified logistic structure on 1 April 2000 with over 43,000 employees of whom about 10,000 are uniformed personnel and its headquarters is at the Ensleigh site in Bath. Annual expenditure is in the region of £4.6 billion.

The DLO's responsibilities will include the through life approach to equipment support and the implementation of Smart Procurement.

NATO Command Structure

The United Kingdom is a member of NATO (North Atlantic Treaty Organisation) and the majority of military operations are conducted in concert with the forces of NATO allies.
In 1993, NATO was reorganised from three into two major Commands. The first is ACLANT (Allied Command Atlantic with headquarters at Norfolk, Virginia (USA) and the second is ACE (Allied Command Europe), with its headquarters at Mons in Belgium.

Operations in the European area in which the United Kingdom was a participant would almost certainly be as part of a NATO force under the command and control of Allied Command Europe (ACE). The current Supreme Allied Commander Europe is General Joseph Ralston.

SACEUR - General Joseph W. Ralston

General Joseph W Ralston was appointed as SACEUR in May 2000 when he replaced General Wesley K Clark who commanded NATO forces during the Kosovo Operation. General Clark had been SACEUR since July 1997.

General Ralston entered the United States Air Force in 1965 through the Reserve Officer Training Corps programme. His career includes operational command at squadron, wing, numbered air force and major command, as well as a variety of influential staff and management positions at every level of the Air Force. He has been closely involved with building the U.S. Air Force of the 21st century, holding a variety of positions related to the requirements and acquisition process. Prior to assuming his current position as SACEUR, he was Vice Chairman of the Joint Chiefs of Staff at the Pentagon in Washington DC and before this he was the commander of US Air Combat Command with headquarters at Langley Air Force Base, Virginia . He is a command pilot with more than 2,500 flying hours, including 147 combat missions over Laos and North Vietnam.

Education

1965 -   Bachelor of arts degree in chemistry, Miami University, Ohio
1976 - Master of arts degree in personnel management, Central Michigan University
1976 - Army Command and General Staff College, Fort Leavenworth, Kansas
1984 - National War College, Fort Lesley J. McNair, Washington D.C.
1989 - John F. Kennedy School of Government, Harvard University, Massachusetts

Assignments

Jul 1965 - Aug 1966	Student, pilot training, Laughlin Air Force Base, Texas
Aug 1966 - Apr 1967	Student, F-105 combat crew training school, Nellis Air Force Base, Nevada.
Apr 1967 - Oct 1969	F-105 combat crew member, 67th Tactical Fighter Squadron, later 12th Tactical Fighter Squadron, Kaden Air Base, Okinawa
Oct 1969 - Dec 1969	Student, F-105 Wild Weasel pilot training, Nhellis Air Force Base, Nevada.
Jan 1970 - Oct 1970	F-105 Wild Weasel pilot, 354th Tactical Fighter Squadron, Takhli Royal Thai Air Force Base, Thailand
Oct 1970 - Dec 1971	F-105 Wild Weasel instructor pilot, 66th Fighter Weapons Squadron, Nellis Air Force Base, Nevada.
Dec 1971 - Jun 1973	Fighter requirements officer and project officer for F-15 and light-weight fighter programmes, Officer of the Deputy Chief of Staff, Requirements, Headquarters Tactical Air Command, Langley Air Force Base, Virginia.
Jun 1973 - Jun 1975	Assistant operations officer, 335th Tactical Fighter Squadron, then chief, Standardisation and Evaluation Division, 4th Tactical Fighter Wing, Seymour Johnson Air Force Base.
Jun 1975 - Jun 1976	Student, Army Command and General Staff College, Fort Leavenworth, Kansas.
Jun 1976 - July 1979	Tactical fighter requirements officer, Office of the Deputy Chief of Staff, Research and Development, Headquarters U.S. Air Force, Washington DC.
Jul 1979 - Jul 1980	Operations officer, then commander, 68th Tactical Fighter Squadron, Moody Air Force Base, Georgia.

General Ralston

Jul 1980 - Aug 1983	Special assistant, then executive officer to the commander, Headquarters Tactical Air Command, Langley Air Force Base, Virginia.
Aug 1983 - Jun 1984	Student, National War College, Fort Lesley J. McNair, Washington, DC.
Jun 1984 - Feb 1986	Special assistant for low observable technology to the deputy chief of staff for research, development and acquisition, Headquarters U.S. Air Force, Washington DC.
Feb 1986 - Mar 1987	Commander, 56th Tactical Training Wing, MacDill Air Force Base, Florida.
Mar 1987 - Jun 1990	Assistant deputy chief of staff for operations, then deputy chief of staff, requirements, Headquarters Tactical Air Command, Langley Air Force Base, Virginia.
Jun 1990 - Dec 1991	Director of tactical programmes, Office of the Assistant Secretary of the Air Force for Acquisition, Washington, DC.
Dec 1991 - Jul 1992	Director of operational requirements, Office of the Deputy Chief of Staff for Plans and Operations, Headquarters U.S. Air Force, Washington DC.
Jul 1992 - Jul 1994	Commander, Alaskan Command, Alaskan North American Aerospace Defence Command Region, 11th Air Force; and Joint Task Force Alaska, Elmendorf Air Force Base, Alaska
Jul 1994 - Jun 1995	Deputy chief of staff for plans and operations, Headquarters U.S. Air Force, Washington DC.
Jun 1995 - Feb 1996	Commander, Headquarters Air Combat Command, Langley Air Force Base, Virginia.
Mar 1996 - May 2000	Vice chairman, Joint Chiefs of Staff, Washington D.C
May 2000	Present Supreme Allied Commander Europe.

Allied Command Europe (ACE)
The current organisation of Allied Command Europe is as follows:

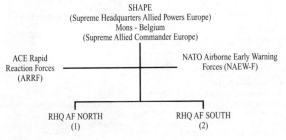

Notes:
(1) Regional Headquarters Allied Forces North Europe (RHQ AFNORTH) with headquarters at Brunssum in the Netherlands and with overall responsibility for military operations in Northern Europe. AFNORTH is further subdivided into four subordinate commands - see next diagram.

(2) Regional Headquarters Allied Forces Southern Europe (RHQ AFSOUTH) with headquarters at Naples in Italy and responsible for military operations in the southern area of NATO responsibility. AFSOUTH is further subdivided into five subordinate commands - see next diagram.

AFNORTH

The 2000 composition of AFNORTH is as follows:

Regional Command North
(Brunssum-Netherlands)

HQ AIRNORTH	JHQ CENT	JHQ NORTH	JHQ NORTHEAST
(Ramstein)	(Heidelberg)	(Stavanger)	(Karup)
Germany	Germany	Norway	Denmark

(1) AIRNORTH is responsible for all air forces in the AFNORTH region.

(2) As an example, the JHQ CENT staff consists of 150 Officers, 140 Non-commissioned Officers and Other Ranks and 20 NATO civilians - a total of 323 headquarters personnel. With Direct Support Units included the total is about 700, and with the supporting Signal Unit, the personnel figure becomes approximately 2,500.

(3) The AFNORTH operational area now includes Norway, Northern Germany and Denmark, extending 800 kms to the south to the Swiss and Austrian borders.

AFSOUTH

The 2000 composition of AFSOUTH is as follows:

Note: JHQs have a defined focus to their primary mission. For example JHQ South in Verona is focused on operations in the area of the Balkans.

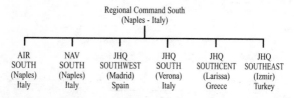

Regional Command South
(Naples - Italy)

AIR SOUTH	NAV SOUTH	JHQ SOUTHWEST	JHQ SOUTH	JHQ SOUTHCENT	JHQ SOUTHEAST
(Naples)	(Naples)	(Madrid)	(Verona)	(Larissa)	(Izmir)
Italy	Italy	Spain	Italy	Greece	Turkey

NATO Reaction Forces

In addition to the forces committed to NATO by the participating countries SACEUR has reaction forces available for crisis response. These reaction forces are multinational, held on a permanent state of readiness and allocated to major NATO commanders as authorised by the North Atlantic Council. They are subdivided into Immediate Reaction Forces (IRF - capable of deployment within 3 to 7 days) and Rapid Reaction Forces (RRF - capable of deployment within 7 to 15 days), and have employment options covering all regions of the Alliance. They may be employed either alone, as part of "joint operations" (with one or more components such as Maritime, Land or Air forces), in "combined operations" (in conjunction with other national, NATO or international forces in the theatre of operations), or with a mixture of both in "combined joint operations".

Allied Command Europe (ACE) reaction forces have the following configuration:

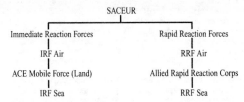

The Allied Rapid Reaction Corps (ARRC)

The concept of the Allied Rapid Reaction Corps was initiated by the NATO Defence Planning Committee in May 1991 and confirmed during November 1991. The concept called for the creation of Rapid Reaction Forces to meet the requirements of future challenges within the alliance. The ARRC provides the Supreme Allied Commander Europe with a multinational corps in which forward elements can be ready to deploy in Western Europe within 14 days.

Currently the ARRC trains for missions across the spectrum of operations from deterrence and crisis management to regional conflict. The formation has to be prepared to undertake Peace Support Operations - both peacekeeping and peacemaking. Belgium, Canada, Denmark, Germany, Greece, Italy, The Netherlands, Norway, Portugal, Spain, Turkey, the United Kingdom and the United States all contribute to the Corps. Ten divisions are assigned to the ARRC and up to four of them could be placed under command for any specific operation. These divisions range from heavily armoured formations to lighter air-portable units more suited to mountainous or difficult terrain. Some of these formations are National Divisions, some are Framework Divisions, where one nation takes the lead and another contributes, and two are Multinational Divisions where the member nations provide an equal share of the command, staff and combat forces.

Headquarters ARRC is located in Rheindahlen, Germany with a peace time establishment of 400 personnel. It comprises staff from all the contributing nations. A French liaison officer is officially accredited to the Headquarters. As the Framework Nation, the UK provides the infrastructure, administrative support, communications and 60% of the staff.

The Commander (COMARRC) and Chief of Staff are UK 3 Star and 2 Star generals and the Deputy Commander is an Italian 2 Star general. The other appointments, as with the training and exercise costs, are shared among the contributing nations.

During early 1996, HQ ARRC deployed to Sarajevo in the Former Yugoslavia to command the NATO Implementation Force (IFOR). In 1999 HQ ARRC was responsible for operations in Kosovo.

Outline Composition of the ARRC (ACE Rapid Reaction Corps)

The assigned divisions fall into three categories:
National Divisions. National divisions are provided from: Greece, the 2nd (GR) Mechanised Division (Edessa, Greece) and Turkey, 1st (TU) Mechanised Division (Ankara, Turkey). Spain will also provide a divisional sized force (the Spanish Rapid Reaction Division - RRD) based in Madrid, Spain under special bi-lateral co-ordination agreements with NATO.

Framework Divisions. Framework divisions fall under the lead of one nation but have other nation's forces assigned for ARRC operations. The 7th (GE) Armoured Division (Düsseldorf, Germany) has assigned a Polish Brigade; The 3rd (IT) Mechanised Division (Milan, Italy) has assigned a Portuguese Parachute Brigade; the 1st (UK) Armoured Division (Herford, Germany) has assigned the Danish Reaction Brigade and the Czech Rapid Reaction Brigade; the 3rd (UK) Mechanised Division (Bulford, England) has assigned the Italian 132 Ariete Brigade; and the 1st (US) Armoured Division (Bad Kreuznach, Germany) has assigned a Hungarian Mechanised Brigade.

Multinational Divisions (MND). Multinational Division Central (MND(C)) comprises brigades from Belgium, Germany, the Netherlands and the United Kingdom. It has a permanent multinational headquarters collocated with HQ ARRC in Rheindahlen, Germany and is under the operational command of COMARRC. The assigned brigades are held as national assets until command authority is transferred to NATO. Multinational Division South (MND(S)) is not yet formed as a standing headquarters but could contain brigades from Italy, Greece and Turkey.

With the exception of Headquarters MND(C) which is under his operational command, COMARRC has no command authority over these divisions in peace. However, he exercises co-ordinating authority over them which enables him and his staff to maintain a continual liaison with divisional commanders and their staffs. HQ ARRC and the assigned divisions train regularly together and hold joint seminars and study days. Common procedures have been established and headquarters work in a single language (English) so that the Corps can be operationally effective from the outset.

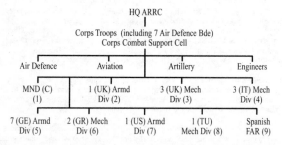

Notes: (1) MND(C) - Multinational Division - Central; (2) Resident in Germany (3) Resident in the UK (4) IT - Italy (5) GE - Germany (6) GR - Greece (7) US - United States (8) TU - Turkish (9) FAR - Spanish Rapid Action Force.

The operational organisation, composition and size of the ARRC would depend on the type of crisis, area of crisis, its political significance, and the capabilities and availability of lift assets, the distances to be covered and the infrastructure capabilities of the nation receiving assistance. It is considered that a four-division ARRC would be the maximum employment structure.

The main British contribution to the ARRC is 1 (UK) Armoured Division that is stationed in Germany and there is also a considerable number of British personnel in both the ARRC Corps HQ and Corps Troops. In addition, in times of tension 3(UK) Mechanised Division and 16 Air

Assault Brigade will move to the European mainland to take their place in the ARRC's order of battle. In total, we believe that if the need arises, some 50,000 British soldiers could be assigned to the ARRC (20,000+ resident in Germany) together with substantial numbers of Regular Army Reservists and formed TA Units.

The Finances of Defence

"You need three things to win a war,
  Money, money and more money".
Trivulzio (1441-1518)

In general terms defence is related to money, and a nation's ability to pay for its defence is linked to its GDP (Gross Domestic Product) as measured by the sum of all economic activity within a country. Estimates for the world's top six GDP rankings for 1999 (in billions of US$ and the latest year for which accurate figures are available) are as follows:

United States	$9,200 billion
Japan	$4,300 billion
Germany	$1,900 billion
United Kingdom	$1,400 billion
France	$1,400 billion
Italy	$1,100 billion

In the 2000-2001 Financial Year (FY) the UK Government planned to spend £22.80 billion on defence.

For comparison purposes defence expenditure is often expressed as a percentage of GDP. Expenditure in FY 2000-2001 represents about 2.6 per cent of GDP and is expected to fall to around 2.4 per cent of GDP in FY 2001-02. In 1985 UK defence expenditure represented 5.2% of GDP.

The total Central Government Expenditure plans for the FY 2000-2001 was budgeted at £365 billion and for comparison purposes the Government's major expenditure programmes during that period are as follows:
Note: For clarity figures have been rounded upwards.

Social Security	£103 billion
Health	£54 billion
Education	£46 billion
Defence	£23 billion
Law and Order	£20 billion
Housing & Environment	£14 billion
Transport	£9 billion
Industry & Agriculture	£15 billion
Debt Interest	£28 billion
Other Expenditure	£53 billion
Total	£365 billion

Defence Budgets - NATO Comparison

The nations of the North Atlantic Treaty Organisation (NATO), spent some US$438 billion on defence during 2000. Of this total the European members of NATO spent US$139.54 billion. For ease of conversions from national currencies, amounts are shown in US$.

Country	2000 Budget
United States	$291.2 billion
Canada	$7.6 billion
Czech Republic	$1.153 billion
Denmark	$2.3 billion
France	$27.0 billion
Germany	$23.3 billion
Greece	$3.3 billion
Hungary	$791 million
Iceland	No defence budget
Italy	$16.0 billion
Luxembourg	$100 million
Netherlands	$6.2 billion
Norway	$2.9 billion
Poland	$3.2 billion
Portugal	$1.6 billion
Spain	$7.0 billion
Turkey	$7.7 billion
United Kingdom	$34.5 billion
TOTAL	**$438.144 billion**

Note: Iceland has no military expenditure although it remains a member of NATO.

An interesting comparison is made by the total national defence budget divided by the total number of full time personnel in all three services. 1997/98 figures for the top six world defence spending nations are as follows:-

Ranking	Nation	2000 Defence Budget	Total Service Personnel	Cost per Serviceman
1	USA	US$291.2 billion	1,365,000	US$213,333
2	Japan	US$45.6 billion	236,000	US$193,220
3	UK	US$34.5 billion	211,000	US$165,507
4	France	US$27.0 billion	294,000	US$91,836
5	Germany	US$23.3 billion	321,000	US$72,585
6	Russia	US$29.0 billion	1,004,000	US$28,884

UK Defence Budget - Top Level Budget Holders

Under the early 1990s "New Management Strategy" the UK defence budget was allocated to a series of "Top Level Budget Holders" each of whom were allocated a budget with which to run their departments. The money allocated to these Top Level Budgets (TLBs) constitutes the building bricks upon which the whole defence budget is based.

Top Level Budgets 2000-2001

Naval Operational Areas (C-in-C Fleet)	£1,105 million
Army Operational Areas (C-in-C Land Command)	£3,166 million
General Officer Commanding (Northern Ireland)	£545 million
Air Force Operational Areas (AOC RAF Strike Command)	£1,609 million
Chief of Joint Operations	£335 million
Chief of Defence Logistics	£4,854 million
Second Sea Lord/Naval Home Command	£588 million
Adjutant General (Army) Personnel & Training Commanding	£1,261 million
Air Officer Commanding RAF Personnel & Training Command	£618 million
Second Permanent Under Secretary of State Centre	£2,069 million
Defence Procurement Agency (1)	£635 million
Defence Systems Procurement	£5,617 million
Major Customers Research Budgets	£435 million
Less Grants and Repayments	£9 million
Total:	**£22,800 million**

Note: (1) Includes operating costs and nuclear warhead and fissile material programmes.

Equipment Expenditure

Inside these figures for TLBs there is an Equipment Procurement Budget that totalled £10,082 million during 2000-2001. This figure can be broken down as follows:

Research	£562 million
Development	£1,856 million
Production, repairs & spares	£7,920 million
Other	£143 million

From the equipment budget the MoD Procurement Executive's business units were allocated money under the following headings:

Sea Equipment	£2,279 million
Land Equipment	£1,620 million
Air Equipment	£3,640 million
General Support	£887 million

Some of the more interesting equipment expenditure figures for the 2000-2001 Financial Year (the latest year for which the figures are available) are amongst the following:

Navy

Ships, hulls and machinery	£517 million
Naval weapon systems	£525 million
Ship equipment & support services	£101 million
Ship/weapon maintenance stores & equip	£666 million
Dockyard services	£470 million

Army

Guns, small arms and NBC defence stores	£25 million
Ammunition, mines and explosives	£135 million
Fighting vehicles	£357 million

Load carrying vehicles	£198 million
Engineering equipment	£53 million
Guided weapons	£90 million
Communications	£274 million
Surveillance equipment	£65 million
Maintenance	£423 million

Air Force

Aircraft, engines & aircraft equipment	£2,271 million
Guided weapons & electronic equipment	£1,369 million

Defence Personnel Totals
Total Service and Civilian Personnel Strength (1 April 2000)

UK service personnel	211,700
UK civilian personnel	115,100
Locally entered/engaged service personnel	4,100
Locally entered/engaged civilian personnel	14,700
Royal Irish (Home Service)	4,200
	349,800

For comparison: Total Service and Civilian Personnel Strength (1 April 1990)

UK service personnel	305,700
UK civilian personnel	141,400
Locally entered/engaged service personnel	9,000
Locally entered/engaged civilian personnel	30,900
	487,000

Note: In 1990, the figures for the then Ulster Defence Regiment (full time personnel) were included in the UK service personnel total.

Strength of UK Regular Forces (1 April 2000)

Royal Navy	Officers	Other Ranks
Trained	6,600	31,700
Untrained	1,100	3,500
Army	Officers	Other Ranks
Trained	12,800	83,700
Untrained	1,100	12,500
Royal Air Force	Officers	Other Ranks
Trained	9,800	41,200
Untrained	1,200	2,500

Deployment in Budgetary Areas (1 April 2000)

Naval Operational Areas	Officers	Other Ranks
Naval Aviation	600	2,800
Fleet Infrastructure	300	700
Surface Fleet	1,100	9,200
Submarines	400	2,600
Royal Marines	500	5,400
	2,900	**20,700**
Army Operational Areas	Officers	Other Ranks

Joint Helicopter Command	1,200	9,600
1st (UK) Armoured Division	1,300	15,800
2nd Division	300	2,100
3rd UK Division	1,100	14,700
4th Division	600	4,200
5th Division	300	1,700
UK Support Command (Germany)	200	300
GOC Northern Ireland	900	9,600
Command and Training	1,500	14,000
Land Support	400	400
	7,600	**72,300**

Air Force Operational Areas	Officers	Other Ranks
1 Group	1,200	9,700
2 Group	1,600	9,000
3 Group	700	4,600
Chief of Staff	1,000	3,200
	4,500	**26,500**

Overseas Deployment (1 April 2000)

Continental Europe

Royal Navy/Royal Marines	522
Army	23,620
Royal Air Force	3,483
Civilians	1,321

Gibraltar

Royal Navy/Royal Marines	544
Army	110
Royal Air Force	116
Civilians	66

Cyprus

Royal Navy/Royal Marines	7
Army	2,462
Royal Air Force	1,162
Civilians	284

Other Mediterranean, Gulf & Near East

Royal Navy/Royal Marines	1,464
Army	244
Royal Air Force	665
Civilians	21

Far East

Royal Navy/Royal Marines	52
Army	236
Royal Air Force	3
Civilians	21

Other Locations

Royal Navy/Royal Marines	1,810
Army	4,771
Royal Air Force	1,437
Civilians	2,690

Note: These tables include personnel on detachment from units in the UK and the final list (Other Locations) includes personnel on detachment to the Falkland Islands plus Defence Attachés and their military staff.

Recruitment of UK Regular Forces (1999-2000)

	Officers	Other Ranks
Royal Navy	408 (665)	4,545 (4,704)
Army	1,047 (1,525)	15,436 (18,743)
Royal Air Force	484 (936)	3,613 (6,078)

For Comparison - 1985-86 figures are in brackets.

Outflow of UK Regular Forces (1999-2000)

	Officers	Other Ranks
Royal Navy	570 (771)	5,226 (7,232)
Army	1,079 (1,985)	15,011 (19,316)
Royal Air Force	601 (983)	4,019 (6,234)

For Comparison - 1985-86 figures are in brackets.

Reserve Forces

In an emergency the UK MoD could call upon a tri-service reserve component of some 292,000 personnel (mid-2000 figure). This figure is composed of Regular Reserves and Volunteer Forces as follows:

Naval Regular Reserves	24,200
Naval Volunteer Reserves	4,100
Regular Army Reserves	175,200
Territorial Army	44,800
Royal Air Force Regular Reserves	41,900
Royal Air Force Volunteer Reserves	1,800

Regular Reserves (241,300) comprise ex-service personnel who have completed regular service and have a reserve liability in civilian life. The Volunteer Forces (50,700) comprise volunteers who may not have had prior regular service and train on a part time basis, generally at establishments close to their homes.

Cadet Forces

In mid 2000, there were 131,900 in the cadet forces of the three services. Single service cadet force numbers (including Combined Cadet Force but excluding officers and administrative staff) are as follows:

Royal Navy	19,700
Army	68,500
Royal Air Force	43,700

Chapter 2 - THE ROYAL NAVY

Royal Naval Summary

42,800: Strategic Forces: 4 x Vanguard Class Submarines each equipped with 16 x Trident D5 SLBM; 12 x Tactical Submarines; 3 x Aircraft Carriers; 1 x Helicopter Carrier; 32 x Destroyers and Frigates; 21 x Mine Counter Measures Vessels; 3 x Assault Ships; 23 x Patrol Craft; 3 x Harrier Squadrons; 10 x Helicopter Squadrons; 3 x Commando Groups and 1 x Logistic Unit (Royal Marines). Royal Fleet Auxiliary - 7 x Tankers; 4 x Fleet Replenishment Ships; 1 x Aviation Training Ship; 5 x Landing Ships; 1 x Forward Repair Ship; 1 x Ice Patrol Ship; 6 x Survey Ships; 2 x Ro Ro Cargo Ships.

The total personnel strength of the Royal Navy at 1 October 2000 was 42,800:

	Trained	Untrained
Officers	6,600	1,100
Other Ranks	31,700	3,500
	38,300	4,600

Figures include approximately 5,900 Royal Marines.

Composition of the Fleet

Submarines			Home Base
Trident	4	Vanguard, Victorious, Vigilant, Vengeance	Faslane
Fleet	7	Tireless, Torbay, Trafalgar Turbulent, Trenchant, Talent, Triumph	Devonport
	5	Sceptre, Spartan, Splendid, Superb, Sovereign.	Faslane
Carriers	3	Invincible, Illustrious, Ark Royal	Portsmouth
Destroyers (Type 42)	11	Cardiff, Exeter, Manchester Newcastle, Nottingham, Southampton Glasgow, Liverpool, York, Gloucester, Edinburgh	Portsmouth
Frigates (Type 23)	16	Norfolk, Sutherland, Monmouth Northumberland, Somerset, Argyll, Montrose, Richmond, Lancaster, Iron Duke, Westminster, Grafton, Marlborough, Kent, Portland, St Albans	Devonport/ Portsmouth
(Type 22)	6	Campbeltown, Chatham, Cornwall, Coventry, Cumberland, Sheffield	Devonport
Assault Ships	1	Fearless	Portsmouth

Helicopter Carrier	1	Ocean	Devonport
Offshore Patrol (Castle Class)	2	Dumbarton Castle, Leeds Castle	Portsmouth
(Island Class)	5	Alderney, Guernsey, Anglesey, Lindisfarne, Shetland	Portsmouth
Minehunters (Hunt Class)	12	Brocklesby, Chiddingford, Dulverton, Ledbury, Middleton, Quorn, Atherstone, Cattistock, Cottesmore, Hurworth, Brecon, Bicester	Portsmouth
(Sandown Class)	12	Inverness, Cromer, Sandown, Faslane/Walney, Bridport, Penzance, Pembroke, Grimsby, Bangor, Ramsay, Blythe, Shoreham	Portsmouth
Patrol Craft	1	Orwell	Devonport
Coastal Training Craft	16	Biter, Blazer, Archer, Charger, Dasher, Smiter, Puncher, Pursuer, Example, Explorer, Express, Exploit, Loyal Watcher, Loyal Chancellor, Tracker, Raider.	

(These 16 vessels are operated by Royal Naval University Training Units).

Search & Rescue Craft	2	Ranger, Trumpeter	Gibraltar
Ice Patrol	1	Endurance	Portsmouth
Survey Ships	5	Beagle, Herald, Scott Bulldog, Roebuck	Devonport
	1	Gleaner	Portsmouth

Note: Not all of these ships will be available for operations at any one time and there will always be ships in refit or engaged on trials or training. One of the ASW Carriers is generally in refit and on average 5-7 destroyers/frigates from a total force of 32 will be in refit/standby.

Royal Fleet Auxiliary Large Fleet Tankers	2	Olna, Olwen	
Small Fleet Tankers	3	Black Rover, Gold Rover, Grey Rover	

Support Tankers	4	Bayleaf, Brambleleaf, Oakleaf, Orangeleaf	
Replenishment Ships	4	Fort George, Fort Austin, Fort Rosalie, Fort Victoria.	
Aviation Training Ship	1	Argus	
Landing Ship	5	Sir Galahad, Sir Geraint, Sir Bedivere, Sir Percivale, Sir Tristram	
Forward Repair Ship	1	Diligence	
Ro-Ro Cargo Ship	2	Sea Crusader, Sea Centurion	

Fleet Air Arm

Air Defence Recce/Attack	Sea Harrier F/A2	7	800 Sqn
	Sea Harrier F/A2	7	801 Sqn
	Sea Harrier Mk 2/T8	14	899 Sqn
Anti-Submarine	Merlin HM Mk 1	4	700 Sqn
	Merlin HM Mk 1	8	824 Sqn
	Sea King HAS 5/6	9	810 Sqn
	Sea King HAS 5/6	6	814 Sqn
	Sea King HAS 5/6	9	819 Sqn
	Sea King HAS 5/6	7	820 Sqn
Anti-Submarine/ Anti-Ship	Lynx HAS 3, HMA 8	36	815 Sqn (1)
	Lynx HAS 3, HMA 8	12	702 Sqn
Airborne Early Warning	Sea King AEW 2	9	849 Sqn
Commando Assault	Sea King HC4	10	845 Sqn
	Sea King HC4	10	846 Sqn
	Sea King HC4	9	848 Sqn
	Lynx AH7	6	847 Sqn
	Gazelle	9	847 Sqn
Aircrew Training	Jetstream T2	7	750 Sqn
	Jetstream T3	2	750 Sqn
Search & Rescue	Sea King HAS Mk5	5	771 Sqn

Note: The figure for 815 Sqn includes six aircraft with squadron HQ. The remainder of the aircraft are in flights of one or two aircraft and in the main, on board ships at sea.

Royal Marines
1 x Commando Brigade Headquarters
1 x Brigade Air Squadron
3 x Royal Marine Commando (Battalion Size)
1 x Commando Regiment Royal Artillery
1 x Commando Artillery Battery (Volunteer)
1 x Commando Squadron Royal Engineers
1 x Commando Squadron Royal Engineers (Volunteer)
1 x Commando Light Helicopter Squadron (847 Sqn)
1 x Commando Logistic Regiment
1 x Special Boat Service Squadron
2 x Assault Squadrons (Landing Craft)
1 x Security Unit for National Strategic Deterrent

The Merchant Navy
Merchant Naval Vessels Registered in the UK, Crown Dependencies and Overseas Territories: 101 x Tankers; 80 x General Cargo Ships; 44 x Refrigerated Cargo Ships; 78 x Cellular Container Ships; 45 x Ro-Ro Ships; 7 x Passenger (Cruise) Ships; 12 x Large Tugs.

Note: This listing refers to vessels of 500 gross tons and over. The total tonnage is 4,670,000 gross tons.

The Admiralty Board
The routine management of the Royal Navy is the responsibility of The Admiralty Board, the composition of which is as follows:

The Secretary of State for Defence
Minister of State (Armed Forces)
Minister of State (Defence Procurement)
Parliamentary Under-Secretary of State for Defence
Chief of the Naval Staff and First Sea Lord
Commander in Chief Fleet
Second Sea Lord and Commander in Chief Naval Home Command
Second Permanent Under Secretary of State and Secretary of the Admiralty Board
Chief of Fleet Support
Controller of the Navy
Assistant Chief of Naval Staff
Decisions made by The Defence Council or the Admiralty Board are acted upon by the naval staff at the various headquarters throughout the defence chain of command. The First Sea Lord is the officer responsible for the Royal Navy's contribution to the national defence effort and he maintains control through the commander and the staff branches of each of these headquarters.

First Sea Lord and Chief of the Naval Staff
Admiral Sir Nigel Essenhigh KCB

Admiral Sir Nigel Essenhigh was born in 1944 and joined the Royal Navy in 1963. He qualified as a principal Warfare Officer in 1972 and specialised in navigation.

He spent the majority of his career at sea, serving in a wide variety of ships ranging from patrol

Admiral Essenhigh

boats to aircraft carriers, including command of the Type 42 Destroyers HMS NOTTINGHAM and HMS EXETER. He has seen active service in the Far East and Middle East including Operation Desert Shield and Desert Storm in the Gulf war.

He is a graduate of the Royal Naval Staff Course, the Higher Command and Staff Course and the Royal College of Defence Studies.

Admiral Essenhigh's previous recent appointments include Hydrographer of the Navy, Assistant Chief of Defence Staff (Programmes) and the most recent, Commander-in-Chief Fleet. He assumed the appointment of Chief of the Naval Staff on 16 January 2001.

He lives in Devon with his wife Susie. He is a Younger Brother of Trinity House, a Fellow of the Royal Institute of Navigation, a Member of the Honourable Company of Master Mariners and a Fellow of the Nautical Institute.

Royal Naval Chain of Command
Commander-in-Chief Fleet

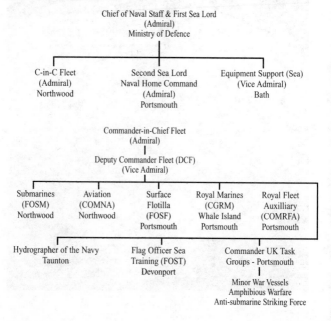

Notes:
FOSM - Flag Officer Submarines
COMNA - Commodore Naval Aviation
FOSF - Flag Officer Surface Flotilla
CGRM - Commandant General Royal Marines
COMRFA - Commander Royal Fleet Auxiliary
FOST - Flag Officer Sea Training.

Naval Home Command

Second Sea Lord & Commander-in-Chief
Naval Home Command (Admiral)
(HMS Victory)

Chief of Staff

| Command Secretary | Training & Recruiting | Naval Secretary | Personnel Support | Strategy & Plans | Medical Director |

Equipment Support (Sea)

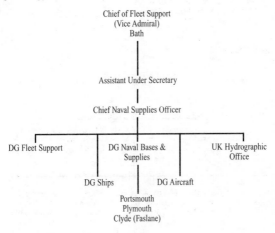

Chief of Fleet Support
(Vice Admiral)
Bath

Assistant Under Secretary

Chief Naval Supplies Officer

DG Fleet Support   DG Naval Bases & Supplies   UK Hydrographic Office

DG Ships   DG Aircraft

Portsmouth
Plymouth
Clyde (Faslane)

Note: DG (Director General) is usually a Rear Admiral.

Fleet Disposition

Submarine Flotilla

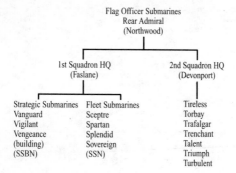

```
                          Flag Officer Submarines
                              Rear Admiral
                              (Northwood)
                                    |
                 _____|_____
                |                                       |
          1st Squadron HQ                        2nd Squadron HQ
            (Faslane)                              (Devonport)
                |
    _____|_____                          Tireless
   |                         |                         Torbay
Strategic Submarines   Fleet Submarines               Trafalgar
Vanguard               Sceptre                         Trenchant
Vigilant               Spartan                         Talent
Vengeance              Splendid                        Triumph
(building)             Sovereign                       Turbulent
(SSBN)                 (SSN)
```

SSBN - Nuclear powered ballistic missile submarine.
SSN - Nuclear powered attack submarine.

Surface Flotilla

```
                          Flag Officer Surface Flotilla
                                 Vice Admiral
                                 (Portsmouth)
                                      |
         _____|_____
        |                             |                             |
   2nd Frigate Sqn                                             3rd Destroyer Sqn
    (Devonport)                                                  (Portsmouth)
   Type 22 Batch 1 & 3                                             Type 42
```

| 4th Frigate Sqn (Portsmouth) Type 23 | 5th Destroyer Sqn (Portsmouth) Type 42 | 6th Frigate Sqn (Devonport) Type 23 | Fishery Protection Sqn | Survey Sqn (Devonport) | MCM Flotilla (Faslane) |

34

Mine Counter Measures Flotilla

HQ Mine War Vessels and Mine Warfare
Commodore
(Faslane)

| 1st Squadron | 2nd Squadron | 3rd Squadron |
| (Portsmouth) | (Portsmouth) | (Faslane) |

Fishery Protection Squadron (Portsmouth)
Island Class Offshore Patrol Vessels: Angelsey, Alderney, Guernsey, Shetland, Lindisfarne.
Castle Class Offshore Patrol Vessels: Leeds Castle, Dumbarton Castle.

Surveying Squadron (Devonport)
Coastal Survey Vessels: Bulldog, Beagle, Roebuck.
Ocean Survey Ships: Herald, Scott.
Ice Patrol Ship: Endurance.
Hydrographic Survey Vessel: Gleaner.

1st Patrol Boat Squadron
Archer Class - Fast Training Boats: Blazer, Puncher, Archer, Smiter, Dasher, Pursuer, Charger, Biter, Northella, Loyal Chancellor, Loyal Watcher, Express, Orwell, Example, Explorer, Exploit, Tracker, Raider.

Gibraltar Squadron
Archer Class - Fast Training Boats: Ranger, Trumpeter.
Surveying Flotilla - Headquarters at Devonport

Outline Organisation of a Frigate

The organisation of a typical RN frigate is the result of hundreds of years of evolution and above all, the ship is organised to fight. The four major departments in a modern frigate are the following:

Commanding Officer

Second in Command

| Operations Department | Marine Engineering Department | Weapons Engineering Department | Supply Department |

Operations Department - This department basically "fights" the ship and is the direct descendant of the Seaman Branch which manned the guns in earlier generations. There is usually a helicopter embarked on the frigate and the flight commander reports to the Head of the Operations Department.

Marine Engineering Department - Runs the machinery of the ship ie. the main propulsion units that drive the vessel (gas turbines or diesels), the electrical power supplies and all of the ancillary machinery required.

Weapons Engineering Department - Responsible for the efficient functioning of all of the ship's highly complex sensors and weapons.

Supply Department - Responsible for the logistic arrangements in the ship ie. catering, spares for all of the weapons, general stores, sensors and machinery spares and for all pay and accounting matters.

All the departments are inter-dependent and each has a head of department - known collectively as "the HODs". These HODs meet at regular intervals and agree such matters as programmes, training and the efficient administration of everything on board. Whilst each HOD is responsible directly to the commanding officer for the efficiency of his department, the Head of the Operations Department generally leads the HODs and is the Second-in-Command - he is known as the First Lieutenant and is a Lieutenant Commander. The other HODs are also likely to be Lieutenant Commanders and, even if senior to the First Lieutenant, are subordinate to him - the First Lieutenant is the man who takes over if the Commanding Officer is unable to perform his duties.

The cleaning of the ship and all the general tasks are shared by the departments, and the HODs would discuss these matters at their meetings - for example, they would agree how many sailors would be required from each department for a storing at sea operation. A recent development is the presence on board many RN ships of female personnel. These females share all the duties of their male counterparts but, of course, have separate living quarters.

The Commanding Officer is usually a Commander RN (with a background in the Operations Department) and he is known as "The Captain". In command of a squadron frigates, an officer with the rank of Captain RN will be found who doubles the duties both of "Captain" of his ship and Captain (F) to whom the "Captains" of the frigates in his squadron report.

The complement of a frigate relates to the requirement to man the ship for battle. A Batch 3 Type 22 has a total of 232 (13 officers) and a newer Duke Class Type 23 has a complement of 169 (12 officers).

Royal Naval Shore Establishments

HMS Cambridge	Plymouth	Gunnery
HMS Cochrane	Rosyth	Naval Base
HMS Collingwood	Fareham	Weapons Engineering
HMS Daedalus	Lee-on-Solent	Air Engineering & RNAS

Dartmouth BRNC	Dartmouth	Officer Training
HMS Dolphin	Gosport	Submarine Training
HMS Drake	Devonport	Naval Base
HMS Dryad	Fareham	Maritime Operations
HMS Forest Moor	Harrogate	Communications Base
HMS Gannet	Prestwick	RN Air Station
HMS Heron	Yeovilton	RN Air Station
HMS Inskip	Preston	Communications Base
HMS Nelson	Portsmouth	Naval Base
HMS Neptune	Faslane	Submarine Base
HMS Raleigh	Torpoint	Training Base
HMS Seahawk	Helston	RNAS Culdrose
HMS Sultan	Gosport	Marine Engineering
HMS Victory	Portsmouth	C-in-C Home Command
HMS Warrior	Northwood	C-in-C Fleet
HMS Excellent	Portsmouth	Operations and Training

Royal Naval Reserve Units

There are Royal Naval Reserve Units located at:

HMS Calliope	Gateshead
HMS Cambria	Penarth
HMS Caroline	Northern Ireland
HMS Dalriada	Greenock
HMS Eaglet	Liverpool
HMS Flying Fox	Bristol
HMS Forward	Birmingham
HMS Northwood	Northwood
HMS President	London
HMS Scotia	Pitreavie
HMS Sherwood	Nottingham
HMS Vivid	Devonport
HMS King Alfred	Portsmouth

The 1998 Strategic Defence Review (SDR) announced that the size of the Royal Naval Reserve was to be increased to 3,850. On 1 April 2000, this force consisted of 4,100 personnel.

Strategic Deterrent

The United Kingdom's Strategic Deterrent is operated by the Royal Navy and submarine launched ballistic missiles (SLBM) have been installed in Royal Naval submarines since the late 1960s, with operational patrols commencing in 1969. The first class of SSBN (Nuclear Powered Ballistic Missile Submarine) was the Resolution Class with 4 x vessels of the type:

HMS Resolution	(Commissioned 1967)
HMS Repulse	(Commissioned 1968)
HMS Renown	(Commissioned 1968)
HMS Revenge	(Commissioned 1969)

Resolution Class submarines carried the Polaris 3-TK missile, armed with 6 x 150 kT MRV (Multiple Re-entry Vehicle) warheads. The 3-TK system was believed to have a range of approximately 4,500 km.

The Resolution Class SSBNS have been replaced by the Vanguard Class, and HMS Vanguard, the lead vessel of the class commenced its first patrol in late 1994/early 1995. The Trident Class submarines, of which there are four, are armed with 16 x US Trident II D5 missiles and each missile has the capability of carrying up to 12 x MIRV (Multiple Independently Targeted Re-entry Vehicle) warheads making a possible total of 192 warheads per submarine. However, in late 1998, the UK MoD announced that Resolution Class vessels would only deploy with 48 warheads. In general terms it is believed, that in UK service the Trident II D5 will carry eight warheads per missile.

The UK is believed to have purchased 58 x Trident 2D-5 missile bodies from the United States and the range of the missile is believed to be in excess of 9,000 km with a CEP (Circular Error Probable) of about 100 metres.

The second vessel in the class, HMS Victorious, reached operational deployment status at the end of 1995 and the third vessel, HMS Vigilant, was ready for operational deployment in early 1997. The fourth vessel of the class, HMS Vengeance, was commissioned in November 1999.

Plans are for at least one of these SSBN to be on patrol constantly and because of their high speed, long endurance underwater, and advanced sensor and electronic equipment, they have little fear of detection under water.

These large submarines displace over 16,000 tonnes, have a length of 150 metres and the three decks offer accommodation for the crew of 130 which is unusually spacious for a submarine. Good domestic facilities are provided for the crew and the air purification system enables them to remain submerged for long periods without any outside support. Each submarine has two crews, known as Port and Starboard; when one crew is away on patrol the other crew is training or taking leave.

Following the 1998 Strategic Defence Review (SDR) the UK MoD revealed that it was no longer necessary to have a stockpile of 300 warheads and that the stockpile was being reduced to 200 operationally available warheads. In addition, the 58 missile bodies already purchased are sufficient to maintain a credible deterrent. The MoD confirmed that there will be one SSBN on patrol at any one time but carrying a reduced load of 48 warheads. The submarine's missiles will not be "targeted" and will be at several days "notice to fire".

Stocks of fissile materials will be reduced. Current (2000) stocks are 7.6 tonnes of plutonium, 21.9 tonnes of highly enriched uranium and 15,000 tonnes of other forms of uranium. The reduction in warheads will allow 0.3 tonnes of weapons-grade plutonium to be placed under international safeguards.

Name	Date Commissioned
Vanguard	1993
Victorious	1995
Vigilant	1996
Vengeance	1999

Fleet Submarines

The Royal Navy operates two classes of Nuclear Powered Attack Submarines (SSN) as follows:

SWIFTSURE CLASS	Commissioned
Sovereign	1974
Superb	1976
Sceptre	1978
Spartan	1979
Splendid	1981

Dimensions: Length 82.9m; Beam 9.8m; Draught 8.2m; Displacement 4,200 tons surfaced and 4,500 tons dived; Propulsion - 1 x Rolls Royce pressurised water-cooled reactor supplying steam to two sets of General Electric geared turbines delivering 15,000 shp to one shaft; Performance - Max Speed 20 kts surfaced and 30+ kts dived; diving depth 400m (operational) and 600m maximum; Complement 12 officers and 85 ratings; Torpedoes - 5 x 533 mm (21") tubes for 20 x Mk 24 Tigerfish wire-guided and Mk 8 anti-ship torpedos; Mines - up to 50 x Mk 5 Stonefish or Mk 6 Sea Urchins instead of torpedoes; Missiles - 5 x UGM-84A Sub Harpoon tube-launched anti-ship missiles.

TRAFALGAR CLASS	Commissioned
Trafalgar	1983
Turbulent	1984
Tireless	1985
Torbay	1987
Trenchant	1989
Talent	1990
Triumph	1991

Dimensions: Length 85.4m; Beam 9.8m; Draught 8.2m; Displacement 4,700 tons surfaced and 5,200 tons dived; Propulsion - 1 x Rolls Royce pressurised water-cooled reactor supplying steam to two sets of General Electric geared turbines delivering 15,000 shp to one shaft; Performance - Max Speed 20 kts surfaced and 32 kts dived; diving depth 400m (operational) and 600m maximum; Complement 12 officers and 85 ratings; Torpedoes - 5 x 533mm (21") tubes for 20 x Mk 24 Tigerfish wire-guided and Mk 8 anti-ship torpedoes; Mines - up to 50 x Mk 5 Stonefish or Mk 6 Sea Urchins instead of torpedoes; Missiles - 5 x UGM-84A Sub Harpoon tube-launched anti-ship missiles.

These nuclear-powered fleet submarines are armed with homing torpedoes (range approx 15km+) that can be used against other submarines or surface vessels. The Sub Harpoon long-range anti-ship missile (range 110 kms) is now in service as the principal anti-surface ship weapon in these submarines.

Both classes are capable of continuous patrols at high underwater speed, independent of base support, and can circumnavigate the globe without surfacing. Their long endurance and sophisticated weapon systems make them formidable adversaries. There are three decks and although space is restricted, living conditions are comfortable.

Tomahawk Cruise Missiles

In 1995, the UK MoD announced that a total of seven in-service SSNs (two Swiftsure class and five Trafalgar class) will be modified for the Tomahawk cruise missile. By 2003 the RN aims to have five TLAM-capable boats fully operational at any one time. The UK is acquiring an initial 65 x Tomahawk Block III missiles built by Hughes Missile Systems Company under a US Foreign Military Sales (FMS) agreement worth £180 million.

Under the terms of the 1998 SDR it was announced that the nuclear powered attack submarine force would be reduced from 12 to 10 "in the longer term" and that all 10 submarines would now be fitted with the Tomahawk land attack cruise missile. The Tomahawk TLAM-C (Tactical Land Attack Missile - Conventional) has a range of about 950 km.

HMS Splendid began a six-month Capability Upgrade Period (CUP) in October 1997 designed to allow the submarine to operate Tomahawk Land Attack Cruise Missile (TLAC-M). The CUP package, the first of its kind, enabled HMS Splendid to conduct the RN's first live firing of TLAM at a Pacific test range off San Diego in November 1998.

HMS Splendid took part in operations against Kosovo during April and May 1999. During some extremely bad weather HMS Splendid was the only European unit available to contribute to the attack element of the campaign.

The submarine remained under United Kingdom (rather than NATO) control throughout the operation, and according to some reports from the UK MoD, is understood to have fired 20 of the 238 TLAC-Ms used in the operation. Overall, 198 of these hit their target, and this success rate of 83% was matched by the 85% success rate (17 out of 20) claimed for the UK-launched rounds.

In total 7 x Trafalgar Class and 2 x Swiftsure Class submarines will be made TLAC-M capable by 2006, with HMS Triumph, HMS Trafalgar, HMS Spartan and HMS Torbay all TLAC-M capable by the end of 2001. The total cost of the TLAC-M programme is believed to be £300 million.

Astute Class Submarines

In June 1997, the MoD awarded GEC-Marconi a contract worth approximately £2 billion for its VSEL shipbuilding subsidiary to build the first 3 x Astute Class nuclear-powered attack submarines for the Royal Navy. These initial vessels, in the past referred to as the Batch 2 Trafalgar Class, will enter service from 2005 to replace the oldest of the five Swiftsure-class boats that were commissioned between 1974 and 1981. The MoD plans to order a further two Astute-class SSNs after 2000 to succeed the remaining Swiftsure Class submarines.

The 6,000-tonne Astute Class SSNs will be faster and quieter than the Trafalgar Class boats, and their PWR-2 nuclear reactors will not require refuelling over the 25 to 30 years that the vessels will be in service. Each will carry a total of 36 weapons - a mix of Spearfish heavyweight torpedoes, Harpoon anti-ship missiles, and Tomahawk TLAC-M.

The first three submarines in the class are planned to enter service as follows:

	Laid Down	Commissioned
Astute	1999	2005

Ambush	2001	2007
Artful	2002	2008

Initial specifications include:
Dimensions: 97m x 10.7m x 10m; Displacement, tons: 6,500 surfaced; 7,200 tons dived; Speed: 29 knots dived; Complement: 98 (including 12 officers).

Aircraft Carriers

The Royal Navy operates 3 x Aircraft/ASW Carriers of which two are generally available and one is in refit at any one time: These vessels are:

	Commissioned
Invincible	1980
Illustrious	1982
Ark Royal	1985

Major Characteristics - Speed 28 knots; Displacement 16,800 tons (standard) 19,000 (full load); Engines 4 x Rolls Royce Olympus TM3B Gas Turbines delivering 112,000 shp to two shafts; Length 206.6m; Beam 27.5m; Draught 7.3m; Flight Deck Length 167.8m; Complement 131 officers and 870 rates plus an air group of 320.

The primary task of this class of ship is to act as the command ship of anti-submarine warfare forces. They are also effective and flexible command ships for air operations and aircraft from the carriers Invincible and Illustrious were involved in operations in the former Yugoslavia during 1995 and more recently, in the Persian Gulf during late 1997 - early 1998 and off Sierra Leone during 2000.

All three carriers carry Sea King anti-submarine (ASW) helicopters, Sea King airborne early warning (AEW) helicopters and Sea Harrier aircraft. A typical embarked "air group" could consist of:

> 6 x Sea Harriers
> 6 x Sea King HAS.6 (ASW)
> 3 x Sea King HAS.2 (AEW)

Note: RAF Chinook helicopters have recently been operating from HMS Invincible and HMS Illustrious. Also see notes in the Fleet Air section regarding the formation of the Joint Force Harrier (JFH).

The Sea Dart medium-range surface-to-air missile is fitted for air defence (with a secondary anti-ship role) and the Phalanx or Goalkeeper rapid-firing gun systems have been fitted to enhance the close-range anti-missile defence capability. A 'ski-jump' launching ramp is fitted to improve the operational take-off performance of the Sea Harrier. The vessels are powered by Rolls-Royce Olympus gas-turbine engines and on average these ships took approximately 6-7 years to build.

In May 1999 HMS Ark Royal entered Rosyth Dockyard for a two year refit and should be out by mid 2001. Following the refit the vessel will be capable of accommodating Royal Air Force Harrier GR.7 strike aircraft alongside her existing air group of Sea Harrier FA.2s, and will be equipped to operate the new Merlin HM.1 anti-submarine warfare helicopter. HMS Invincible was adapted for the above configuration earlier in 2000.

New Aircraft Carriers

Following the 1998 SDR, the UK MoD announced its intention to replace the Royal Navy's current carrier force with two larger vessels once the current vessels have reached the end of their planned life. Invitations to tender for the future aircraft carrier CV(F) were issued on 25 January 1999 to six companies, including BAe Defence Systems, Boeing, Lockheed Martin, Marconi Electronic Systems (now merged with British Aerospace), Raytheon, and Thomson-CSF.

These tender invitations are for a one-year assessment phase, for which £5 million study contracts are expected to be awarded to three of the companies during early 2001. Two of the companies will then be shortlisted and the prime contractor should be selected in 2003.

The intention is to acquire two CV(F)s with the first unit entering service in 2012. Each will be capable of operating up to 50 aircraft (implying a displacement of some 40,000 tonnes) and would have a crew of some 1,000, including the air group. In addition to strike aircraft belonging to the RN/Royal Air Force Joint Force 2000 organisation, the CV(F) will be required to support helicopter and UAV (unmanned aerial vehicle) operations.

The vessel's exact dimensions and costs depend on the choice of future carrier-borne aircraft (FCBA), a selection decision for which is due in 2001. The short take-off and vertical landing (STOVL) variant of the US JSF (Joint Strike Fighter) is the UK's preferred choice for its Future Carrier Borne Aircraft requirement to replace the Sea Harrier FA2 and Harrier GR7.

According to sources in the UK Ministry of Defence, the government will require the ships to be built in the UK. This means that the work would almost certainly go to either Harland & Wolf (Belfast) or Kvaerner (Govan), the two shipyards that are capable of constructing vessels of this size. It is possible that Marconi Marine and Land Systems could develop an appropriate dock at Barrow in Furness, and it also owns the former Cammell Laird shipyard at Birkenhead. There is also a chance that Birkenhead could figure. Planning permission is believed to have been applied for, to build a suitable dry dock specifically to support the CV(F) at the former Swan Hunter yard at Wallsend.

In the interim, HMS Ocean, an LPH (Landing Platform Helicopter) has joined the fleet. The hull of the ship was built to Merchant Navy standards at a cost of some £170 million. The ship is capable of carrying an air group of 12 x Sea King HAS.4 troop lift helicopters and 6 x Lynx HAS.8 attack helicopters (although these will probably be replaced by EH 101 and Apache during the next five years). HMS Ocean has a crew of 250 and the ship is capable of carrying a complete Marine Commando (up to 850 personnel).

Assault Ships

Major Characteristics - Speed 21 knots; Displacement 11,582 tons; Engines 2 x sets of English Electric geared steam turbines delivering 22,000 shp to 2 props; Length 158m; Beam 24.3m; Draught 6.2m; Complement 50 officers and 50 rates plus air group of 3 officers and 85 rates.

	Commissioned
Fearless	1965

This vessel is a versatile (but somewhat ageing) amphibious warfare platform that proved its worth in the Falklands Campaign. The ship is capable of supporting a Naval Assault Group/Brigade HQ from which naval and military personnel, working in close co-operation, can mount and control an amphibious operation.

In addition the vessel can transport a military force complete with full supporting armour. four Mk 4 landing craft capable of transporting 35 troops or a 5.5 ton vehicle are carried in davits and the well deck can carry two main battle tanks or 100 tons of stores and 4 x LCM (landing craft). Four more main battle tanks can be carried on the tank deck. The ship can also operate a flight of four helicopters and is armed with modern close-range guns for air defence. HMS Fearless is fitted with the Phalanx close-in weapon system to enhance the air defence. In an emergency, the ship could carry up to 1,000 troops. The sister ship HMS Intrepid was disposed of in 1999.

New Assault Ships

In a July 1996 order to VSEL worth £450 million, two replacement assault vessels were ordered. These vessels, carrying the names of Albion and Bulwark are due to be launched in March 2001 and Dec 2001 respectively. Both ships should be in commission by mid 2003.

The new ships will be 176 metres in length, displacing 19,000 tons and diesel propulsion will give a top speed of 20 knots. The vessel's range will be 8,000 miles at 15 knots. There will be 2 flight deck places for EH 101 helicopters plus Chinooks, 4 x LCU landing craft in the well deck and another 5 x landing craft in davits. The crew will total some 325 and 650 embarked troops will be carried.

Type 42 Destroyers

There are currently 11 x Type 42 Guided Missile Destroyers (DDG) whose primary role is to provide air defence for naval task group operations.

	Commissioned	
Cardiff	1979	Batch 1
Newcastle	1978	Batch 1
Glasgow	1979	Batch 1
Exeter	1980	Batch 2
Southampton	1981	Batch 2
Nottingham	1982	Batch 2
Liverpool	1982	Batch 2
Manchester	1982	Batch 3
Gloucester	1985	Batch 3
Edinburgh	1985	Batch 3
York	1985	Batch 3

Major Characteristics - Speed 29 knots on Olympus turbines or 18 knots on Tyne turbines; Range 7,400 kms at 18 kts; Displacement Batch 1 & 2 - 4,350 tons full load and Batch 3 - 5,350 tons at full load; Engines - COGOG Type system with 2 x Rolls Royce Olympus TM3B gas turbines delivering 56,000 shp and 2 x Rolls Royce Tyne RM1A gas turbines delivering 8,500 shp to two shafts; Length 125.6m Batch 1 & 2 and 141.1m for Batch 3; Beam 14.3m Batch 1 & 2 and 14.9m Batch 3; Draught 5.8m; Complement 24 officers and 229 rates (max total 312); Aircraft Carried - Sea Lynx with Sea Skua and or Stingray torpedoes.

In general, these vessels are armed with the Sea Dart medium-range air-defence missile system, which also has an anti-ship capability (1 x twin launcher for 24 x Sea Dart SAM for Batch 1 & 2 with Batch 3 carrying 40 missiles). The automatic rapid-fire 114mm (4.5 inch) gun with a range of 21 km, anti-submarine torpedo tubes and the Phalanx rapid-firing gun system for close-range anti-missile defence. They also carry the high-speed multi purpose Lynx helicopter armed with anti-submarine weapons and the Sea Skua anti-ship missile which is controlled by the Sea Spray search radar. The latest communication and sensor equipment is fitted in all Type 42 Destroyers.

All the Type 42 Destroyers are based at Portsmouth.

Type 45 Destroyers

On 11 July 2000 the UK MoD announced the commencement of the Royal Navy's Type 45 destroyer programme. The intention is to order a first batch of three ships worth more than £1 billion from the prime contractor, BAE Systems.

The contract is expected to be awarded in early 2001 and it is believed that a second batch of three will be ordered in 2004.

It is expected that design and construction of the first three ships will be split between BAE Systems Marine and Vosper Thornycroft. Overall project management is the responsibility of BAE Systems. Two of the ships will probably be assembled at Scotstoun and the other by Vosper Thornycroft.

Plans are believed to include 12 x Type 45 destroyers that should be in service by the end of 2014, with the entire programme budgeted at about £6 billion. The Type 45, displacing around 7,200 tons, will be equipped with the UK variant of the Principal Anti-Air Missile System (PAAMS).

The Type 45 will have the ability to land and hangar a Merlin HM.1 helicopter, however, the Type 45 will operate with the smaller Lynx HMA.8 when the vessels first enter service. A main gun is to be fitted and this will initially be a standard Mk 8 Mod 1 4.5in mounting. In the longer term there will be provision for installation of the future 155 mm gun.

First ships of the class will be HMS Daring, due for launching in 2005 and HMS Dauntless, due for launching in 2007. Other ship names may include Defender, Dorsetshire, Dover, Dragon, Demon, Duncan, Dreadnought, Diamond, Despatch and Decoy.

Broadsword Class Frigates (Type 22)

From 1 Jan 2001, it would appear that the Royal Navy will be operating 6 x Type 22 Frigates whose primary role is anti-submarine warfare:

	Commissioned	
Sheffield	1988	Batch 2
Coventry	1988	Batch 2
Cornwall	1988	Batch 3
Cumberland	1988	Batch 3
Campbeltown	1989	Batch 3
Chatham	1989	Batch 3

The Batch 1 ships, HMS Broadsword, Battleaxe, Brilliant and Brazen, all commissioned between 1979 and 1982 were sold to the Brazilian Navy between 1995 and 1997.

Major Characteristics - Speed 30 kts+ on Olympus turbines or 18 knots on Tyne turbines; Range 8,370 km at 18 kts; Displacement 4,600 tons full load; Engines - COGOG Type system with 2 x Rolls Royce Spey SM1A gas turbines delivering 18,770 shp and 2 x Rolls Royce Tyne RM1A gas turbines delivering 8,500 shp to two shafts; Length 143.6m; Beam 14.8m; Draught 6.0m; Complement 23 officers and 302 rates; Aircraft Carried - 1 or 2 x Sea Lynx with Sea Skua and or Stingray torpedoes or 1 x Sea King HAS.6.

Type 22 Frigates of both Batch 2 and Batch 3 are capable of not only anti-submarine operations (their primary role) but also anti-aircraft and anti-ship roles. Equipped with the latest computer-assisted sonar systems and communications equipment, these vessels are highly efficient maritime hunters. Two Lynx anti-submarine helicopters can be carried and anti-submarine torpedo tubes are fitted. Batch 2 vessels carry the Exocet MM38 surface-to-surface missile (range 65 km) and the Batch 3 vessels carry the Harpoon surface to surface missile (range 110 km). Sea Wolf close-range air-defence missile systems provide an all-round defence capability and the 30mm Goalkeeper gives defence against incoming missiles. The automatic rapid-fire Vickers Mk 8 DP 114mm (4.5-inch) gun with a range of 21 kms is fitted to the Batch 3 ships.

All the ships have controllable-pitch propellers and stabilisers. This class is the first in the Royal Navy to be designed to the metric system.

<u>Duke Class Frigates (Type 23)</u>

Although designed for anti-submarine operations like most new surface combatants of this size, this is really a multi purpose vessel. There are currently 15 ships of this class in service with another one being built.

	Commissioned
Norfolk	1990
Argyll	1991

Marlborough	1991
Lancaster	1991
Iron Duke	1992
Monmouth	1993
Montrose	1993
Westminster	1993
Northumberland	1994
Richmond	1994
Somerset	1996
Grafton	1997
Sutherland	1997
Kent	2000
St Albans	2001
Portland	2002 (building)

Major Characteristics - Speed 28 kts+; Range 14,400 km at 15 knots; Displacement 3,500 tons standard; Engines - CODLAG type system with 2 x Rolls Royce Spey SM1A gas turbines delivering 18,770 shp each; For vessels after HMS Westminster (1994) 2 x Rolls Royce Spey SM1C delivering 26,150 shp each; Length 133m; Beam 16.2m; Draught 5.5m; Complement 12 officers and 157 rates; Aircraft carried - 1 x Sea Lynx with Sea Skua and Stingray torpedoes.

Designed primarily for the anti-submarine (ASW) role, and fitted with the latest radar and communications systems and towed array sonar. Air defence is provided with a vertical launch Sea Wolf system and the surface armament includes the Harpoon missile system (range 110 km) and the 114mm (4.5-inch) gun for naval gun fire support. From 1999, the Lynx helicopter was replaced on some of the vessels by the EH 101 Merlin helicopter. HMS Norfolk, the first of this class, was commissioned in 1990, the latest to be accepted into service being HMS St Albans in January 2001. One more vessel, HMS Portland remains to be commissioned.

These ships are powered by a CODLAG system (Combined diesel-electric and gas-turbine propulsion) and the diesel-electric is used for minimum underwater noise during ASW operations. This class will form the backbone of the frigate fleet in the short to medium term.

Hunt Class - Mine Counter Measures Vessels (MCMV)

	Commissioned		Commissioned
Brecon	1979	Chiddingford	1984
Ledbury	1981	Hurworth	1985
Cattistock	1982	Bicester	1986
Cottesmore	1983	Atherstone	1987
Brocklesby	1982	Quorn	1989
Middleton	1984		
Dulverton	1983		

Major Characteristics - Speed 17 knots+; Dispacement 625 tons standard; Engines 2 x Rushton Paxman Deltic 9-59K Diesels; Length 57m; Beam 10m; Draught 2.2m; Complement 6 officers and 39 rates:

The first of this advanced class of GRP-built mine countermeasures vessels, HMS Brecon, entered service in 1979, twelve are now in service, and are due a mid-life update that started in 2000. They are equipped with Remote Control Mine Disposal System (RCMDS1) and are fitted with Influence Sweeps and a 30mm gun.

Single Role Minehunter

	Commissioned		Commissioned
Sandown	1989	Grimsby	1998
Inverness	1991	Bangor	2000
Cromer	1991	Ramsey	2000
Walney	1993	Blyth	2001
Bridport	1993	Shoreham	Launched Feb 2001
Penzance	1997		
Pembroke	1997		

Major Characteristics - Speed 15 knots+; Displacement 378 tons lights; Engines 2 x Paxman Valentia 6RPA 200-EM 1500 Diesels; Range 2,600 km at 11 knots; Length 52.7m; Beam 10.5m; Draught 2.30m; Complement 5 officers and 29 rates:

HMS Sandown, the first of the new Single Role Minehunter class entered service in 1989, and HMS Blythe, the latest, entered service in January 2001. They are built of GRP, capable of operating in deep and exposed waters and complement the Hunt Class MCMVs. Sandown Class vessels are equipped with a minehunting sonar and mine disposal equipment making them capable of dealing with mines at depths of up to 200m. Each ship carries 2 x Mk2 Remote Control Mine Disposal Systems (Submersibles) capable of identifying and disposing of mines up to 300m depth. One 30mm Oerlikon gun is carried for local defence. When the final order for HMS Shoreham is completed in 2001 there will be 12 vessels of this class in service.

Fishery Protection and Offshore Patrol Vessels

Fishery protection and patrolling Britain's offshore gas and oilfield installations is carried out by the Royal Navy's Fishery Protection Squadron.

Island Class

	Commissioned
Alderney	1979
Guernsey	1977
Anglesey	1979
Lindisfarne	1978
Shetland	1977

Major Characteristics - Speed 16.5 knots+; Displacement 998 tons standard; Engines 2 x Rushton 12 RK 3CM diesels; Range 11,000 kms at 12 knots; Length 61m; Beam 11m; Draught 4.27m; Complement 5 officers and 29 rates:

Five Island Class patrol vessels form the Offshore Division (a sixth HMS Orkney was sold in 1999) which, in addition to their fishery protection tasks outside the 12-mile coastal limit, carry out regular surveillance patrols of the offshore gas and oilfield installations. The vessels are armed with 1 x 40mm Bofors AA Gun.

Castle Class

	Commissioned
Leeds Castle	1981
Dumbarton Castle	1982

Major Characteristics - Speed 20 knots; Displacement 1,350 tons standard; Engines 2 x Rushton 12 RK 320DM Diesels; Range 10,000 km at 12 knots; Length 81m; Beam 11.5m; Draught 3.42m; Complement 6 officers and 39 rates plus 25 Royal Marines as required.

The two Castle Class patrol vessels which are in service with the Offshore Division have a landing deck and fuelling facilities for the Sea King helicopter. Armament consists of 1 x 30mm Oerlikon and 2 x 7.62mm MG. One of these vessels is generally on patrol around the area of the Falkland Islands.

Survey Ships

The Royal Navy's Surveying Service has been operating throughout the world since the formation of the Hydrographic Department in 1795 and the information from oceanographic surveys is used for producing Admiralty charts and nautical publications which have a world-wide sale and are used by ships of many nations.

The Surveying Flotilla consists of ocean-going ships, coastal vessels and inshore craft. In addition to surveying in overseas areas, many of the flotilla are constantly engaged in updating the charts covering the waters around the United Kingdom.

To carry out these wide-ranging task the latest surveying techniques are employed, including digitised echo sounders, side scan sonar, automated plotting and recording of position, depth, gravity and magnetic parameters. Satellite and inertial navigation systems are used when out of range of shore-based position fixing systems.

	Commissioned	
Scott	1997	Ocean Survey
Herald	1974	Ocean Survey

Major Characteristics (HMS Herald) - Speed 14 knots+; Displacement 2,510 tons standard; Engines 3 x Paxman Ventura 12YJCZ diesels; Range 12,000 km at 11 knots; Length 79.3m; Beam 14.9m; Draught 4.0m; Complement 12 officers and 116 rates.

Major Characteristics (HMS Scott) - Speed 17 knots+; Displacement 13,500 tons at full load; Engines 2 x Krupp MaK 9M32 9-cyclinder diesels; Length 131.1m; Beam 21.5 m; Draught 9.0m; Complement 12 officers and 50 rates.

The silhouette refers to HMS Herald, an improved Hecla Class vessel.

HMS Scott was ordered in 1995 and replaced HMS Hecla in the Survey Squadron. The vessel has an ice strengthened bow and a strengthened foredeck to allow for helicopter operations. HMS Scott can also be used as an MCMV support ship.

Beagle	1968	Coastal Survey Vessels
Bulldog	1968	Coastal Survey Vessels

Major Characteristics - Speed 15 knots ; Displacement 800 tons standard; Engines 4 x Lister Blackstone ERS-8-M Diesels; Range 4,600km at 12 knots; Length 60.9m; Beam 11.43m Draught 3.6m; Complement 5 officers and 34 rates.

Roebuck	1986	Coastal Survey Vessels

Major Characteristics - Speed 15 knots ; Displacement 1,059 tons standard; Engines 4 x Mirrles ES-8 Mk 1 Diesels; Range 4,000 km at 10 knots; Length 63.8m; Beam 13m; Draught 3.65m; Complement 8 officers and 34 rates.

Gleaner	1983	Surveying Motor Vessel

Major Characteristics - Speed 14 kts ; Displacement 20 tons standard; Length 14.8m; Complement 1 officer and 4 rates.

Echo Class Survey Vessels

A contract was signed in late 2000 for two new survey vessels with a MCMV secondary support function. The first vessel (probably HMS Echo) should be launched in 2002 and the second (probably HMS Enterprise) in early 2003. A third vessel may be ordered in 2001.

Ice Patrol Ship

Major Characteristics - Speed 12 knots; Displacement 6,500 tons standard; Engines 2 x Ulstein Bergen BRM-8 Diesels; Range 5,000 km at 12 knots; Length 91m; Beam 17.9m; Draught 6.5m; Complement 15 officers and 97 rates and 15 Royal Marines.

In service with the Royal Navy since 1991, HMS Endurance (previously MV Polar Circle) supports British interests in the South Atlantic and Antarctic waters, working alongside members of the British Antarctic Survey Team, carrying out hydrographic surveying, meteorological work and research programmes. It has a flight deck and hangar for Lynx helicopters. The hull is painted red for easy recognition in the ice.

Training Ships

Major Characteristics - Speed 22.5 knots ; Displacement 44 tons standard; Engines Perkins CVM 800T Diesels; Range 500km at 15 knots; Length 20.8m; Beam 5.8m; Draught 1.8m; Complement 11-15 total; Armament 1 x 20mm AA Gun and 2 x 7.62mm MG (Ranger and Trumpeter only).

	Commissioned		Commisssioned
Archer	1985	Puncher	1988
Biter	1985	Charger	1988
Smiter	1985	Ranger	1988
Pursuer	1985	Trumpeter	1988
Blazer	1988	Example	1985
Dasher	1988	Explorer	1985
Exploit	1988	Express	1988
Tracker	1998	Raider	1998

Sixteen Fast Training vessels are in service with the Inshore Training Squadron (ITS) based at Rosyth. The Archer and Example Class supported by the Fleet Tenders Loyal Watcher and Loyal Chancellor are mainly used as University Training Ships. HMS Ranger and Trumpeter are used as Gibraltar Search and Rescue Craft.

The final vessels of the class HMS Tracker and HMS Raider were delivered in 1998 and are used by the Oxford and Cambridge University Officer Training Units.

Royal Fleet Auxiliary Service

The Royal Navy describes the Royal Fleet Auxiliary Service as "The specialist front-line support force for the Royal Navy that replenishes warships at sea with fuel, stores and weapons. The service is unique in that all the Royal Navy's major Auxiliaries are civilian manned. The RFA service is part of the Royal Naval Supply and Transport Service and employs some 2,500 officers and ratings, who follow the traditional paths of the Merchant Navy to obtain their basic qualifications, with a substantial overlay of Royal Naval training to develop the skills needed in an operational environment. The 22 ships of the Fleet include both large and small Fleet tankers, Support tankers, Landing ships Logistic, an Aviation Training Ship, Replenishment Ships and a Forward Repair ship. Since it was formed in 1905, the RFA service has pioneered and perfected the art of Replenishment at Sea (RAS). RFA vessels are now fitted with close range small-calibre self-defence weapons and decoys which are manned and maintained by RFA personnel".

Fleet Tankers

	In-Service
Olwen	1965
Olna	1966
Grey Rover	1970
Gold Rover	1974
Black Rover	1974

RFAs Olwen and Olna are purpose-built fast Fleet Tankers capable of supporting Naval task groups in the front line with fuel, lubricants and a limited range of stores. The ability of each of these vessels is further enhanced by the provisions of facilities to embark and operate the Royal Navy's ASW Sea King and Lynx helicopters. Both ships are capable of speeds of up to 20 knots carrying 18,000 tons of fuel oil, 1,720 tons of diesel, 3,730 tons of aircraft fuel and 130 tons of lube oil.

There are also three smaller fleet tankers of the Rover Class. These relatively fast and highly manoeuvrable vessels are able to replenish warships with fuel and a limited amount of dry cargo and refrigerated stores. Although they do not normally carry their own helicopter, they are fitted with a flight deck, but no hangar, and are capable of providing a forward operating base for deploying helicopters if they require fuel. Rover Class tankers can carry 7,460 cubic metres of fuel; 326 cubic metres of water; 70 cubic metres of lube oil and 600 cubic metres of aviation fuel or gasoline at a sustained speed of 17 knots.

Support Tankers

	In Service
Brambleleaf	1980
Orangeleaf	1982
Bayleaf	1982
Oakleaf	1981

In general the Royal Navy's Support Tankers have the duel role of replenishing warships and fleet tankers at sea and the bulk movement of fuels between naval supply depots. Expect RFA Oakleaf to be able to carry 43,020 cubic metres of fuel in 16 tanks and the remaining three (Appleleaf

Class) tankers approximately 35,000 cubic metres of fuel in 24 tanks. RFA Oakleaf has a crew of 36 and the other three vessels about 65 in total.

Fleet Replenishment Ships

	In Service
Fort Rosalie	1978
Fort Austin	1979
Fort George	1993
Fort Victoria	1994

These vessels are ammunition, food and stores ships capable of operating up to 5 x Sea King helicopters with full maintenance facilities onboard. Fort Victoria and Fort Geogre displace 22,749 tons and are capable of carrying about 12,000 cubic metres in four holds, including 2,300 cubic metres of refrigerated stores. Both of these ships have a crew of 127 RFA personnel, 36 civilian staff and 45 Royal Naval personnel.

Aviation Training Ship

	In Service
RFA Argus	1981

RFA Argus was launched in 1981 and was formerly the container ship MV Contender Bezant. In 1982 the vessel was used as an aircraft transport during the Falklands War and was purchased by the Royal Navy during 1984. The ship operates Lynx and Sea King helicopters and transports Sea Harriers. RFA Argus is managed and operated by the RFA Service but there is a sizeable Royal Naval Aviation Group embarked. In 1991 during the Gulf War, RFA Argus was used as a Primary Casualty Receiving Ship. The complement is generally about 80 x RFA personnel, 30 x permanent RN personnel and a training group of some 130 RN personnel. In an emergency, the ship could probably carry up to 700 troops.

Forward Repair Ship

	In Service
RFA Diligence	1981

Launched in 1981 and named the Stena Inspector, the ship was originally chartered during the Falklands War and taken into Royal Naval Service as RFA Diligence during 1984. RFA Diligence is a general repair and maintenance ship and capable of providing specialised maintenance support across the fleet. The vessel is particularly useful when Task Forces are operating far from home bases and, in the past, has provided particularly valuable support especially in the Gulf during 1991 and alongside in Split (Croatia) during the latter part of the 1990s.

Ro-Ro General Cargo Ship

	In Service
Sea Crusader	1966
Sea Centurion	1998

Sea Crusader entered service in 1996 as a Ro-Ro general cargo vessel having been built to commercial specifications. The vessel is available for use by the Joint Rapid Reaction Force plus general freight duties and there is a requirement for a second vessel (Sea Chieftain). Sea Crusader has 2,300 lane metres of space and a stern ramp capacity of 150 tons. With a complement of 17 and 161 metres in length the vessel is not equipped to enter a war zone.

Sea Centurion was leased from Stena in January 1998 and is available for Joint Rapid Deployment Force (JRDF) operations and has over 2,700 lane metres of vehicle space. Probably six more of these vessels are available for leasing if required.

Landing Ships Logistic

Sir Geraint	1967
Sir Bedivere	1966
Sir Percivale	1967
Sir Tristram	1966 (rebuilt 1985)
Sir Galahad	1988

The five LSLs in service with the RFA are capable of carrying approximately 400 troops and there is a beaching cargo capacity of 3,440 tons. Heavy stores and equipment are carried, including armoured vehicles, and the ships are fitted with bow and stern loading doors and ramps. They are capable of beach landings and the operation of helicopters. During the Falklands Campaign two LSLs sustained heavy damage. RFA Sir Tristram was subsequently redesigned, rebuilt and re-entered service in late 1985. RFA Sir Galahad was later sunk and designated an official War Grave, with a new RFA Sir Galahad entering service in 1988.

Royal Maritime Auxiliary Service (RMAS)

The Royal Maritime Auxiliary Service (RMAS) provides the Royal Navy with the wide variety of waterborne services needed at naval bases. Marine Services has taken its present shape during the past 30 years by combining the areas formerly managed by Captains of Dockyards, senior victualling, armament supply, and naval stores officers. This was followed by the amalgamation in 1975 of the separate Marine Services such as ocean tugs, Admiralty cable ships, trials vessels, and the Mooring and Salvage service into the present organisation.

The RMAS operates about 400 vessels and lighters and is a unified service manned by a civilian staff of some 425 officers and 1,250 junior staff. Tasks include the provision of tugs and pilots for harbour movements, ocean and coastal towing; moorings, salvage and diving operations, the transport of personnel, fuel, water, stores and ammunition; torpedo recovery, degaussing, Fleet trials support, tank cleaning, pollution control, and marine range safety duties.

RMAS vessels are allocated to the UK Naval bases at Portsmouth, Devonport, Rosyth, Portland, the Clyde, Pembroke Dock, Kyle of Lochalsh and Gibraltar. RMAS vessels are easily recognised by their buff-coloured funnels and superstructure and their black hulls, which have an all-round white riband at deck level. They fly the blue ensign, which is defaced in the fly by a yellow anchor above two yellow wavy lines.

Support operations are carried out mainly in UK waters with occasional overseas deployments ranging from the Mediterranean to the Falklands.

Fleet Air Arm

The Fleet Air Arm provides the air support for the Royal Navy and the Royal Marines. Harrier Squadrons are available for embarkation on the three carriers HMS Ark Royal, HMS Illustrious and HMS Invincible, as are detachments of the airborne early warning and anti-submarine Sea King helicopter squadrons. The majority of RN ships of the destroyer/frigate type have their own anti-submarine/anti-ship Lynx aircraft that also serve a vital fleet communications role. Whilst not strictly part of the Fleet Air Arm, the Royal Marines 3 Cdo Bde Air Sqn is a Royal Naval organisation that provides communications and anti-tank helicopter support for Commando forces operating ashore.

On 1 April 2000 the Sea Harrier FA.2 squadrons previously under Royal Naval command became part of the new Joint Force Harrier (JFH) within No 3 Group, RAF Strike Command. This new formation is commanded by Rear Admiral Iain Henderson, who was previously Flag Officer Naval Aviation (FONA). At the same time Admiral Henderson became Air Officer Commanding No 3 Group which operates JFH aircraft plus RAF Nimrods and Sea King (SAR) helicopters. This is the first time that an officer from the Royal Navy has commanded an RAF air formation.

The JFH which combines RN Sea Harriers and RAF Harriers will enhance the Maritime Contribution to Joint Operations. In the future, aircraft embarked on Royal Navy vessels will come from the JFH and will form part of a Tailored Air Group (TAG) that has been specially configured for the mission. A typical TAG might consist of 6 x Sea Harrier FA. 2s (for air defence), 6 x Harrier GR.7s (for ground attack), 4 x Sea King AEW.2 and/or AEW.7 helicopters plus 2 x Sea King HAS.6 helicopters (for anti submarine operations). Other Sea King HAS.6 could be embarked on accompanying vessels.

In 2003 RAF and RN squadrons will be co-located at RAF Cottesmore and the Harrier training unit at RAF Wittering. The Royal Naval Squadrons will still be linked to specific aircraft carriers and the RAF's Harrier squadrons will be attached in rotation to form Joint Air Wings.

The Harrier is likely to be replaced in 2012 and the current front runner is the US/UK short take off and landing (STOL) version of the Joint Strike Fighter (JSF).

The overall current Fleet Air Arm basic structure is as follows:
The majority of 815 Squadron's aircraft are at sea on board RN Frigates/Destroyers. Of the squadron total - about 25-30 aircraft are probably assigned to ships at any one time.

Air Defence/Recce/Attack

800 Sqn	801 Sqn	899 Sqn
Yeovilton	Yeovilton	Yeovilton
7 x Sea Harrier	7 x Sea Harrier	10 x Sea Harrier FRS1, F/A2
FRS1, F/A2	FRS1, F/A2	4 x Harrier T4/T8

Air Defence/Recce/Attack

815 Sqn	702 Sqn
Portland	Portland
Approx 36 x Lynx	12 x Lynx
HAS 2/3, HMA 8	HAS 2/3, HMA 8

Aircraft in these squadrons are often deployed in flights of single or multiple aircraft.

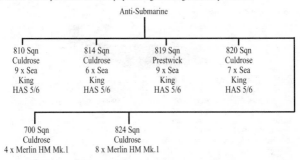

Anti-Submarine

810 Sqn	814 Sqn	819 Sqn	820 Sqn
Culdrose	Culdrose	Prestwick	Culdrose
9 x Sea King	6 x Sea King	9 x Sea King	7 x Sea King
HAS 5/6	HAS 5/6	HAS 5/6	HAS 5/6

700 Sqn	824 Sqn
Culdrose	Culdrose
4 x Merlin HM Mk.1	8 x Merlin HM Mk.1

Note: The Commando Helicopter Force (CHF) was absorbed into the Joint Helicopter Command (JHC) in October 1999. Details of the JHC are given in the Royal Air Force section.

Commando Air Assault

845 Sqn	846 Sqn	848 Sqn
Yeovilton	Yeovilton	Yeovilton
10 x Sea King	10 x Sea King	Training/Special Tasks
HC4	HC4	9 x Sea King HC4

In addition to the above the Fleet Air Arm has the following:-

Airborne Early Warning	849 Sqn	Culdrose	9 x Sea King AEW2
Fleet Support & SAR	771 Sqn	Culdrose	5 x Sea King Mk5
3 Cdo Bde	847 Sqn	Yeovilton	9 x Gazelle & 6 x Lynx AH7
Aircrew Training	750 Sqn	Culdrose	9 x Jetstream T2/3

Sea Harrier
In Service With:

800 Sqn	7 x Sea Harrier F/A2	RNAS Yeovilton
801 Sqn	7 x Sea Harrier F/A2	RNAS Yeovilton
899 Sqn	10 x Sea Harrier F/A2	RNAS Yeovilton
	4 x Sea Harrier Mk 2/T8	RNAS Yeovilton

F/A2 (FRS2) Crew 1; Length overall 14.17m; Wingspan 7.70m; Height 3.71m; Max level speed 1,185 km h (736mph) at low level; Max take-off Weight approx 11,880 kg (26,200lbs); Armament - Able to carry bombs, rockets, guns, missiles and flares attached to 4 x wing weapon pylons and 1 x underfuselage weapon pylon; Engine 1 x Rolls-Royce Pegasus Mk 2 vectored thrust turbofan; Ferry attack radius 463 kms (288 miles).

In service with the Royal Navy since 1979, the Sea Harrier has been improved and updated to cope with the technological changes that the changing threat has posed. The aircraft remains the most advanced ship-borne Short Take Off and Vertical Landing (STOVL) aircraft in the world.

The aircraft has a maritime fighter/reconnaissance/strike role and proved itself as an effective, flexible and reliable aircraft in the Falklands campaign, where 29 aircraft flew over 2,300 sorties and destroyed 22 enemy aircraft in air-to-air combat without loss. The original version in Royal Naval Service was the FRS1 with the newer F/A2 (FRS2) variant entering service in 1994. The FRS2 differs from the earlier model in that it has a Blue Vixen look-down/shoot -down radar combined with the fire and forget Advanced Medium Range Air-to-Air Missile (AMRAAM) which allows the aircraft to engage targets beyond visual range. In addition, the Sea Eagle (anti-ship missile) and laser-guided bombs can be carried.

The STOVL capability of the Sea Harrier enables the aircraft to operate from the flight deck of an aircraft carrier without the use of catapult-assisted take-off and arrester-wire equipment. "Ski-jump" launching ramps that improve the aircraft's take-off performance are fitted to all three of the Royal Navy's aircraft carriers.

Since 1998, 18 x new F/A2 aircraft have entered service and 31 of the remaining aircraft have received their mid-life update to bring them up to the F/A2 standard. The T4 is a two-seat trainer version of the Harrier.

Expect a Sea Harrier Squadron to have 9 established crews.

Sea King
In Service With:

810 Sqn	Sea King HAS 5/6	9
814 Sqn	Sea King HAS 5/6	6
819 Sqn	Sea King HAS 5/6	9

820 Sqn	Sea King HAS 5/6	7
849 Sqn	Sea King AEW 2	9
845 Sqn	Sea King HC4	10
846 Sqn	Sea King HC4	10
848 Sqn	Sea King HC4	9
771 Sqn	Sea King Mk5 HAS	5

HAS Mk 5/6: Crew 2 on flight deck and two in cabin; Fuselage length 17.01m; Width 3.78m; Height 4.72m; Weight (empty) 6201kg; Max take-off weight 9525 kg; Rotor diameter 18.9m; Cruising speed 208 km h (129mph) at sea level; service ceiling 1,220m; Mission Radius (with 2 hours on station and carrying 3 x torpedoes) 231 kms (144 miles); Engines 2 x Rolls Royce Gnome H.1400 1T turboshafts mounted side by side above the cabin; Armament such as 7.62mm MG or 40mm grenade launchers can be fitted where appropriate.

The Westland Sea King is a licence built version of the US Sikorsky S-61 and the Royal Navy's HAS Mark 1 aircraft's first flight was in 1969. Since that time, the aircraft has been extensively upgraded and passed through a series of Marks.

The current situation is that the Royal Navy operates the HAS Mk 5/6 in the anti submarine role. The aircraft can remain on station for long periods up to 100 miles from the ship and can search for submarine targets using either its own sonar-bouys or those dropped by maritime patrol aircraft such as Nimrods. Targets that have been located are then attacked with torpedoes or depth charges.

The AEW 2 is used for airborne early warning and is a Sea King HAS Mark 2 fitted with a Thorn EMI Search Water radar carried in a radardome that can be swivelled down underneath the aircraft for operational searches. A detachment of three AEW 2 aircraft generally deploys with each aircraft carrier.

The Sea King HC4 (Commando) is a tactical military helicopter capable of transporting 28 fully equipped troops or 6,000 lbs (2,720 kg) as an internal load. Carrying 28 troops the aircraft has a range of about 246 miles (396 km). The first HC4 deliveries were made to the Royal Navy in 1979.

The Mk 5 aircraft in service with 771 Sqn are SAR aircraft (Search & Rescue). RN SAR aircraft are stationed at Prestwick, Culdrose and Portland.

Lynx

In Service With:

815 Sqn	Lynx HAS 3, HMA 8	36
702 Sqn	Lynx HAS 3, HMA 8	12
847 Sqn	Lynx AH 7	6

Crew - 2 on the flight-deck and up to 2 mission crew in the fuselage; Length Fuselage 11.92m:

Height 3.2m: Rotor diameter 12.8m: Max speed 144mph (232km h) at sea level: Ferry range 1,046 km (650 miles) with max internal and external fuel tanks; Engines 2 Rolls-Royce Gem Mk 42 Turboshafts; Weight (max take-off) 4,876kg (10,750lbs).

Lynx aircraft are at sea with all frigates and destroyers to provide anti-surface surveillance and anti-submarine warfare (ASW) capabilities. With the introduction into service of the first of the upgraded 44 x HAS 3, HMA 8 aircraft in late 1994 the Lynx in Royal Naval service has been turned from an anti-submarine helicopter into a dedicated maritime attack aircraft. Capable of carrying anti-submarine torpedoes (range 10km) and anti-ship Sea Skua missiles (range 20km) the HMA 8 is capable of integrating its navigational, communications and fighting systems through a 1553B databus.

Typical combat mission profiles in the anti-submarine role could be a patrol out to 60 miles, a two hour loiter in the search area carrying torpedoes and smoke markers etc and return.

EH 101 Merlin HAS Mk1
In Service With:

700 Sqn	Merlin Mk 1	4
824 Sqn	Merlin Mk 1	8

Service ceiling 4,572 m; Range 550 n miles (1,019 km); Sensors; GEC-Marconi Blue Kestrel 5000 radar, Thomson Marconi Flash AQS 960 dipping sonar, GEC-Marconi sonobuoy acoustic processor AQS-903, Racal Orange Reaper ESM; Weapons: ASW - 4 x Stingray torpedoes or Mk 11 Mod 3 depth bombs plus anti-ship missiles.

The Royal Navy has 44 x EH 101 Merlin ASW helicopters on order in a contract worth £1.5 billion. The "in service date" was 1998 and by the early part of the next decade the Merlin should have replaced the ASW Sea Kings and some of the ASW Lynx in Royal Naval service. Extensive sea trials were held on HMS Iron Duke in 1993 and the first production aircraft came off the production line in 1996.

Plans are for 824 Sqn to become the first operational squadron in October 2001 (probably assigned to HMS Ark Royal). This will be followed by the commissioning of 829 Sqn that will parent the ship's flights on Type 23 frigates. At the same time 829 Sqn will become the second aircraft carrier squadron. A carrier squadron will normally consist of 6 aircraft.

<u>**Royal Naval Missiles**</u>

Exocet MM38
Length 5.21m; Diameter 0.45m; Total weight 750 kgs; Range 45 kms.

Exocet MM38 is a medium range surface launched anti-ship missile and is carried in the Type 22 Batch 2 frigates. The guidance system is active radar terminal homing.

Sea Wolf
Length 1.91m; Diameter 0.18m; Total weight 79.8 kgs; Range 6/7,000m; Altitude 3/4000m.

Sea Wolf is a ship-based, surface-to-air missile designed for the defence of point targets. This is a highly efficient system thought to be capable of dealing with aircraft, missiles and even artillery rounds. The guidance system is semi-automatic command to line of sight with radar and/or infra-red missile and target tracking.

Sea Skua
Length 2.85m; Diameter 0.22m; Total weight 147 kg; Range 20km approx.

Sea Skua is a short-range, anti-ship missile that has been in Royal Naval service since 1982. The missile is currently carried as the main armament of the Lynx aircraft flying from RN destroyers/frigates. The guidance system is semi-active terminal homing.

Sea Dart
Length 4.40m; Diameter 0.42m; Total weight 549 kg; Range 80km+ approx.

Sea Dart is a surface-to-air missile system with a long range (probably in excess of 80kms) and employs a two-stage system with a primary booster rocket powering the warhead and ramjet on their way to the target. There is a limited surface-to-surface capability out to a range of about 28km and the guidance system is a semi-active homing radar.

Harpoon

Length 3.84m: Diameter 0.343m: Total weight 526kg: Warhead weight 225kg: Range 110kms.

Harpoon, manufactured by McDonnell-Douglas of the USA, is an extremely powerful anti-shipping missile that is fitted to the Type 22 and Type 23 Frigates. The Sub Harpoon (UGM-84A) is fitted to the Trafalgar and Swiftsure Class submarines. The latest versions of this missile have extremely sophisticated electronic counter measures (ECM), and the ability to fly a sea-skimming course on a dog-leg path through three pre-programmed way points. The warhead is extremely powerful and a hit from Harpoon is almost certain to result in the destruction or disablement of a major surface vessel.

Other Missiles

Missiles in Royal Naval Service such as: AMRAAM, Sea Eagle and Sidewinder are also in RAF service and the relevant entries are in the RAF Section (Part 4).

The Royal Marines

Although the Royal Marines (RM) are part of the Royal Navy, they are trained and equipped for warfare or operations on land, and because of their role it is very likely that they could be involved in operations and exercises with allied marine and army units. The Royal Marines number approximately 500 officers and 5,400 men and, until recently, the primary task for the bulk of the Corps was the reinforcement of Norway and NATO's Northern Flank, should a threat develop in that area. Events have moved on since the end of the Cold War, and of late, the Corps appears to have reverted to its tradition role of being ready for operations anywhere in the world. In 2000 the Royal Marines were in the forefront of the UK's contribution to the operation in Sierra Leone.

The Royal Marines also have detachments on 12 ships at sea and a number of smaller units worldwide with widely differing tasks. However, the bulk of the manpower of the Royal Marines is grouped in battalion-sized organisations known as Commandos (Cdo). There are 3 Commando Groups and they are part of a larger formation known as 3 Commando Brigade (3 Cdo Bde).

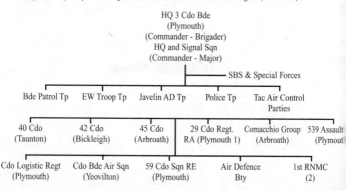

Note:
(1) 29 Cdo Regt RA has one battery stationed at Arbroath with 45 Cdo.
(2) 1st Bn The Royal Netherlands Marine Corps is part of 3 Cdo Bde for NATO assigned tasks.
(3) The air defence troop is equipped with Rapier.
(4) There are three regular Tactical Air Control Parties and one reserve.
(5) 539 Assault Sqn has hovercraft, landing craft and raiding craft.
Note: A troop (Tp) equates to an army platoon. Each rifle company has three troops. A Royal
Marine rifle company is generally commanded by a Captain RM.

Royal Marine Listing

Headquarters Royal Marines	Portsmouth
HQ 3 Commando Brigade	Plymouth (Stonehouse)
3 Commando Bde HQ & Signal Sqn	Plymouth (Stonehouse)
3 Commando Bde Air Sqn RNAS	Yeovilton
40 Commando	Taunton
42 Commando	Plymouth (Bickleigh)
45 Commando	Arbroath (Condor)
Commando Logistic Regiment	Plymouth (Marsh Mills)
539 Assault Sqn	Plymouth (Turnchapel)
Comacchio Group	Arbroath (Condor)
Commando Training Centre	Lympstone
Royal Marines Stonehouse	Plymouth
Royal Marines Poole	Poole
Amphibious Training & Trials Unit	Bideford

There are Royal Marine Reserve Units in London, Bristol, Birkenhead, Glasgow and Newcastle
Upon Tyne that form 'T' Company of the Royal Marine Reserve (RMR).

Army Commando Reserve units are:
289 Commando Battery RA (Volunteers)
131 Independent Squadron RE (Volunteers)

Special Boat Service (SBS)
This organisation is the Naval equivalent of the Army's SAS (Special Air Service). Personnel are all volunteers from the mainstream Royal Marines and vacancies are few with competition for entry fierce. Generally speaking only about 30% of volunteers manage to complete the entry course and qualify. The SBS specialises in mounting clandestine operations against targets at sea, in rivers or harbours and against occupied coastlines.

Comacchio Company
This specialist company was formed in 1980, and has the task of guarding the UK's oil rigs and other associated installations from a variety of threats - in particular terrorist attacks.

CHAPTER 3 - THE BRITISH ARMY

British Army Major Units

(at 1 Jan 2001)	Germany	UK	Elsewhere	TA
Armoured Regts	5	2	-	-
Armoured Recce Regts	1	2	-	-
Yeomanry Regts	-	-	-	4
Armoured Infantry Bns	6	2	-	-
Mechanised Bns	-	6	-	-
Air Assault Bns	-	3(1)	-	-
Parachute Bns	-	3	-	2
Light Role Bns	-	13	15	-
Northern Ireland Resident Bns	-	6(2)	-	-
Gurkha Bns	-	1	1	-
Land Warfare Bn	-	1(3)	-	-
Home Service Regts	-	6	1(4)	-
SAS Regts	-	1	-	2
Army Air Corps Regts	1	4	-	1
Artillery Field Regts	3	6	-	2
Air Defence Regts	1	3	-	4
Commando Regt	-	1	-	-
Surveillance & Target Acquisition	-	1	-	-
HAC	-	-	-	1
Engineer Regts	4	7	-	5
Signals Regts	3	5	1	11
EW Regt	-	1	-	-
Equipment Support Bns	3	3	-	4
Equipment Support Bn (Aviation)	-	1	-	-
Logistic Regts	5	15	2	7
Medical Regts	1	4	-	-
Field Ambulances	-	-	-	4
Hospitals	-	3	-	11

(1) Includes two in-role parachute battalions.
(2) Includes one battalion stationed in either England or Scotland designated as the Province reserve.
(3) This battalion provides the Land Warfare training battlegroup at the Combined Arms Training Centre (Warminster).
(4) Royal Irish and Royal Gibraltar Regiment

Personnel

The personnel strength of the British Army on 1 October 2000 was:

	Trained	Untrained	Total
Officers	12,800	1,100	13,900
Other Ranks	83,700	12,500	96,200
	96,500	**13,600**	**110,100**

Note: The above figures do not include 2,974 x Gurkhas, 351 x Royal Gibraltar Regiment and personnel of the Royal Irish Regiment (Home Service).

British Army Equipment Summary

Armour: 410 x Challenger 1 - 386 Challenger 2 on order (probably 189 in service on 1 Jan 2001); 139 x Sabre (approx); 88 x Striker; 332 x Scimitar; 748 x Fv 432; 726 x MCV 80 Warrior; 103 x Spartan; 610 x Saxon; 11 x Fuchs NBC recce vehicles.

Artillery: 179 x AS 90; 63 x 227mm MLRS ; 44 x FH 70; 165 x 105mm Light Gun; 540 x 81mm Mortar (including 112 SP); 2,093 x 51mm Light Mortar.

Air Defence: 40 x Rapier Fire Units; 374 x Javelin Launchers; 147 x Starstreak HVM SP.

Army Aviation: 110 x Lynx (some armed with TOW); 144 Gazelle; 7 x BN-2; 67 x Apache on order; Helicopters available from RAF - 31 x Chinook; 33 x Puma.

The Army Board

The routine management of the Army is the responsibility of The Army Board, the composition of which is as follows:

The Secretary of State for Defence
Minister of State (Armed Forces)
Minister of State (Defence Procurement)
Parliamentary Under-Secretary of State for the Armed Forces
Chief of the General Staff
Second Permanent Under-Secretary of State
Adjutant General
Quartermaster General
Master General of the Ordnance
Commander in Chief (Land Command)
Commander UK Support Command (Germany)
Assistant Chief of the General Staff

Decisions made by The Defence Council or the Army Board are acted upon by the military staff at the various headquarters worldwide. The Chief of the General Staff is the officer responsible for the Army's contribution to the national defence effort and he maintains control through the commander and the staff branches of each of these headquarters.

General Walker

Chief of The General Staff (1 Jan 2001)

General Sir Michael Walker KCB CMG CBE ADC Gen

General Sir Michael Walker was born on 7 July 1944 in Salisbury, Southern Rhodesia. He was educated partly in Rhodesia and partly in Yorkshire. On leaving school he taught at a preparatory school for 18 months before attending the Royal Military Academy, Sandhurst. He was commissioned into the Royal Anglian Regiment in 1966 and served with the 1st Battalion as a platoon commander in Celle and Catterick. In 1969 he was posted to Cyprus as an ADC to the GOC Near East Land Forces. He returned to his battalion in 1971 and during the course of the next five years served in Northern Ireland, Cyprus and Tidworth variously as Operations Officer, Regimental Signals Officer and Adjutant. In 1975 he was posted to the Ministry of Defence as a Staff Officer.

He attended the Army Staff Course at Shrivenham and Camberley, returning to his battalion in Tidworth as a Company Commander. At the end of 1979 he was posted back to the Ministry of Defence to the Directorate of Military Operations. On promotion to Lieutenant Colonel he was appointed Military Assistant to the CGS from 1982 to 1985. He then commanded his battalion in Londonderry and Gibraltar. He commanded 20 Armoured Brigade in Detmold from December 1987 and after three years in command was appointed Chief of Staff 1 (British Corps) in Bielefeld (Germany). General Walker assumed the appointment of GOC North East District and Command 2 Infantry Division on 30 September 1991 and then GOC Eastern District on 1 April 1992. In December 1992 he returned to the Ministry of Defence as Assistant Chief of the General Staff.

In December 1994, as a Lieutenant General, he assumed command of the ARRC in Rheindahlen, Germany, and deployed with HQ ARRC to Bosnia Herzegovina from December 1995 to November 1996 to command the multinational land component of IFOR. On relinquishing command of the ARRC he became the Commander-in-Chief Land Command, based at Wilton in Wiltshire and became Chief of the General Staff on 14 April 2000.

Chain of Command

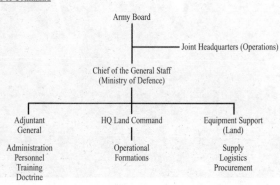

Army Board

Joint Headquarters (Operations)

Chief of the General Staff
(Ministry of Defence)

Adjutant
General

HQ Land Command

Equipment Support
(Land)

Administration
Personnel
Training
Doctrine

Operational
Formations

Supply
Logistics
Procurement

The Army is controlled from the MoD via the above three subsidiary headquarters and a number of smaller headquarters worldwide. The diagram illustrates this chain of command as at 1 Jan 2001.

Operations in Northern Ireland are controlled directly from the MoD.

HQ Land Command

Following the MoD's "Front Line First" study, plans were drawn up to reorganise HQ United Kingdom Land Forces (HQ UKLF) in a new formation designated HQ Land Command that became operational on 1 April 1995. HQ Land Command is located at Erskine Barracks, Wilton near Salisbury and controls about 75% of the troops in the British Isles and almost 100% of its fighting capability.

Land Command's role is to deliver and sustain the Army's operational capability, whenever required throughout the world, and the Command comprises all operational troops in Great Britain, Germany, Nepal and Brunei, together with the Army Training Teams in Canada, Belize and Kenya.

Land Command has almost 70,000 trained Army personnel - the largest single Top Level Budget in Defence, with a budget of over £3 billion. It contains all the Army's fighting equipment, including attack helicopters, Challenger 2 tanks, Warrior Infantry Fighting Vehicles, AS90 and the Multi-Launched Rocket System (MLRS).

Land Command is one of the three central commands in the British Army, the other two being the Adjutant General (with responsibility for administration, personnel and training) and Equipment Support (Land) responsible for supply and logistics. The Command is responsible for providing all the Army's fighting troops throughout the world. These are organised into eight formations and are commanded by Major Generals.

The Structure of Land Command

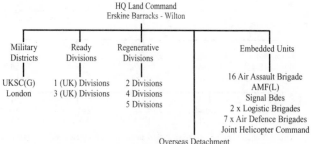

Note: Overseas Detachments include Belize, Canada, Brunei, Nepal and Kenya. Garrisons in Cyprus and the Falkland Islands are commanded from the MoD via PJHQ.

Ready Divisions

There are two "Ready" Divisions: the 1st (UK) Armoured Division, based in Germany, and the 3rd (UK) Division in the United Kingdom. Both these divisions are earmarked to form part of the Allied Command Europe Rapid Reaction Corps (ARRC), NATO's premier strategic formation; but they also have the flexibility to be employed on rapid reaction tasks or in support of other Defence Roles.

In addition to their operational roles, they also command the Army units in specified geographic areas: in the case of the 1st Division, this area is made up of the garrisons in Germany where the Division's units are based; and in the case of the 3rd Division, the South West of England.

Composition of 1(UK) Armoured Division

1 (UK) Armoured Division has its headquarters at Herford in Germany (about 50 kms from Hanover) and the three Armoured Brigades under command are located at Osnabruck, Bergen-Hohne and Paderborn. The divisional personnel strength is 1,300 officers and 15,800 other ranks. 1 January 2001 equipment totals are as follows:

> 152 x Challenger MBT
> 434 x Warrior Armoured Fighting Vehicles
> 1,079 x Armoured Personnel Carriers
> 96 x 155 mm AS 90
> 18 x Armoured Vehicle Launched Bridges
> 35 x Helicopters

Divisional Structure

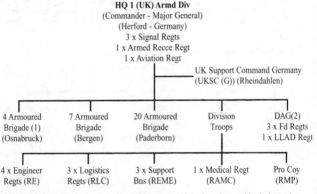

Note: (1) Current plans appear to be for all three armoured brigades to have an identical organisation. (2) DAG (Divisional Artillery Group) This DAG could be reinforced by Rapier Air Defence and MLRS units from the UK as necessary. This Division could provide the Headquarters (HQs) for 9 x Battlegroups.

1 (UK) Armoured Division - Armoured Brigade Organisation (From mid 2001)

The following diagram illustrates the possible composition of an Armoured Brigade in 1(UK) Armd Div on operations.

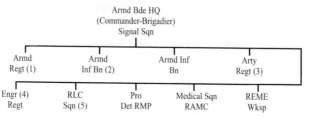

Totals: 58 x Challenger MBT (possibly)
       104 x Warrior AIFV
       350 x Armoured Personel Carriers
       32 x AS 90 SP Gun
       Approx 4,500 personnel

Notes: (1) Armoured Regiment with approx 50 x Challenger MBT; (2) Armoured Inf Battalion with approx 52 x Warrior and approx 40 x FV432; (3) Artillery Regiment with 32 x AS90 SP Guns; (4) Engineer Regiment with an HQ Sqn, Armd Engr Sqn, Mechanised Field Sqn and possibly additional resources dependent upon task; (5) Brigade Support Squadron RLC with approximately 60 -70 x trucks; (6) Depending upon task the Brigade could expect to be reinforced with Medium Reconnaissance, Aviation and Air Defence Units. This Brigade could provide the HQs for 3 Battlegroups.

The 1998 SDR stated that in the future 3 of the 6 armoured regiments in 1 (UK) Division during 1998 will be returned to the UK. As a result there are now 3 armoured regiments in 1(UK) Division (one with each brigade). Each of these regiments will have 58 x MBT and 600 personnel, but will hold 30 x MBT for peacetime training. These arrangements will be complete by mid 2001.

UKSC(G) - The United Kingdom Support Command (Germany) has responsibility for British Army troops on the Continent of Europe that are not part of 1(UK) Armoured Division. Its headquarters replaces that of the British Army of the Rhine, whose sign it has adopted. The new headquarters is located at Rheindahlen and has 500 personnel under command.

Composition of 3 (UK) Division

Following plans for the reorganisation of NATO Forces on the Central Front during 1992, the HQ of the 3rd (UK) Armoured Division moved from its old location at Soest in Germany to Bulford in Wiltshire, where it became 3 (UK) Division part of the NATO ARRC (Allied Rapid Reaction Corps). In the event of hostilities, it will move to the ARRC area of operations on the European mainland or worldwide as necessary.

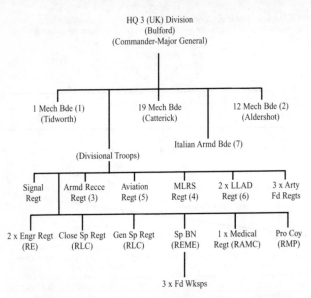

HQ 3 (UK) Division
(Bulford)
(Commander-Major General)

1 Mech Bde (1)
(Tidworth)

19 Mech Bde
(Catterick)

12 Mech Bde (2)
(Aldershot)

Italian Armd Bde (7)

(Divisional Troops)

Signal Regt

Armd Recce Regt (3)

Aviation Regt (5)

MLRS Regt (4)

2 x LLAD Regt (6)

3 x Arty Fd Regts

2 x Engr Regt (RE)

Close Sp Regt (RLC)

Gen Sp Regt (RLC)

Sp BN (REME)

1 x Medical Regt (RAMC)

Pro Coy (RMP)

3 x Fd Wksps

Note: (1) 1 Mechanised Brigade; (2) 12 Mech Bde has replaced 5 Airborne Brigade which has been redesignated as 16 Air Assault Brigade and moved to Colchester; (3) Armoured Reconnaissance Regiment; (4) Artillery Regiment with Multi-Launch Rocket System; (5) Army Air Corps Regiment with Lynx & Gazelle; (6) Air Defence Regiments with Rapier and Javelin/Starstreak missiles; (7) Under Allied Rapid Reaction Corps framework agreements this division could be reinforced by an Italian Armoured Brigade (Ariete).

3 Commando Brigade, a Royal Naval formation, is available to support 3(UK) Div if necessary. Details of the organisation of 3 Cdo Bde are given in Chapter 2 (Royal Navy). 3 Cdo Bde is not under the command of 3 (UK) Div.

During operations 3 (UK) Div equipment totals (excluding 3 Cdo Bde) could resemble the following (as at 1 Jan 2001).

Main Battle Tanks (MBT) - Approx 150 x Challenger.
Armoured Infantry Fighting Vehicles (AIFV) - Approx 210 x Warrior
Armoured Personnel Carriers (APCs) - Approx 172 x Saxon.
Self-Propelled (SP) Artillery - Approx 96 x AS90.
Multi-Launch Rocket System (MLRS) - Approx 18 Launchers
Lynx Helicopters armed with TOW missiles - approx 24

3 (UK) Div - Mechanised Brigade Organisation

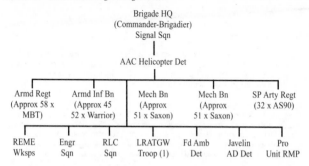

Note: (1) Long Range Anti-Tank Guided Weapons - Currently Striker/Swingfire. (2) Two of the three brigades have 1 x armoured infantry battalion. The third brigade has 3 x mechanised battalions (with Saxon).

The Battlegroup

A division usually consists of 3 brigades. These brigades are further sub divided into smaller formations known as battlegroups. The Battlegroup is the basic building brick of the fighting formations.

A battlegroup is commanded by a Lieutenant Colonel and the infantry battalion or armoured regiment that he commands provides the command and staff element of the formation. The battlegroup is then structured according to task, with the correct mix of infantry, armour and supporting arms.

The battlegroup organisation is very flexible and the units assigned can be quickly regrouped to cope with a change in the threat. A typical battlegroup fighting a defensive battle might be composed of one armoured squadron and two armoured infantry companies, containing about 600 men, 12 tanks and about 80 armoured personnel carriers.

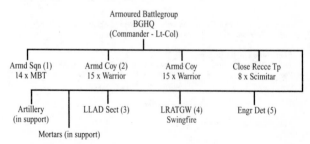

(1) Armoured Squadron
(2) Armoured Infantry Company
(3) LLAD-Low Level Air Defence - Javelin
(4) LRATGW - Long Range Anti-Tank Guided Weapon - Swingfire.
(5) Engineer Detachment

The number of battlegroups in a division and a brigade could vary according to the task the formation has been given. As a general rule you could expect a division to have as many as 9 battlegroups and a brigade to have up to 3. The diagram shows a possible organisation for an armoured battlegroup in either 1(UK) Armd Div or 3(UK) Div.

Regenerative Divisions
There are three Regenerative Divisions, based on older UK military districts. These are the 2nd Division with its Headquarters at Edinburgh, the 4th Division with its Headquarters at Aldershot, and the 5th Division with its Headquarters at Shrewsbury. These Regenerative Divisions are responsible for all Army units within their boundaries and could provide the core for three new divisions, should the Army be required to expand to meet a major international threat.

Composition of 2nd Division
The 2nd Division has responsibility for the whole of Scotland and Northern England. Though the Division was first formed in 1809 to fight in the Peninsular War, the crossed keys sign was not adopted until 1940 when it was reconstituted in England after Dunkirk. Its most famous engagement was during the Burma Campaign in 1944 when, at the battle for Kohima, the tide against the Japanese Army finally turned. The Divisional Headquarters is in Edinburgh. The 2nd Division comprises four brigades and a garrison:

15 (North East) Brigade, with its HQ in York, responsible for units in the North East of England

42 (North West) Brigade, with its HQ in Preston, responsible for units in the North West of England

51 (Highland) Brigade, with its HQ in Perth, responsible for all units north of Stirling including Shetland and the Western Isles

52 (Lowland) Brigade, with its HQ in Edinburgh, responsible for units in Central and Southern Scotland

Catterick Garrison, including units in Ripon, Topcliffe and Dishforth. Catterick Garrison also hosts 19 (Mechanised) Brigade which is under operational command of 3rd (UK) Division

Composition of 4th Division
The 4th Division has military responsibility for South East England, including Bedfordshire, Essex and Hertfordshire and its headquarters is in Aldershot. It was based in Germany until 1992 as an armoured division. The divisional symbol is the Tiger.

The division now has three brigades under command:

2 Brigade based in Shorncliffe

24 Brigade in Colchester

145 Brigade in Aldershot

Composition of 5th Division

The 5th Division has responsibility for military units and establishments in Wales, the West Midlands and the North West of England and the Headquarters is in Shrewsbury. The Division emblem, inherited from Wales and Western District, depicts the Welsh Dragon, the cross of St Chad (7th Century Bishop of Mercia), and the Red Rose of Lancaster. The 5th Division fought at Waterloo and played a significant part in the endeavours of the BEF in both World Wars. The following brigades are under command:

42 Inf Bde based at Preston

143 Inf Bde based at Shrewsbury

160 Inf Bde based at Brecon

11 (ARRC) Signals Brigade

Northern Ireland

The military presence in Northern Ireland is commanded by HQ Northern Ireland (HQNI) situated at Lisburn just outside Belfast and there are three Brigades under command.

HQ Northern Ireland
Lisburn

| 39 Bde | 8 Bde | 3 Bde |
| Belfast | Londonderry | Armagh |

During early 2001 under the operational command of these brigades were:

	6 x Resident Infantry Battalions*
	2 x Infantry Battalions on short 6 month tours
	1 x Engineer Regiment
	1 x Royal Signals Regiment
	1 x Army Air Corps Regiment
	6 x Home Service Battalions of the Royal Irish Regiment
	1 x RLC Logistic Support Regiment
	1 x REME Workshop
	1 x Military Hospital manned by the Army Medical Services
RAF:	1 x Puma Squadron
	1 x RAF Regiment Squadron

If the present ceasefire holds the number of units will almost certainly be reduced.

Districts

From 1st April 2000 two Districts will remain: London (although subordinated to 4th Division for budgetary purposes), and the United Kingdom Support Command (Germany). London is responsible for all Army units within the M25 boundary the United Kingdom Support Command (Germany) with its Headquarters at Rheindahlen has similar responsibilities, but also provides essential support functions for the 1st Division and the Headquarters of the ARRC.

These divisional and district areas are further sub-divided into brigades and garrisons, which also have a varying mix of operational and infrastructure support responsibilities. As a result of the Defence Costs Studies, some brigade headquarters, which previously had purely operational functions, have been amalgamated with garrison headquarters to achieve savings and greater efficiency.

Embedded into this structure are all the other force elements which represent Land Command's operational capability. They include:

16 Air Assault Brigade, based in Colchester and under the command of the Joint Helicopter Command from 1st April 2000.

The United Kingdom element of the Allied Command Europe Mobile Force (Land), with its Headquarters and logistic elements at Bulford and an infantry battalion at Dover.

Allied Command Europe Mobile Force Land (AMF(L)) contingent is the UK's contribution to the Allied Command Europe Mobile Force (AMF) which is tasked with the reinforcement of the flanks of NATO. On mobilisation, operations would probably take place in either Norway or Turkey and the UK MoD has recently stated that the UK's contribution to the AMF will be retained. The AMF is a Brigade+ NATO formation with about 6,000 men and 1,500 vehicles. The UK AMF(L) has its Headquarters and logistic elements at Bulford and an infantry battalion at Dover.

Three Signal Brigades (one of which is in Germany).

Two Combat Service Support Groups (one of which is in Germany).

Various additional units which are earmarked for the ACE Rapid Reaction Corps or for National Defence tasks.

The overseas detachments in Canada, Belize, Brunei and Nepal are commanded directly from Headquarters Land Command at Wilton. The Review of the Army Command Structure recommended that the Army should be organised into three central commands and that doctrine and training should be the responsibility of the Adjutant General rather than the Command-in-Chief. Therefore Headquarters Doctrine and Training at Upavon, Wiltshire, does not form part of Land Command (although it was part of United Kingdom Land Forces until 1993).

Although Land Command is not responsible for running operations in Northern Ireland, Cyprus and the Falkland Islands (a responsibility of PJHQ), it will provide the operational troops for these areas. Some 12,000 troops are involved in Northern Ireland at present, either deployed in the Province or training for deployment; and a further 5,000 are deployed to Cyprus and the Falklands.

National operations and operations in support of the United Nations/NATO, the most significant of which are 6,000 troops deployed in Bosnia and Kosovo

Some 500 troops are involved at any one time in MoD-sponsored equipment trials, demonstrations and exhibitions. Public Duties in London taking up two/three battalions at any one time. All troops not otherwise operationally committed are also available to provide Military Aid to the Civil Authorities in the United Kingdom.

16 Air Assault Brigade

Nearly 10,000 personnel form the personnel component of 16 Air Assault Brigade. It should be able to punch deep and fast into enemy territory, radically changing Britain's ability to react rapidly to conflicts. Using everything from the latest Apache helicopter to air-mobile artillery equipment and high velocity air defence missiles, the new Brigade marks a considerable leap forward in Britain's defence capability.

The Brigade capitalises on the combat capabilities of the former 24 Airmobile Brigade and 5 Airborne Brigade, including two parachute battalions with an increase in combat service support. The introduction of the Apache attack helicopter, due in operational servvice within the next two years, will provide a new generation of weapons systems bringing major improvements in military capability.

The newly launched Brigade is expected to be fully capable in the air manoeuvre role in June 2004, when the last Aviation Regiment is combat-ready.

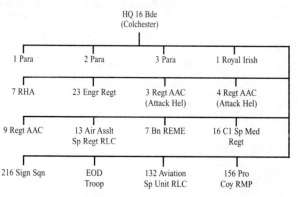

Note: Although much of the brigade in already in locations around the Colchester area, some units will be arriving at various stages during 2001/2002. 23 Engineer Regiment is forming and as yet we have no date for when it will join the brigade.

Support helicopters are provided by the RAF and the Brigade would normally expect to operate with 18 x Chinook and 18 x Puma. An airmobile infantry battalion can be moved by 20 x Chinook equivalents. Each airmobile infantry battalion is equipped with 42 x Milan firing posts - a total of 84 within the Brigade.

<u>Units of the Army (Situation at 1 August 1998)</u>
<u>The Cavalry</u>

Apart from the Royal Tank Regiment, which was formed in the First World War with the specific task of fighting in armoured vehicles, tank forces in the British Army are provided by the regiments which formed the cavalry element of the pre-mechanised era. Following the "Options for Change" restructuring in January 1995 there were 11 regular armoured regiments and 4 TA Yeomanry Regiments. One of these regiments forms The Household Cavalry and the remaining regiments are known collectively as The Royal Armoured Corps (RAC).

Of the 11 regular armour roled units remaining in the British Army post SDR there are four in Germany, three MBT regiments equipped with Challenger 2 and a Recce regiment. In the UK there will be the remaining three MBT regiments equipped with Challenger 2, three Recce Regiments and the Joint NBC Regiment.

In the UK there are two regular armoured regiments equipped with Challenger MBT stationed in Tidworth and one in Catterick. All three of these regiments are under the operational command of 3 (UK) Division that has a role in support of the ARRC. There are also three regular armoured reconnaissance regiments stationed in the UK one of which, based at Bovington doubles as the armoured training regiment at the RAC Training Centre. In addition to these armoured forces the Household Cavalry Mounted Regiment is stationed in London and provides mounted troops for ceremonial duties.

The Territorial Army has four Yeomanry Regiments. These units form national defence regiments with a reconnaissance role.

The Cavalry accounts for about 6% of the strength of the Army and Regimental Titles are as follows:

The Household Cavalry

The Household Cavalry Regiment	HCR
The Household Cavalry Mounted Regiment	HCMRD

The Royal Armoured Corps

1st The Queen's Dragoon Guards	QDG
The Royal Scots Dragoon Guards	SCOTS DG
The Royal Dragoon Guards	RDG
The Queen's Royal Hussars	QRH
9th/12th Royal Lancers	9/12L
The King's Royal Hussars	KRH
The Light Dragoons	LD
The Queen's Royal Lancers	QRL
1st Royal Tank Regiment	1 RTR
2nd Royal Tank Regiment	2 RTR

Armoured Regiment Wiring Diagram
The following diagram shows the current structure of an Armoured Regiment equipped with Challenger 1. Regiments equipped with Challenger 2 will in the future be equipped with 58 tanks and have 600 personnel.

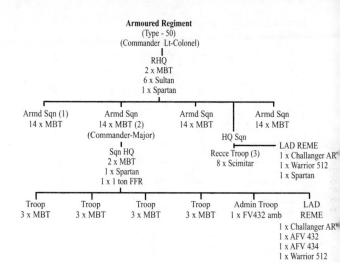

Armoured Regiment
(Type - 50)
(Commander Lt-Colonel)

RHQ
2 x MBT
6 x Sultan
1 x Spartan

Armd Sqn (1)
14 x MBT

Armd Sqn
14 x MBT (2)
(Commander-Major)

Sqn HQ
2 x MBT
1 x Spartan
1 x 1 ton FFR

Armd Sqn
14 x MBT

Armd Sqn
14 x MBT

HQ Sqn

Recce Troop (3)
8 x Scimitar

LAD REME
1 x Challanger AR
1 x Warrior 512
1 x Spartan

Troop
3 x MBT

Troop
3 x MBT

Troop
3 x MBT

Troop
3 x MBT

Admin Troop
1 x FV432 amb

LAD REME
1 x Challanger AR
1 x AFV 432
1 x AFV 434
1 x Warrior 512

Totals: 58 x MBT (Challenger 1), 8 x Scimitar, 5 x ARV, 558 men.

Notes: (1) Armoured Squadron; (2) Main Battle Tank; (3) We believe that this recce troop of 8 x Scimitar is normally held in HQ Sqn but on operations comes under the direct control of the commanding officer; (4) The basic building brick of the Tank Regiment is the Tank Troop of 16 men and four tanks. The commander of this troop will probably be a Lt or 2/Lt aged between 20 or 23 and the second-in-command will usually be a sergeant who commands his own tank. The remaining tank in the troop will be commanded by a senior corporal; (5) A Challenger tank has a crew of 4 - Commander, Driver, Gunner and Loader/Operator.

The Infantry
The British Infantry is based on the well tried and tested Regimental System that has been justi-fied regularly on operational deployment. It is based on battalions, which when they number more than one are grouped together to form a "large Regiment". Most Regiments now comprise one Regular and one TA Battalion and Regiments are then grouped together within Divisions, which provide a level of administrative command.

The Division of Infantry is an organisation that is responsible for all aspects of military adminis-tration, from recruiting, manning and promotions for individuals in the regiments under its wing, to the longer term planning required to ensure continuity and cohesion. Divisions of Infantry have no operational command over their regiments, and should not be confused with the operational divisions such as 1(UK) Armd Div and 3 (UK) Div.

The Divisions of Infantry are as follows:

The Guards Division	- 5 regular battalions
The Scottish Division	- 6 regular battalions
The Queen's Division	- 6 regular battalions
The King's Division	- 6 regular battalions
The Prince of Wales Division	- 7 regular battalions
The Light Division	- 4 regular battalions

Not administered by Divisions of Infantry but operating under their own administrative arrangements are the following:

The Parachute Regiment	- 3 regular battalions
The Brigade of Gurkhas	- 2 regular battalions
The Royal Irish Regiment	- 1 regular battalion

TA battalions are under the administrative command (from mid 1999) of the following:

The Guards Division	- Nil
The Scottish Division	- 2 TA battalions
The Queen's Division	- 3 TA battalions
The King's Division	- 3 TA battalions
The Prince of Wales Division	- 3 TA battalions
The Light Division	- 2 TA battalions
The Parachute Regiment	- 1 TA battalion
The Royal Irish Regiment	- 1 TA battalion

In total the British Army has 40 regular battalions available for service and this total combined with the 15 TA battalions could give a mobilisation strength of 55 infantry battalions.

Outside the above listed Regiments are three companies of guardsmen each of 110 men, who are provided to supplement the Household Division Regiments while on public duties in London, to allow them to continue to carry out normal training on roulement from guard duties. Gibraltar also has its own single battalion of the Gibraltar Regiment comprising one Regular and two volunteer companies.

At the beginning of 2001 the infantry is located as follows:

United Kingdom	- 31 battalions (5 Resident in Northern Ireland)
Germany	- 6 battalions
Cyprus	- 2 battalions
Falkland Islands	- 1 company group on detachment
Bosnia	- 1 composite battalion on detachment
Kosovo	- 1 composite battalion on detachment
Brunei	- 1 battalion (Gurkha)

As explained previously, it would be most unusual for the Infantry to fight as battalion units especially in armoured or mechanised formations. The HQ of an infantry battalion will generally be the HQ of a battle group, and the force will be provided with armour, artillery, engineers and possibly aviation to enable it to become a balanced all arms grouping.

The Infantry accounts for about 25% of the Army

The Guards Division

1st Bn The Grenadier Guards	1 GREN GDS
1st Bn The Coldstream Guards	1 COLM GDS
1st Bn The Scots Guards	1 SG
1st Bn The Irish Guards	1 IG
1st Bn The Welsh Guards	1 WG

There are generally three battalions from the Guards Division on public duties
in London at any one time. When a Regiment is stationed in London on public duties it is given
an extra company to ensure the additional manpower required for ceremonial events is available.

The Scottish Division

1st Bn The Royal Scots	1 RS
1st Bn The Royal Highland Fusiliers	1 RHF
1st Bn The King's Own Scottish Borderers	1 KOSB
1st Bn The Black Watch	1 BW
1st Bn The Argyll & Sutherland Highlanders	1 A & SH
1st Bn The Highlanders	1 HLDRS

The Queen's Division

1st Bn The Princess of Wales's Royal Regiment (Queen's and Royal Hampshire)	1 PWRR
2nd Bn The Princess of Wales's Royal Regiment (Queen's and Royal Hampshire)	2 PWRR
1st Bn The Royal Regiment of Fusiliers	1 RRF
2nd Bn The Royal Regiment of Fusiliers	2 RRF
1st Bn The Royal Anglian Regiment	1 R ANGLIAN
2nd Bn The Royal Anglian Regiment	2 R ANGLIAN

The King's Division

1st Bn The King's Own Royal Border Regiment	1 KINGS OWN BORDER
1st Bn The King's Regiment	1 KINGS
1st Bn The Prince of Wales's Own Regiment of Yorkshire	1 PWO
1st Bn The Green Howards	1 GREEN HOWARDS
1st Bn The Queen's Lancashire Regiment	1 QLR
1st Bn The Duke of Wellington's Regiment	1 DWR

The Prince of Wales Division

1st Bn The Devonshire & Dorset Regiment	1 D and D
1st Bn The Cheshire Regiment	1 CHESHIRE
1st Bn The Royal Welch Fusiliers	1 RWF
1st Bn The Royal Regiment of Wales	1 RRW
1st Bn The Royal Gloucestershire, Berkshire and Wiltshire Regiment	1 RGBW
1st Bn The Worcestershire & Sherwood	1 WFR

Foresters Regiment
1st Bn The Staffordshire Regiment   1 STAFFORDS

The Light Division
1st Bn The Light Infantry   1 LI
2nd Bn The Light Infantry   2 LI
1st Bn The Royal Green Jackets   1 RGJ
2nd Bn The Royal Green Jackets   2 RGJ

The Brigade of Gurkhas
1st Bn The Royal Gurkha Rifles   1 RGR
2nd Bn The Royal Gurkha Rifles   2 RGR

The Parachute Regiment
1st Bn The Parachute Regiment   1 PARA
2nd Bn The Parachute Regiment   2 PARA
3rd Bn The Parachute Regiment   3 PARA

The Royal Irish Regiment
1st Bn The Royal Irish Regiment   1 R IRISH
3rd/4th/5th/7th/8th/9th Royal Irish Regiment*   3-9 R IRISH

* The 3rd to 9th Bns The Royal Irish Regiment are employed exclusively in
Northern Ireland and were formerly battalions of The Ulster Defence Regiment. The 4/5 Rangers
is a TA Battalion stationed in Northern Ireland and wearing the Royal Irish cap badge.

The Special Air Service Regiment
The 22nd Special Air Service Regiment   22 SAS

The SAS can be classed as an infantry unit but the members of the regiment are found from all
arms and services of the Army after exhaustive selection tests.

Infantry Organisations

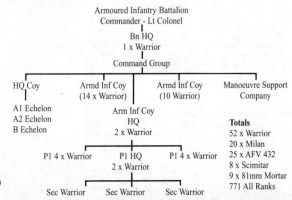

Armoured Infantry Battalion
Commander - Lt Colonel

Bn HQ
1 x Warrior

Command Group

HQ Coy   Armd Inf Coy   Armd Inf Coy   Manoeuvre Support
          (14 x Warrior)   (10 Warrior)   Company

A1 Echelon
A2 Echelon
B Echelon   Arm Inf Coy
                 HQ
                 2 x Warrior   **Totals**
                                            52 x Warrior
                                            20 x Milan
    P1 4 x Warrior   P1 HQ   P1 4 x Warrior   25 x AFV 432
                      2 x Warrior   8 x Scimitar
                                                 9 x 81mm Mortar
    Sec Warrior   Sec Warrior   Sec Warrior   771 All Ranks

80

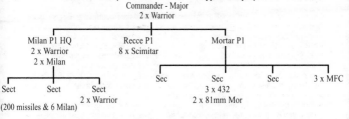

Armoured Infantry Battalion - Manoeuvre Support Company
Commander - Major
2 x Warrior

Milan P1 HQ
2 x Warrior
2 x Milan

Recce P1
8 x Scimitar

Mortar P1

Sect   Sect   Sect
2 x Warrior
(200 missiles & 6 Milan)

Sec   Sec   Sec   3 x MFC
3 x 432
2 x 81mm Mor

Note: (1) There are 8 x Armoured Infantry Battalions, 6 of which are in Germany with 1 (UK) Armoured Division and the remaining 2 in the UK with 3 (UK) Division - following the 1998 SDR an extra armoured infantry battalion has been allocated to 3 (UK) Division.. (2) There are longer term intentions to replace the AFV 432s on issue to armoured infantry battalions by other versions of Warrior or equivalent vehicles such as mortar carrier, ambulance, command vehicle etc.(3) Another 4 Milan firing posts are held by the section that is only activated on mobilisation.

Light Role Infantry Battalion
Commander - Lt Colonel
Bn HQ

HQ Coy
A1 Echelon
A2 Echelon
B Echelon
Assault Pioneers

Rifle Coy
(only 2 plas)

Rifle Coy
HQ

P1   P1   P1

Rifle Coy

Manoeuvre Support Coy

Totals
6 x Milan
6 x 81mm mortars
620 Personnel

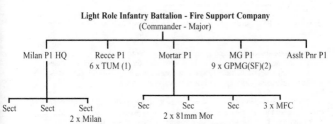

Light Role Infantry Battalion - Fire Support Company
(Commander - Major)

Milan P1 HQ

Recce P1
6 x TUM (1)

Mortar P1

MG P1
9 x GPMG(SF)(2)

Asslt Pnr P1

Sect   Sect   Sect
2 x Milan

Sec   Sec   Sec   3 x MFC
2 x 81mm Mor

Notes: (1) TUM is the abbreviation for Truck-Utility-Medium; (2) General Purpose Machine Guns mounted on tripods with a range of up to 1,800 metres.

The Royal Regiment of Artillery (RA)

The Royal Regiment of Artillery (RA) provides the battlefield fire support and air defence for the British Army in the field. Its various regiments are equipped for conventional fire support using field guns, for area and point air defence using air defence missiles and for specialised artillery locating tasks. There are now three Regiments equipped with the Multiple Launch Rocket System (MLRS) which have now taken their place in the Order of Battle and these weapons were used with great effect during the 1991 war in the Gulf. In October 1993 1st Royal Horse Artillery became the first regiment to be equipped with the AS 90 self propelled howitzer. By 1999 the AS 90 self propelled howitzer was the primary 155 mm artillery weapon of the British Army and the towed 155 mm FH 70 has been retired from service.

Following the Strategic Defence Review of 1990 the RA remains one of the larger organisations in the British Army with 17 Regiments included in its regular Order of Battle. It has the following structure in both the UK and Germany (ARRC).

	UK	Germany	
Field Regiments (AS 90 SP Guns)	3	3	
Field Regiments (Light Gun)	2(1)	-	
Depth Fire Regiments (MLRS)	2(2)	-	
Air Defence Regiments (Rapier)	2	-	
Air Defence Regiment (Javelin)	1	-	HVM from mid 2001
Air Defence Regiment (HVM)	-	1	
Training Regiment (School Assets Regt)	1	-	
The Kings Troop (Ceremonial)	1	-	

Note:
(1) Of these 2 Regiments one is a Commando Regiment (29 Cdo Regt) and the other is an Air Assault Regiment (7 PARA RHA*). This Regt has one battery in the Parachute role but the Regt is assigned to the 16th Air Assault Bde at Colchester. Both of these regiments are equipped with the Light Gun. Either of these Regiments can be called upon to provide Manoeuvre Support Artillery to the AMF. On deployment of the AMF it is 29 Cdo Regt RA which forms the AMF Arty HQ and the Commanding Officer is CO Force Arty.
* 7 RHA will, incidentally, keep the designation "PARA" as well as the word "Horse" in their title. 7 RHA Battery titles are those of the famous horse drawn batteries at Waterloo,

(2) The third MLRS Regiment is now a TA Regt with 12 Launch vehicles in peace uprateable to 18 in war.

(3) Although the artillery is organised into Regiments, much of a "Gunner's" loyalty is directed towards the battery in which they serve. The guns represent the Regimental Colours of the Artillery and it is around the batteries where the guns are held that history has gathered. A Regiment will generally have three or four gun batterys under command.

The Royal Horse Artillery (RHA) is also part of the Royal Regiment of Artillery and its three regiments have been included in the totals above. There is considerable cross posting of officers and soldiers from the RA to the RHA, and some consider service with the RHA to be a career advancement.

Artillery training is carried out at the Royal School of Artillery at Larkhill in Wiltshire. After initial training officers and gunners will be posted to RA units worldwide, but soldiers will return to the RSA for frequent career and employment courses. Artillery recruits spend the first period of recruit training (Common Military Syllabus) at the Army Training Regiment - Litchfield.

Air Defence is a vital part of the role of the Royal Artillery and updates to the Rapier system continue, with batterys being upgraded to Field Standard B2 and Field Standard C. During 1994 a Starstreak HVM Regiment became operational in the UK. In addition, the air defences have been enhanced by the Air Defence Alerting Device for Javelin and Starstreak.

The Royal Artillery provides the modern British armoured formation with a protective covering. The air defence covers the immediate airspace above and around the formation, with the field artillery reaching out to approximately 30km in front and across the flanks of the formation. An armoured formation that moves out of this protective covering is open to immediate destruction by an intelligent enemy as the Egyptians discovered in 1973.

Divisional Artillery Group (DAG)

An armoured or mechanised division has it own artillery under command. This artillery usually consists of 3 Close Support Regiments, with a number of units detached from the Corps Artillery and could include TA reinforcements. In war the composition of the DAG will vary according to the task.

The following is a diagram of the artillery support available to a UK division. Expect each brigade in the division to have one Close Support Regiment with AS90 under command.

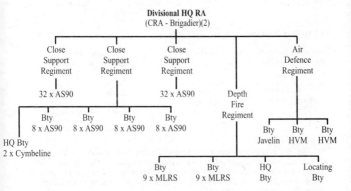

Divisional HQ RA
(CRA - Brigadier)(2)

Notes:
(1) Air defended areas (ADAs) are provided by Rapier.
(2) The Staff of an armoured or mechanised division includes a Brigadier of Artillery known as the Commander Royal Artillery (CRA). The CRA acts as the artillery adviser to the Divisional Commander, and would probably assign one of his Close Support Regiments to support each of the Brigades in the division. These regiments would be situated in positions that would allow

most of their batterys to fire across the complete divisional front. Therefore, in the very best case, a battlegroup under extreme threat could be supported by the fire of more than 96 guns.

The number of batterys and final number of guns per battery in an AS90 Close Support Regiment appears to have been finally resolved at 4 batterys of eight guns per battery to enable the 4 battlegroups in each brigade to be fully supported. Although a battery has eight guns on establishment only six guns will be manned in peacetime.

Royal Artillery Regiments

1st Regiment RHA	1 RHA	(Field)
3rd Regiment RHA	3 RHA	(Field)
4th Regiment RA	4 REGT	(Field)
5th Regiment RA	5 REGT	(MLRS)
7th Regiment RHA	7 RHA	(Parachute)
12th Regiment RA 1	2 REGT	(Air Defence)
14th Regiment RA	14 REGT	(Training)
16th Regiment RA	16 REGT	(Air Defence)
19th Regiment RA	19 REGT	(Field)
22nd Regiment RA	22 REGT	(Air Defence)
26th Regiment RA	26 REGT	(Field)
29th Commando Regiment	RA 29 REGT	(Field)
32nd Regiment RA	32 REGT	(MLRS)
39th Regiment RA	39 REGT	(MLRS)
40th Regiment RA	40 REGT	(Field)
47th Regiment RA	47 REGT	(Air Defence)

TA Artillery Regiments

The Honourable Artillery Coy	London	STA and Special Ops
100 Fd Regt RA (V)	Luton	Reinforcement Regt
101 Fd Regt RA (V)	Newcastle	MLRS (12 in peace)
103 Fd Regt RA (V)	Liverpool	Javelin
104 Fd Regt RA (V)	Newport	Javelin
105 Fd Regt RA (V)	Edinburgh	Javelin
106 Fd Regt RA (V)	London	Individual Reinforcements

Army Air Corps

The Army obtains its aviation support from the Army Air Corps (AAC), which is an Army organisation with 5 separate regiments and a number of independent squadrons. The AAC also provides support for Northern Ireland on a mixed resident and roulement basis and the two squadrons concerned are sometimes referred to as the sixth AAC Regiment, although the units would disperse on mobilisation and have no regimental title.

1 Regiment - Germany	(651,652 & 661 Sqns)
3 Regiment - Wattisham	(653,662 & 663 Sqns)
4 Regiment - Wattisham	(654,659 & 669 Sqns)
5 Regiment - Aldergrove	(655 & 665 Sqns)
7 Regiment - Netheravon	(658 & 666(V) Sqns)

9 Regiment - Dishforth   (656, 657 & 664 Sqns)

The HQ of 2 (Trg) Regiment is at Middle Wallop and there are TA Flights at Netheravon, Turnhouse and Shawbury.

In addition to the Regiments in the UK and Germany there are small flights in Cyprus, Bruggen (Germany), Brunei, Suffield (Canada) and the Falkland Islands.

The AAC Centre at Middle Wallop in Hampshire acts as a focal point for all Army Aviation, and it is here that the majority of training for pilots and aircrew is carried out. From1997, elementary flying training for all three services has been carried out at RAF Shawbury in Shropshire.

Although the AAC operates some fixed-wing aircraft for training, liaison flying and radar duties, the main effort goes into providing helicopter support for the ground forces. About 350 AAC helicopters are used for anti-tank operations, artillery fire control, reconnaissance, liaison flying and a limited troop lift.

Army Air Corps - Regimental Designations   AAC

1st Regiment	1 REGT AAC
3rd Regiment	3 REGT AAC
4th Regiment	4 REGT AAC
7th Regiment	7 REGT AAC
9th Regiment	9 REGT AAC

AAC Regimental Organisation

Organisations for the individual AAC Regiments appear to be in a state of flux. The following wiring diagram outlines the organisation of 3 Regiment AAC in early 2000. 3 Regiment AAC supports the Colchester based, 16 Air Assault Brigade and various regimental organisations are a variation on this theme.

A Regiment of this type could act as the core formation of an airborne battlegroup. If necessary an infantry aviation company consisting of 3 x rifle platoons and a Milan anti-tank platoon will be attached. The infantry could be moved in RAF Chinooks or Pumas.

4 Regiment AAC joined 3 Regiment in Wattisham during early 1995 and it is believed that both regiments will have a similar organisation. Wattisham is also the home of 7 Bn REME - a unit configured as an aircraft workshops. By the end of 2003 we would expect both of these regiments to be equipped with AH-64 Apache.

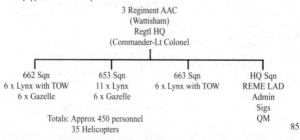

3 Regiment AAC
(Wattisham)
Regtl HQ
(Commander-Lt Colonel

662 Sqn	653 Sqn	663 Sqn	HQ Sqn
6 x Lynx with TOW	11 x Lynx	6 x Lynx with TOW	REME LAD
6 x Gazelle	6 x Gazelle		Admin
			Sigs
			QM

Totals: Approx 450 personnel
35 Helicopters

Corps of Royal Engineers

The engineer support for the Army is provided by the Corps of Royal Engineers (RE). This large corps, currently composed of 17 regiments filled with highly skilled tradesmen is currently organised as follows:

	Germany	UKLF
Engineer Regiments	4	6
EOD Regiment	-	1
Resident N Ireland Regiment	-	1
TA Engineer Regiments	-	5

There are also a number of independent engineer squadrons worldwide.

The Royal Engineers provide specialist support to the combat formations and engineer detachments can be found at all levels from the Combat Team/Company Group upwards. Combat Engineers tasks are amongst the following:

a. **Defence:** Construction of field defences; laying anti-tank mines; improvement and construction of obstacles.

b. **Attack:** Obstacle crossing; demolition of enemy defences (bunkers etc); mine clearance; bridge or ferry construction.

c. **Advance:** Building or strengthening roads and bridges; removal of booby traps; mine clearance; airfield construction; supply of water; survey.

d. **Withdrawal:** Demolition - of airfields, roads and bridges, fuel, ammunition and food dumps, railway tracks and rolling stock, industrial plant and facilities such as power stations; route clearance; laying anti-tank mines; booby trapping likely enemy future positions and items that might be attractive to the enemy. Often among the first soldiers into battle, and still involved in dangerous tasks such as mine clearance in the former Yugoslavia, the Sappers can turn their hands to almost any engineering task.

Recent UN tasks have highlighted the importance of combat engineers. Tasks for which engineer support was requested stretched the resources of the Corps to its limit and the first priority in almost any call from the UN for support is for engineers. Tracks have to be improved, roads must be built, wells dug and clean water provided together with camps for refugees. All of these are engineer tasks that soak up large amounts of manpower.

Engineer Organisations

The smallest engineer unit is the field troop which is usually commanded by a Lieutenant and consists of approximately 44 men. In an armoured division a field troop can be expected to have up to four sections and each section is mounted in an APC. Engineer Regiments in UKLF may have only three sections and may be mounted in wheeled vehicles such as Land Rovers and 4 ton Trucks. An engineer troop will carry equipment, stores and explosives to enable it to carry out its immediate battlefield tasks.

(1) This Regiment would send most of its soldiers to man the engineer detachments that provide support for a division's battlegroups; (2) Field Squadron (expect a field squadron to have approximately 68 vehicles and some 200 men; (3) Support Squadron; (4) Medium Girder Bridge; (5) Combat Engineer Tractor; (6) This whole organisation is highly mobile and built around the AFV 432 and Spartan series of vehicles; (7) In addition to the regimental REME LAD each squadron has its own REME section of approximately 12 - 15 men.

Armoured Divisional Engineer Regiment (1)
RHQ
(Commander Lt Colonel)

HQ Sqn	Fd Sqn (2)	Fd Sqn	Fd Sqn	Sp Sqn (3)	REME LAD

HQ Sqn:
- Sp Tp
- Fd Tp
- Fd Tp
- Fd Tp

5 x CET (5)
1 x Digger
3 x Tractors
1 x Stalwart

Sp Sqn:
- Bridging Tp — 2 x MGB (4)
- Plant Tp — 1 x Crane, Tractors, Diggers
- Resources Tp — 3 x Cranes, 3 x 10 Ton

Strength: Approx 650 All Ranks

Engineer amphibious capability and specialist support is provided by elements of 28 Engineer Regiment in Germany and a TA Regiment in the UK.

The UK Engineer Field Regiment (Regular & TA) is generally a wheeled organisation that might be expected to have 2 Field Squadrons, a Support Squadron and possibly an Airfield Damage Repair (ADR) Squadron. Engineer regiments supporting 3(UK) Division could be structured along the lines of the Armoured Divisional Engineer Regiment.

Royal Engineers - Regimental Designations

1st RSME Regiment	1 RSME REGT RE
3rd RSME Regiment	3 RSME REGT RE
21st Engineer Regiment	21 ENGR REGT
22nd Engineer Regiment	22 ENGR REGT
23rd Engineer Regiment	23 ENGR REGT
25th Engineer Regiment	25 ENGR REGT
28th Engineer Regiment	28 ENGR REGT
32nd Engineer Regiment	32 ARMD ENGR REGT
33rd Engineer Regiment	33 ENGR REGT (EOD)
35th Engineer Regiment	35 ENGR REGT
36th Engineer Regiment	36 ENGR REGT
38th Engineer Regiment	38 ENGR REGT
39th Engineer Regiment	39 ENGR REGT

The Royal Corps of Signals

The Royal Corps of Signals (R Signals) provides the communications throughout the command system of the Army. Individual battlegroups are responsible for their own internal communications, but all communications from Brigade level and above are the responsibility of the Royal Signals.

Information is the lifeblood of any military formation in battle and it is the responsibility of the Royal Signals to ensure the speedy and accurate passage of information that enables commanders to make informed and timely decisions, and to ensure that those decisions are passed to the fighting troops in contact with the enemy. The rapid, accurate and secure employment of command, control and communications systems, maximises the effect of the military force available and consequently the Royal Signals act as an extremely significant 'Force Multiplier'.

The Royal Corps of Signals provides about 9% of the Army's manpower with 11 Regular (including 1 Training Regiment) and 11 Territorial Army Regiments, each generally consisting of between 3 and up to 6 Sqns with between 400 and 1,000 personnel. In addition, there are 20 Regular and 2 Territorial Army Independent Squadrons, each of which has about 200 men, and 4 Independent Signal Troops of between 10 and 80 men each. Royal Signals personnel are found wherever the Army is deployed including every UK and NATO headquarters in the world. The Headquarters of the Corps is at the Royal School of Signals (RSS) located at Blandford in Dorset.

Royal Signals units based in the United Kingdom provide command, control and communications for forces that have operational roles both in the UK itself, including Northern Ireland, and overseas including mainland Western Europe and further afield wherever the Army finds itself. There are a number of Royal Signals units permanently based in Germany, Holland and Belgium from where they provide the necessary command and control communications and Electronic Warfare (EW) support for both the British Army and other NATO forces based in Europe. Royal Signals units are also based in Cyprus, Hong Kong, the Falkland Islands, Belize and Gibraltar.

Armoured Divisional Signal Regiment Organisation

Notes: (1) SAN - Secondary Access Node (2) A Divisional HQ will have two HQs to allow for movement and possible destruction. The main HQ will be set up for approx 24 hrs with the alternative HQ (Alt HQ) set up 20-30 km away on the proposed line of march of the division. When the Main HQ closes to move to a new location, the Alt HQ becomes the Main HQ for another 24 hour period. (3) Expect a Brigade Sig Sqn to have a Radio Troop and an SAN Troop.

Regiments

1st (UK) Armd Div HQ and Signal Regiment	1 SIG REGT
2nd Signal Regiment	2 SIG REGT
3rd (UK) Div HQ & Signal Regiment	3 SIG REGT
7th (ARRC) Signal Regiment	7 SIG REGT
9th Signal Regiment (Radio)	9 SIG REGT
11th Signal Regiment (Trg Regt)	11 SIG REGT
14th Signal Regiment (Electronic Warfare)	14 SIG REGT
15th Signal Regiment	15 SIG REGT
16th Signal Regiment	16 SIG REGT

| 21st Signal Regiment (Air Support) | 21 SIG REGT |
| 30th Signal Regiment | 30 SIG REGT |

The Royal Logistic Corps (RLC)

The RLC is the youngest Corps in the Army and was formed in April 1993 as a result of the recommendations of the MoD's Logistic Support Review. The RLC results from the amalgamation of the Royal Corps of Transport (RCT), the Royal Army Ordnance Corps (RAOC), the Army Catering Corps (ACC), the Royal Pioneer Corps (RPC) and elements of the Royal Engineers (RE). The Corps makes up about 16% of the Army with 20,000 Regular soldiers and 10,000 Territorial Army soldiers wearing its cap badge.

The RLC has very broad responsibilities throughout the Army that includes the movement of personnel throughout the world, the Army's air dispatch service, maritime and rail transport, operational resupply, and explosive ordnance disposal which includes the hazardous bomb disposal duties in Northern Ireland and in mainland UK, the operation of numerous very large vehicle and stores depots both in the UK and overseas, the training and provision of cooks to virtually all units in the Army, the provision of pioneer labour and the Army's postal and courier service.

The principal field elements of the RLC are the Close Support and the General Support Regiments whose primary role is to supply the fighting units with ammunition, fuel and rations (Combat Supplies).

A division has an integral Close Support Regiment which is responsible for manning and operating the supply chain to Brigades and Divisional units.

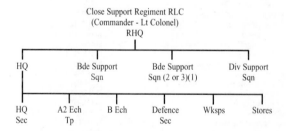

Close Support Regiment RLC
(Commander - Lt Colonel)
RHQ

Note:
(1) A regiment could have two or three brigade support sqns depending upon the size of the division being supported.
(2) Some of these regiments may have a Postal and Courier Squadron.

The General Support Regiment's role is primarily to supply ammunition to the Royal Artillery using DROPS vehicles and to provide Tank Transporters that move armoured vehicles more rapidly and economically than moving them on their own tracks.

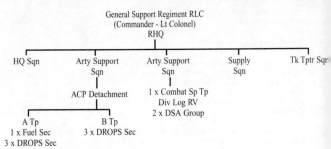

Both types of Regiment have large sections holding stores both on wheels and on the ground. A Division will typically require about 1,000 tons of Combat Supplies a day but demand can easily exceed that amount in high intensity operations.

Regiments

1 General Support Regiment	1 (GS) REGT
2 Close Support Regiment	2 (CS) REGT
3 Close Support Regiment	3 (CS) REGT
4 General Support Regiment	4 (GS) REGT
5 Territorial Army Training Regiment	5 (TRG) REGT
6 Support Regiment	6 (SP) REGT
7 Transport Regiment	7 (TPT) REGT
8 Artillery Support Regiment	8 (ARTY SP) REGT
9 Supply Regiment	9 (SUP) REGT
10 Transport Regiment	10 (TPT) REGT
11 Explosive Ordnance Disposal Regiment	11 (EOD) REGT
12 Supply Regiment	12 (SUP) REGT
13 Air Assault Support Regiment	13 (AIR ASSLT) REGT
14 Supply Regiment	14 (SUP) REGT
17 Port and Maritime Regiment	17 (PORT) REGT
21 Logistic Support Regiment	21 (LOG SP) REGT
23 Pioneer Regiment	23 (PNR) REGT
24 Regiment	24 REGT
27 Transport Regiment	27 (TPT) REGT
29 Regiment	29 REGT
89 Postal and Courier Regiment	89 (PC) REGT

The Royal Electrical & Mechanical Engineers (REME)

The Logistic Support review of 1990 recommended that Equipment Support should remain separate from the other logistic pillar of Service Support and consequently the REME has retained not only its own identity but expanded its responsibilities. Equipment Support encompasses equipment management, engineering support, supply management, provisioning for vehicle and technical spares and financial management responsibilities for in-service equipment.

The aim of the REME is "To keep operationally fit equipment in the hands of the troops" and in the current financial environment it is important that this is carried out at the minimum possible cost. The equipment that REME is responsible for ranges from small arms and trucks to helicopters and Main Battle Tanks. All field force units have some integral REME support which will vary, depending on the size of the unit and the equipment held, from a few attached tradesmen up to a large Regimental Workshop of over 200 men.

In war, REME is responsible for the recovery and repair of battle damaged and unserviceable equipments.

The development of highly technical weapon systems and other equipment has meant that REME has had to balance engineering and tactical considerations. On the one hand the increased scope for forward repair of equipment reduces the time out of action but, on the other hand, engineering stability is required for the repair of complex systems. In 1993, following the Options for Change and Logistic Support Reviews, four extra REME battalions were formed, to provide second line support for the British contribution to the ACE Rapid Reaction Corps (ARRC).

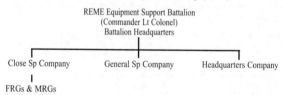

Note: Approx 450 personnel. At the beginning of 2001 there were 6 Regular REME Support battalions, 3 in Germany and 3 in the UK. There are 4 battalions in the TA.

The Close Support Company will normally deploy a number of FRGs (Forward Repair Groups) and MRGs (Medium Repair Groups) in support of brigades. The company is mobile with armoured repair and recovery vehicles able to operate in the forward areas, carrying out forward repair of key nominated equipment often by the exchange of major assemblies. It is also capable of carrying out field repairs on priority equipment including telecommunications equipment and the repair of damage sustained by critical battle winning equipments.

The role of the General Support Company is to support the Close Support Companies and Divisional Troops. Tasks include the regeneration of fit power packs for use in forward repair and the repair of equipment backloaded from Close Support Companies. The General Support Company will normally be located to the rear of the divisional area in order to maximise productivity and minimise vulnerability.

Army Medical Services

Royal Army Medical Corps
In peace, the personnel of the RAMC are based at the various medical installations throughout the world or in field force units and they are responsible for the health of the Army.

The primary role of the Corps is the maintenance of health and the prevention of disease. On operations, the RAMC is responsible for the care of the sick and wounded, with the subsequent evacuation of the wounded to hospitals in the rear areas. Each Brigade has a field ambulance which is a regular unit that operates in direct support of the battlegroups. These units are either armoured, airmobile or parachute trained. In addition, each division has two field ambulance units that may be regular or TA, that provide medical support for the divisional troops and can act as manoeuvre units for the forward brigades when required.

All field ambulance units have medical sections that consist of a medical officer and eight Combat Medical Technicians. These sub-units are located with the battlegroup or units being supported and they provide the necessary first line medical support. In addition, the field ambulance provides a dressing station where casualties are treated and may be resuscitated or stabilised before transfer to a field hospital. These units have the necessary integral ambulance support, both armoured and wheeled to transfer casualties from the first to second line medical units.

Field hospitals may be regular or TA and all are 200 bed facilities with a maximum of 8 surgical teams capable of carrying out life-saving operations on some of the most difficult surgical cases. Since 1990, most regular medical units have been deployed on operations either in the Persian Gulf or the former Yugoslavia.

Casualty Evacuation (CASEVAC) is by ambulance either armoured or wheeled and driven by RLC personnel or by helicopter when such aircraft are available. A Chinook helicopter is capable of carrying 44 stretcher cases and a Puma can carry 6 stretcher cases and 6 sitting cases.

The Queen Alexandra's Royal Army Nursing Corps (QARANC)
On 1 April 1992 the QARANC became an all-nursing and totally professionally qualified Corps. Its male and female, officer and other rank personnel, provide the necessary qualified nursing support at all levels and covering a wide variety of nursing specialities. QARANC personnel can be found anywhere in the world where Army Medical services are required.

Royal Army Dental Corps (RADC)
The RADC is a professional corps that in late 2000 consisted of over just over 290 officers and soldiers. The Corps fulfils the essential role of maintaining the dental health of the Army in peace and war, both at home and overseas. Qualified dentists and oral surgeons, hygienists, technicians and support ancillaries work in a wide variety of military units - from static and mobile dental clinics to field medical units, military hospitals and dental laboratories.

The Adjutant General's Corps (AGC)

The Adjutant General's Corps was formed on 1 April 1992 and its sole task is the management of the Army's most precious resource, its soldiers. The Corps absorbed the functions of six existing smaller corps; the Royal Military Police, the Royal Army Pay Corps, the Royal Army Educational Corps, the Royal Army Chaplain's Department, the Army Legal Corps and the Military Provost Staff Corps.
The Corps is organised into four branches, Staff and Personnel Support (SPS), Provost (PRP), Educational and Training Services (ETS) and Army Legal Services (ALS). In late 2000, the AGC consisted of over 7,000 officers and soldiers.

The Role of SPS Branch
The role of SPS Branch is to ensure the efficient and smooth delivery of Personnel Administration

to the Army. This includes support to individual officers and soldiers in units by processing pay and Service documentation, first line provision of financial, welfare, education and resettlement guidance to individuals and the provision of clerical skills and information management to ensure the smooth day to day running of the unit or department.

AGC (SPS) officers are employed throughout the Army, in direct support of units as Regimental Administrative Officers or AGC Detachment Commanders. They hold Commander AGC(SPS) and SO2 AGC(SPS) posts in district/Divisional and Brigade HQs and fill posts at the Adjutant General's Information Centre (AGIC) and general staff appointments throughout the Army headquarters locations.

AGC(SPS) soldiers are employed as military clerks in direct support of units within the AGC Field Detachments, in fixed centre pay offices, in headquarters to provide staff support and in miscellaneous posts such as embassy clerks, as management accountants or in AGIC as programmer analysts.

Currently, about 62% of AGC(SPS) soldiers are based in UK, 27% in Germany and 11% elsewhere. The majority, currently 70% serving with field force units, with the remaining 30% in base and training units or HQs, such as MoD.

Members of AGC(SPS) are first trained as soldiers and then specialise as Military Clerks. AGC(SPS) officers complete the same military training as their counterparts in other Arms and Services, starting at the Royal Military Academy, Sandhurst. They are required to attend all promotion courses such as the Junior Command and Staff Course, and to pass the standard career exams prior to promotion to the rank of Major.

The Role of the Provost Branch
The Provost Branch was formed from the formerly independent Corps of Royal Military Police (RMP) and the Military Provost Staff Corps (MPSC). Although they are no longer independent they are still known as the AGC (PRO) and AGC (MPS) thus forming the two parts of the Provost Branch.

Royal Military Police
To provide the police support the Army requires the RMP has the following functions:

a. Providing operational support to units in the field.
b. Preventing crime.
c. Enforcement of the law within the community and assistance with the maintenance of discipline.
d. Providing a 24 hour response service of assistance, advice and information.

Operational support includes advising commanders and the staff who produce the operational movement plans. RMP traffic posts are deployed along the main operational movement routes and provide a constant flow of traffic information regarding the progress of front line troops and the logistical resupply. RMP units with a vehicle to man ratio of 1:3 are also a valuable force for the security of rear areas. In addition, there is a highly trained RMP close protection group that specialises in the protection of high risk VIPs.

The RMP provides the day to day police support for both the army in the UK and dependents and

MoD civilians overseas. RMP units are trained and equipped to deal with the most serious crimes. The Special Investigation Branch (SIB) operates in a similar fashion to the civilian CID.

The Military Provost Staff

AGC(MPS) staff recruited from within the Army, are carefully selected for the leadership, management and training skills necessary to motivate the predominantly young offenders with whom they work. The majority of AGC(MPS) personnel are located in the Military Corrective Training Centre (MCTC) at Colchester where offenders sentenced by military courts are confined.

The Role of the ETS Branch

The AGC(ETS) Branch has responsibility for improving the efficiency, effectiveness and morale of the Army by providing support to operations and the developmental education, training, support and resettlement services that the Army requires to carry out its task. ETS personnel provide assistance at almost all levels of command but their most visible task is the manning of Army Education Centres wherever the Army is stationed. At these centres officers and soldiers receive the educational support necessary for them to achieve both civilian and military qualifications.

The Role of the ALS Branch

The AGC(ALS) Branch advises on all aspects of service and civilian law that may affect every level of the Army from General to Private soldiers. Members of the branch are usually qualified as solicitors or barristers.

Smaller Corps

THE INTELLIGENCE CORPS (Int Corps) - The Int Corps deals with operational intelligence, counter intelligence and security.

THE ROYAL ARMY VETERINARY CORPS (RAVC) - The RAVC looks after the many animals that the Army has on strength. Veterinary tasks in today's army are mainly directed towards guard or search dogs and horses for ceremonial duties.

THE ARMY PHYSICAL TRAINING CORPS (APTC) - Consists mainly of SNCOs who are responsible for unit fitness. The majority of major units have a representative from this corps on their strength.

THE GENERAL SERVICE CORPS (GSC) - A holding unit for specialists. Personnel from this corps are generally members of the reserve army.

SMALL ARMS SCHOOL CORPS (SASC) - A small corps with the responsibility for training instructors in all aspects of weapon handling.

The Royal Gibraltar Regiment
Consists of one infantry company and an artillery battery which assists in the defence of Gibraltar.

The Regular Army Reserve

The Regular Reserve

Individual Reservists (IR) are former members of the Regular Army who after completion of their full-time service may be recalled to the Colours, or who volunteer after their legal Reserve obligation has expired. They have varying degrees of liability for recall and training depending upon factors such as period of Regular Army service, age and sex. Categories of IR are described below:

a. The Regular Army Reserve of Officers (RARO). Retired Regular, Army Emergency Reserve or TA Officers. Those granted Commissions from 1 April 1983 have a compulsory training liability for six years after leaving the Active List. Others may volunteer to train;

b. The Regular Reserve. Ex-Regular soldiers (male and female) who have a compulsory training liability (normally for six years after leaving the Colours) or who have volunteered to join it from other categories;

c. The Long-Term Reserve. Men (but not women) who have completed their Regular Reserve liability and who serve in this category until aged 45. They have no training liability;

d. Army Pensioners. Ex-Regular soldiers (male and female) who are in receipt of a Service pension. They have a legal liability for recall to age 60 (but only to age 55 would be invoked). They have no training liability.

Call-out Procedure

IR are required to keep at home an Instruction Booklet (AB 592A), their ID card and a personalised Booklet (AB 592B). The AB 592A provides IR with general instructions on what they have to do if mobilised. It contains a travel warrant and a special cash order. The AB 592A is computer produced and updated quarterly as required to take account of such changes as address, medical category and age. It explained where the reservist is to report on mobilisation and arrangements for pay and allotments, next-of-kin, clothing held etc.

Under present legislation IR may only be mobilised if called-out by Queen's Order. Mobilisation may involve only a few individuals/units or any number up to general mobilisation when all are called out. If mobilisation is authorised Notices of Call-Out are despatched to those IR concerned by Recorded Delivery as the legal notification. Announcements of call-out are also made by the press, radio and television.

Under the proposals for the new Reserve Forces Act, IR will be liable to call-out under the same new provisions as described above for the TA. In addition, the Act will bring the conditions relating to all three Services in line and will include officers and pensioners who are currently covered by separate legislation/Royal Warrants.

In October 2000 the Regular Army Reserve consisted of 34,200 personnel and IR's totalled 141,000.

The Territorial Army (TA)

Strength of the Territorial Army (1 January 2001)

Armour	4 Regiments
Royal Artillery	7 Regiments (1)
Royal Engineers	5 Regiments

Infantry	15 Battalions
Special Air Service	2 Regiments
Signals	11 Regiments
Equipment Support	4 Battalions
Logistics	7 Regiments
Adjutant General's Corps	2 Regiments (2)
Intelligence Corps	1 Battalion
Aviation	1 Regiment
Medical	15 Hospitals & Field Ambulances

Notes: (1) Including HAC (2) Royal Military Police (3) Total is 74 major units.

TA ORDER OF BATTLE

Royal Armoured Corps

Royal Yeomanry
RHQ - London
Squadrons: Swindon; Leicester; Croydon; Nottingham; London.

Royal Wessex Yeomanry
RHQ - Bovington
Squadrons: Bovington; Salisbury; Cirencester; Barnstable.

Royal Mercian and Lancastrian Yeomanry
RHQ - Telford
Squadrons: Dudley; Telford; Chester; Wigan.

Queen's Own Yeomanry
RHQ - Newcastle
Squadrons: York; Ayr; Belfast; Cupar; Newcastle.

Royal Artillery

Honourable Artillery Company
RHQ - London
Squadrons: 5 all based in the City of London.

100 Regiment
RHQ - Luton
Batteries: Luton; Bristol; Nottingham.

101 Regiment
RHQ - Gateshead
Battalions: Blyth; Newcastle; South Shields.

103 Regiment
RHQ - St Helens

Batteries: Liverpool; Manchester; Bolton.

104 Regiment
RHQ - Newport
Batteries: Wolverhampton; Newport; Worcester.

105 Regiment
RHQ - Edinburgh
Batteries: Newtownards; Glasgow; Arbroath.

106 Regiment
RHQ - London
Batteries: Bury St Edmunds; London; Leeds: Southampton.

Central Volunteers HQ RA
London

<u>**Royal Engineers**</u>

Royal Monmouthshire RE (Militia)
RHQ - Monmouth
Squadrons: Cwmbran; Swansea; Warley.

71 Regiment
RHQ - Leuchars
Squadrons: Paisley; Newcastle.

73 Regiment
RHQ - Nottingham
Squadrons: Sheffield; Nottingham; Chesterfield; St Helier (Jersey).

75 Regiment
RHQ - Failsworth
Squadrons: Birkenhead; Stoke on Trent; Walsall.

101 Regiment
RHQ - London
Squadrons: London; Rochester; Tunbridge Wells.

131 Independent Commando Squadron
London.

135 Topographical Squadron
Ewell.

412 Amphibious Engineer Troop
Hameln.

Central Volunteer HQ RE
Camberley.

Royal Signals
31 Signal Regiment
RHQ - London
Squadrons: Coulsdon; Eastbourne; London.

32 Signal Regiment
RHQ - Glasgow
Squadrons: Aberdeen; East Kilbride; Edinburgh.

33 Signal Regiment
RHQ - Huyton
Squadrons: Manchester; Liverpool; Runcorn.

34 Signal Regiment
RHQ - Middlesborough
Squadrons: Leeds; Darlington; Middlesborough.

35 Signal Regment
RHQ - Coventry
Squadrons: Birmingham; Newcastle-Under-Lyme; Rugby; Shrewsbury.

36 Signal Regiment
RHQ - Ilford
Squadrons: Grays; Colchester; Cambridge.

37 Signal Regiment
RHQ - Redditch
Squadrons: Cardiff; Stratford-Upon-Avon; Manchester; Coventry.

38 Signal Regiment
RHQ - Sheffield
Squadrons: Derby; Sheffield; Nottingham.

39 Signal Regiment
RHQ - Bristol
Squadrons: Uxbridge; Banbury; Gloucester.

40 Signal Regiment
RHQ - Belfast
Squadrons: Belfast; Limavady; Bangor.
71 Signal Regiment
RHQ - London
Squadrons: Lincolns Inn; Bexleyheath; Chelmsford.

72 Signal Regiment
RHQ - Oxford

Squadrons: Bath; Windsor; Aylesbury.

1 Signal Squadron
Bletchley.

2 Signal Squadron
Dundee.

5 Communications Company
Chicksands.

63 Signal Squadron (SAS)

<u>Infantry</u>

The Tyne Tees Regiment
Bn HQ - Durham
Companies: Scarborough; Middlesborough; Bishop Auckland; Newcastle upon Tyne; Ashington.

The King's and Cheshire Regiment
Bn HQ - Warrington
Companies: Liverpool; Warrington; Manchester; Crewe.

51st Highland Regiment
Bn HQ - Perth
Companies: Dundee; Peterhead; Inverness; Dunbarton; Stirling.

52nd Lowland Regiment
Bn HQ - Glasgow
Companies: Edinburgh; Ayr; Glasgow; Galashiels.

The East and West Riding Regiment
Bn HQ - Pontefract
Companies: Huddersfield; Barnsley; Hull; York; Wakefield.

The East of England Regiment
Bn HQ - Bury St Edmunds
Companies: Norwich; Lincoln; Leicester; Mansfield; Chelmsford.

The London Regiment
Bn HQ - Battersea
Companies: Westminster; Edgeware; Balham; Camberwell; Mayfair; West Ham.

3rd (Volunteer) Battalion, The Princess of Wales's Royal Regiment (Queen's and Royal Hampshires)
Bn HQ - Canterbury
Companies: Farnham; Brighton; Canterbury.

The Royal Rifle Volunteers
Bn HQ - Reading
Companies: Oxford; Reading; Portsmouth; Milton Keynes.

The Rifle Volunteers
Bn HQ - Exeter
Companies: Gloucester; Taunton; Dorchester; Truro; Exeter.

The West Midlands Regiment
Bn HQ - Wolverhampton
Companies: Birmingham; Kidderminster; Burton upon Trent; Stoke-on-Trent; Shrewsbury.

The Royal Welsh Regiment
Bn HQ - Cardiff
Companies: Wrexham; Swansea; Cardiff; Colwyn Bay.

The Lancastrian and Cumbrian Volunteers
Bn HQ - Preston
Companies: Barrow in Furness; Blackburn; Workington; Preston.

The Royal Irish Rangers
Bn HQ - Portadown
Companies: Newtonards; Newtownabbey.

4th (Volunteer) Battalion, The Parachute Regiment
Bn HQ - Pudsey
Companies: London; Pudsey; Glasgow.

Army Medical Services
201 Field Hospital
RHQ - Newcastle upon Tyne
Squadrons: Newton Aycliffe; Stockton-on-Tees; Newcastle upon Tyne.

202 Field Hospital
RHQ - Birmingham
Squadrons: Birmingham; Stoke on Trent; Oxford; Shrewsbury.

203 Field Hospital
RHQ - Cardiff
Squadrons: Cardiff; Swansea; Abergavenny.

204 Field Hospital
RHQ - Belfast
Squadrons: Belfast; Ballymena; Newtownards; Armagh.
205 Field Hospital
RHQ - Glasgow
Squadrons: Glasgow; Aberdeen; Dundee; Edinburgh.

207 Field Hospital
RHQ - Manchester
Squadrons: Stockport; Blackburn; Bury.

208 Field Hospital
RHQ - Liverpool
Squadrons: Liverpool; Ellesmere; Lancaster.

212 Field Hospital
RHQ - Sheffield
Squadrons: Sheffield; Bradford; Nottingham; Leeds.

243 Field Hospital
RHQ - Keynsham
Squadrons: Keynsham; Exeter; Plymouth; Portsmouth.

256 Field Hospital
RHQ - Walworth, London
Squadrons: Walworth; Hammersmith; Kingston; Bow.

253 Field Ambulance
Belfast.

254 Field Ambulance
Cambridge.

152 Ambulance Regiment
RHQ - Belfast
Squadrons: Londonderry; Belfast; Bridgend.

C (144) Parachute Medical Squadron
London.

B (220) Medical Squadron
Maidstone.

B (250) Medical Squadron
Hull.

B (225) Medical Squadron
Dundee.

C (251) Medical Squadron
Sunderland.

C (222) Medical Squadron
Leicester.

HQ Army Medical Service TA
York.

<u>**Royal Logistic Corps**</u>
150 (Northumbria) Transport Regiment
RHQ - Hull
Squadrons: Hull; Tynemouth; Leeds; Doncaster.

151 (Greater London) Logistic Support Regiment
RHQ - Croydon
Squadrons: Romford; Sutton; Barnet; Southall.

156 (North West) Transport Regiment
RHQ - Liverpool
Squadrons: Liverpool; Birkenhead; Salford; Bootle.

157 (Wales and Midland) Logistic Support Regiment
RHQ - Cardiff
Squadrons: Cardiff; Telford; Swansea; Carmarthen; West Bromwich.

158 (Royal Anglain) Transport Regiment
RHQ - Peterborough
Squadrons: Peterborough; Kempston; Ipswich; Loughborough.

Scottish Transport Regiment
RHQ - Dunfermline
Squadrons: Dunfermline; Glasgow; Edinburgh; Glenrothes; Irvine.

168 Pioneer Regiment
RHQ - Grantham
Squadrons: Grantham; Cramlington; Coulby Newham.

CVHQ and HR RLC TA
Grantham.

<u>**Royal Electrical And Mechanical Engineers**</u>
101 Battalion REME
Bn HQ - Queensferry
Companies: Prestatyn; Coventry; Clifton; Grangemouth.

102 Battalion REME
Bn HQ - Newton Aycliffe
Companies: Newton Aycliffe; Rotherham; Scunthorpe; Newcastle upon Tyne.

103 Battalion REME
Bn HQ - Crawley
Companies: Portsmouth; Redhill; Ashford.

104 Battalion REME
Bn HQ - Bordon
Company: Northampton.

HQ REME TA
Bordon

<u>**Adjutant General's Corps**</u>
4 Regiment, Royal Military Police
RHQ - Aldershot
Companies: West Bromwich; Brixton.

5 Regiment, Royal Military Police
RHQ - Livingston
Companies: Livingston; Stockton-on-Tees.

CVHQ AGC:
Worthy Down.

Intelligence Corps

3 (Volunteer) Military Intelligence Battalion:
BHQ - London
Companies: London; Edinburgh; York; Keynsham; Birmingham.

<u>**Special Air Service**</u>
21 and 23 Regiments SAS

<u>**Army Air Corps**</u>
7 Regiment AAC
Netheravon.

Officer Training Corps
Aberdeen University Officer Training Corps
Birmingham University Officer Training Corps
Bristol University Officer Training Corps
Cambridge University Officer Training Corps
East Midlands University Officer Training Corps
City of Edinburgh University Officer Training Corps
Exeter University Officer Training Corps
Glasgow and Strathclyde Universities Officer Training Corps
Leeds University Officer Training Corps
Liverpool University Officer Training Corps
London University Officer Training Corps
Manchester and Salford University Officer Training Corps
Northumbrian University Officer Training Corps
Oxford University Officer Training Corps
Queens University Officer Training Corps
Sheffield University Officer Training Corps

Southampton University Officer Training Corps
Tayforth University Officer Training Corps
University of Wales Officer Training Corps

Currently the TA has 43,300 personnel and would be reinforced in war by 34,200 Individual Reservists (IRs) to a fully mobilised establishment of 77,500. The TA acts as a General Reserve to the Army, with a secondary but vitally important function being the promotion of a nationwide link between the military and civilian community.

The MoD describes the role of the TA as follows:

a. To reinforce the Regular Army, as and when required, with individuals, sub-units and units, either in the UK or overseas;
b. To provide the framework for bringing units up to full War Establishment strength and the basis for forming new units in times of national emergency.

Current plans appear to place a large part of the defence of mainland UK in the hands of the TA. TA soldiers have been assigned national defence roles such as, guarding vital installations, under-taking reconnaissance and early warning, providing communications and damage control. In early 1995, a composite TA platoon served alongside the regular infantry component of the Falkland Islands garrison, and in Bosnia and Kosovo during the past 3 years an average of over 200 TA soldiers at any one time has been serving alongside their regular counterparts as individual reinforcements. In the longer, term TA Soldiers on short term contracts will almost certainly prove to be a valuable addition to regular units where manpower is at a premium.

TA Infantry Units have a General Purpose structure which will give them flexibility of employment across the spectrum of military operations. All Infantry Battalions, including Parachute Battalions, have a common establishment of three Rifle Companies and a Headquarters Company. In addition there are four Fire Support Battalions, each with a Headquarters and two Heavy Weapons Companies. Each company will have Milan, Mortar and Machine Gun Platoons. These battalions will provide operational and training support to all TA Battalions.

The 1998 SDR produced a TA with an emphasis on reducing the old Home Defence Role and a new priority of providing highly trained and properly resourced units to support the Regular Army worldwide.

Major Army Equipment

Fv 4030/4 Challenger 1
(Phased out of operational service in November 2000 - being replaced by Challenger 2.
Armament 1 x 120mm L11A7 gun: 2 x 7.62mm Machine Guns: 2 x 5 barrel smoke dischargers:
Engine Rolls-Royce CV12: Ammunition capacity 44 rounds of 120mm: 6,000 rounds of 7.62mm:
Engine power 1,200 bhp at 2,300 rpm: engine capacity 26.1 litres: Max road speed 56km/h:
Weight loaded 62,000kg: Length Hull 9.87m: Length Gun Forward 11.55m: Height 3.04m: Width
3.42m: Ground clearance 0.5m: Crew 4: Ground pressure 0.96 kg/cm2: Fording depth (no prep)
1.07m.

Produced by the Royal Ordnance Factory in Leeds, the first Challenger 1's were delivered to the British Army in 1983.

Challenger 1 was a development of the Centurion/Chieftain line which was modified to produce the Shir Iran 2 originally planned for service with the Iranian forces. After the Iranian Revolution the Shir Iran 2 project was taken over by the British Army and the end result was Challenger, later redesignated as Challenger 1.

The main differences between Challenger 1 and its predecessor Chieftain (the MBT that it replaced) were in the engine and armour. The Challenger engine, which produces 1,200 bhp at 2,300 rpm was far more powerful than the Chieftain engine, and the Chobham Armour carried is believed to give protection from almost all types of anti-tank weapon. Chobham armour is thought to consist of several layers of nylon micromesh, bonded on both sides by sheets of titanium alloy, in addition to several other layers of specialised armour and ceramics. Challenger 1 is believed to have cost about £2 million per vehicle at 1987 prices.

The main armament on all Challenger 1's is currently being upgraded by the installation of the L30 CHARM gun. In addition to firing the existing range of ammunition, this gun fires a new armour piercing fin stabilised discarding sabot round with a depleted uranium warhead, which should be able to defeat the armour on all known MBTs. An additional improvement is the ACTAS (Active Cupola Target Acquisition System) which has been retrofitted to all Challenger 1's. This system permits the use of the commander's cupola for target acquisition and designation to the gunner.

The only nation known to be operating Challenger 1 other than the UK is Jordan, where the 274 tanks in service are known as Khalid. Under an agreement signed in March 1999, another 288 Challenger 1s are to be supplied to Jordan over a three-year period to enable the Jordanian fleet of Centurion MBTs (locally called Tariq) to be replaced.

In the short term the UK will continue to operate approximately 40 Challenger 1 ARV's and 8 Challenger 1 driver training tanks.

Challenger 2

(386 Challenger 2 on order) Crew 4; Length gun forward 11.55m; Hull length 8.32m; Height to Turret roof 2.49m; Width 3.52m; Ground clearance 0.50m; Combat weight 62,500 kg; Main Armament 1 x 120mm L30 CHARM Gun; Ammunition carried 52 rounds - APFSDS, HESH, Smoke, DU; Secondary armament Co-axial 7.62mm MG; 7.62mm GPMG Turret mounted for Air Defence; Ammunition Carried 4,000 rounds 7.62mm; Engine CV12TCA 12 cylinder - Auxiliary Engine Perkins 4.108 4-stroke diesel; Gearbox TN54 epicyclic - 6 forward gears and 2 reverse; Road speed 56 km/h; Cross country speed 40 km/h; Fuel capacity 1,797 litres.

In July 1991, the UK MoD announced an order for 127 x Challenger 2 MBT and 13 driver train-ing tanks. This initial order was followed in July 1994 by a further contract for 259 vehicles to make a total of 386. Under original plans this figure would have been enough to equip 8 regi-ments with the vehicle and allow 82 tanks for training and reserve when plans were for regiments to have 38 tanks in three squadrons. However under the new 1998 SDR proposals there will be 6 regiments each with 58 tanks (total 348).

Challenger 2 is manufactured by Vickers Defence Systems and production is being undertaken at its factories in Newcastle-Upon-Tyne and Leeds. At 1995 prices, Challenger 2 was believed to cost £2.5 million per vehicle.

Although the hull and automotive parts of the Challenger 2 are based upon that of its predecessor Challenger 1, the new tank incorporates over 150 improvements aimed at increasing reliability and maintainability. The whole of the Challenger 2 turret is of a totally new design and the vehicle has a crew of four - commander, gunner, loader/signaller and driver. The 120mm rifled Royal Ordnance L30 gun fires all current tank ammunition plus the new depleted uranium (DU) round with a stick charge propellant system.

The design of the turret incorporates several of the significant features that Vickers had developed for its Mk 7 MBT (a Vickers turret on a Leopard 2 chassis). The central feature is an entirely new fire control system based on the Ballistic Control System developed by Computing Devices Company (Canada) for the US Army's M1A1 MBT. This second- generation computer incorporates dual 32-bit processors with a MIL STD 1553B databus and has sufficient growth potential to accept Battlefield Information Control System (BICS) functions and navigation aids (a GPS satnav system). The armour is an uprated version of Challenger 1's Chobham armour.

The first production models of the Challenger 2 were taken into service by the Royal Scots Dragoon Guards in mid 1994 and the regiment was the first to deploy to Germany with the new tank in mid 1995. The actual in service date (ISD) for the vehicle was December 1995 and we would expect to see all 386 Challenger 2's in service with the British Army by the end of 2002. Production of the UK's Challenger 2 contract should be complete by the end of 2001.

The only export order so far is an Omani order for 18 x Challenger 2 MBTs, 2 x Driver Training Vehicles and 4 x Challenger Armoured Repair and Recovery Vehicles, signed during 1993. However, Vickers Defence Systems has high hopes for the vehicle in the remainder of the world market during the next ten years.

A contract has also been signed for 66 x Engineer Tank Systems (ETS) based on a modified Challenger 2 MBT chassis with design, development and production being undertaken by Vickers Defence Systems from 2003 with an in-service date of 2005.

There will be two versions of the ETS, the first is the Titan bridge-laying vehicle and the second the Trojan flexible obstacle/ mineclearing vehicle. Titan will be able to carry and lay the current in-service 26 m and 13.5 m long aluminium bridges with the crew under complete protection.

It is expected that VDS will win a contract for the supply of 32 Challenger 2-based Heavy Armoured Repair and Recovery Vehicles to enable the replacement of the remaining Chieftain armoured recovery vehicles. This order has been postponed but is expected to be placed when sufficient funds are available and vehicles could be in service in 2004.

MCV - 80 Fv 510 (Warrior)
(789 In Service) Weight loaded 24,500kg: Length 6.34m: Height to turret top 2.78m: Width 3.0m: Ground Clearance 0.5m: Max Road Speed 75km/h: Road range 500km: Engine Rolls Royce CV8 diesel: Horsepower 550hp: Crew 2 (carries 8 infantry soldiers): Armament L21 30mm Rarden

Cannon: Coaxial EX-34 7.62mm Chain Gun: Smoke Dischargers Royal Ordnance Visual and Infra Red Screening Smoke (VIRSS).

Warrior is an armoured infantry fighting vehicle (AIFV) that replaced many of the AFV 432 in the armoured infantry battalions. Following drawdown, the original buy of 1,048 vehicles was reduced and in early 1993, it was announced that the total buy had been reduced to 789 units. The vehicle is in service with 2 armoured infantry battalions in the UK (with 3 (UK) Div) and 6 armoured infantry battalions in Germany (with 1 (UK) Armd Div). Warrior is armed with the 30mm Rarden cannon that gives the crew a good chance of destroying enemy APCs at ranges of up to 1,500m. The vehicle carries an infantry section of seven men.

The vehicle is NBC proof, and a full range of night vision equipment is included as standard. The basic Warrior is part of a family of vehicles which include a Milan ATGW carrier, a mechanised recovery vehicle, an engineer combat version and an artillery command vehicle to name but a few. Examination of the contract details reveal that each vehicle cost approximately £550,000 at 1990 prices.

The vehicle has seen successful operational service in the Gulf (1991) and with the British contingent serving in Bosnia and Kosovo. The vehicle has proven protection against mines, and there is dramatic BBC TV footage of a Warrior running over a Serbian anti-tank mine in Bosnia with little or no serious damage to the vehicle.

The Kuwait MoD has signed a contract for the purchase of Warrior vehicles some of which are Recce vehicles armed with a 90mm Cockerill gun. Industry sources confirm that the Kuwait contract is for 230 vehicles.

Following the 1998 SDR, an extra Warrior battalion has been formed to act as the armoured infantry battalion for the new 12th Mechanised Brigade.

AT - 105 Saxon

(500 of 664 Saxon believed to be in operational service) Weight 10,670kg: Length 5.16m: Width 2.48m: Height 2.63m: Ground Clearance (axles) 0.33m: Max road speed 96km/h: Max Road Range 510km: Fuel capacity 160 litres: Fording 1.12m: Gradient 60 degrees: Engine Bedford 600 6-cylinder diesel developing 164bhp at 2,800rpm: Armour proof against 7.62mm rounds fired at point blank range: Crew 2 + 10 max.

The Saxon was manufactured by GKN Defence and the first of the 664 units for the British Army were delivered in late 1983. The vehicle, which can be best described as a battlefield taxi is designed around truck parts and does not require the extensive maintenance of track and running gear normally associated with APCs/AIFVs. Capable of travelling across very rough terrain and fording over 3 feet of water, the Saxon is a welcome addition to the inventory of infantry units in UKLF providing much needed battlefield mobility. The vehicle is fitted with a 7.62mm machine gun for LLAD.

Each vehicle cost over £100,000 at 1984 prices and they are on issue to 6 mechanised infantry battalions assigned to 3 (UK) Division. The vehicle has been used very successfully by British mechanised battalions serving with the UN in Bosnia where the addition of an L37 turret has enhanced its firepower.

During 1993 the British Army took delivery of the Saxon Patrol vehicle for service in Northern Ireland. This new vehicle has a Cummins BT 5.1 engine instead of the Bedford 6 cyclinder installed on the APC version and other enhancements for internal security operations such as roof-mounted searchlights, improved armour, a barricade removal device and an anti-wire device.

Saxon Patrol comes in two versions, troop carrier and ambulance. The troop carrier carries ten men and the ambulance 2 stretcher cases. Industry sources suggest that this contract was for 137 vehicles at a cost of some £20 million resulting in a unit cost per vehicle of approximately £145,000.

Milan 2
Missile - Max range 2,000m; Mix range 25m; Length 918mm; Weight 6.73kg; Diameter 125mm; Wing span 267mm; Rate of fire 3-4rpm; Warhead - Weight 2.70kg; Diameter 115mm; Explosive content 1.79kg; Firing Post- Weight 16.4kg; Length 900mm; Height 650mm; Width 420mm; Armour penetration 352mm; Time of flight to max range 12.5 secs; Missile speed 720km/h; Guidance semi-automatic command to line of sight by means of wires:

Milan is a second generation, anti-tank weapon, the result of a joint development project between France and West Germany, with British Milan launchers and missiles built under licence in the UK by British Aerospace Dynamics. We believe that the cost of a Milan missile is currently in the region of £15,000 and that to date, the UK MOD has purchased over 50,000 missiles. The Milan comes in two main components, which are the launcher and the missile. It is then a simple matter to clip both items together and prepare the system for use. On firing, the operator has only to keep his aiming mark on the target and the SACLOS guidance system will do the rest.

Milan was the first of a series of infantry anti-tank weapons that seriously started to challenge the supremacy of the main battle tank on the battlefield. During fighting in Chad in 1987, it appears that 12 Chadian Milan post mounted on Toyota Light Trucks were able to account for over 60 Libyan T-55s and T-62s. Reports from other conflicts suggest similar results.

Milan is on issue throughout the British Army and an armoured infantry battalion could be expected to be equipped with 24 firing posts and 200 missiles. Milan is in service with 36 nations worldwide and it is believed that are over 1,000 firing posts in service with the British Army.

There are longer term plans to replace Milan with either the US Javelin or the Israeli Gill anti tank missiles. Quantities of these systems have been purchased by the UK Defence Procurement Agency (DPA) for missile trials in late 2001. These are the only two contenders for the UK Light

Forces Anti-Tank Guided Weapon System (ATGWS), which will initially replace Milan in service with rapid reaction formations such as the army's 16 Air Assault Brigade and Royal Marines 3 Commando Brigade.

It is expected that the initial requirement will be for at least 100 firing posts and 2,000 missiles with an in-service date of 2005. The requirement stipulates that a two-man crew be capable of carrying a firing post and two missiles for up to 20km. In addition to being capable of defeating main battle tanks (MBTs) from all aspects it is also required to have a secondary capability against other battlefield targets such as fixed defences.

5.56mm Individual Weapon (IW) (SA 80)

Effective Range 400m: Muzzle Velocity 940m/s: Rate of Fire from 610-775rpm: Weight 4.98kg (with 30 round magazine): Length Overall 785mm: Barrel Length 518mm: Trigger Pull 3.12-4.5kg:

Designed to fire the standard NATO 5.56mm x 45mm round the SA 80 is fitted with an X4 telescopic (SUSAT) sight as standard. Although some modification work is still in progress, the British Army is now totally equipped with this weapon. The total buy for SA 80 is for 332,092 weapons. Issues of the weapon are believed to be as follows: Royal Navy 7,864; Royal Marines 8,350; Royal Air Force 42,221; MoD Police 1,878; Army 271,779. At 1991/92 prices the total cost of the SA80 contract was in the order of £384.16 million. By mid-1995 some 10,000 SA 80 Night Sights and 3rd Generation Image Intensifier Tubes had been delivered, completing the contract.

The weapon has had a mixed press and much has been made of the 32 modifications that have been made to the SA80 since 1983. Although there are many critics outside of the services, in the main the serving soldiers that we have spoken to have praised the weapon, and those that have had experience on both the SLR and SA80 are unstinting in their praise for the newer system.

AS 90

(179 in service) Crew 5: Length 9.07m: Width 3.3m: Height 3.0m overall: Ground Clearance 0.41m: Turret ring diameter 2.7m: Armour 17mm: Calibre 155mm: Range (39 cal) 24.7km (52 cal) 30km: Recoil length 780mm: Rate of fire 3 rounds in 10 secs (burst) 6 rounds per minute (intense) 2 rounds per minute (sustained): Secondary armament 7.62mm MG: Traverse 6,400 mills: Elevation -89/+1.244 mills: Ammunition carried 48 x 155mm projectiles and charges (31 turret & 17 hull): Engine Cummins VTA903T turbo-charged V8 diesel 660hp: Max speed 53 km/h: Gradient 60 degrees: Vertical obstacle 0.75m: Trench crossing 2.8m: Fording depth 1.5m: road range 420km.

AS 90 is manufactured by Vickers Shipbuilding and Engineering (VSEL) at Barrow in Furness and in 1992 was the subject of an order for 179 guns under a fixed price contract for £300 million. These 179 guns are equipping 5 field regiments, completely replacing the Abbot and M109

in British service. The first Regiment to receive AS 90 was 1st Regiment Royal Horse Artillery (1 RHA) in October 1993, followed by issues to 3 RHA, 4 Regt, 40 Regt and 26 Regt. Each Regiment will received 4 batterys of eight guns, of which six will be manned in peacetime. Three of these Regiments are under the command of 1(UK) Armoured Division in Germany and two under the command of 3 (UK) Div in the United Kingdom. Production of AS 90 was complete in late 1995.

AS 90 is currently equipped with a 39 calibre gun which fires the NATO L15 unassisted projectile out to a range of 24.7 km (RAP range is 30km). It is believed that in the future models may have the 52 calibre gun with ranges of 30km (unassisted) and 40kms (assisted projectile).

AS 90 has been fitted with an autonomous navigation and gun-laying system (AGLS), enabling it to work independently of external sighting references. Central to the system is an inertial dynamic reference unit (DRU) taken from the US Army's MAPS (Modular Azimuth Positioning System). The bulk of the turret electronics are housed in the Turret Control Computer (TCC) which controls the main turret functions, including gunlaying, magazine control, loading systems control, power distribution and testing.

Following the 1998 SDR, it was announced that a light gun regiment would be re-roled and equipped with AS 90 to provide the fire support for the new 12th Mechanised Brigade. At this stage it is not clear if extra AS 90 are to be purchased, or if the deficit in the number of guns available to form 6 x 32 gun regiments will be met by having 6 x 24 gun regiments.

227 mm MLRS

(62 launchers in service - 54 operational in 3 Regiments): Crew 3: Weight loaded 24,756kg: Weight unloaded 19,573kg: Length 7.167m: Width 2.97m: Height (stowed) 2.57m: Height (max elevation) 5.92m: Ground clearance 0.43m: Max road speed 64km/h: Road range 480km: Fuel Capacity 617 litres: Fording 1.02m: Vertical obstacle 0.76m: Engine Cummings VTA-903 turbo-charged 8 cylinder diesel developing 500 bhp at 2,300 rpm: Rocket diameter 227mm: Rocket Length 3.93m: M77 Bomblet rocket weight 302.5kg: AT2 SCATMIN rocket weight 254.46kg: M77 Bomblet Range 11.5 -32km: AT2 SCATMIN Rocket range 39km: One round "Fire for Effect" equals one launcher firing 12 rockets: Ammunition carried 12 rounds (ready to fire).

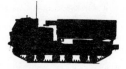

The British Army has purchased MLRS to replace the M107 SP Guns that were previously deployed with Corps Artillery Heavy Regiments. The MLRS is based on the US M2 Bradley chassis and the system is self loaded with 2 x rocket pod containers, each containing 6 x rockets. The whole loading sequence is power assisted and loading takes between 20 and 40 minutes. There is no manual procedure.

A single round "Fire for Effect" (12 rockets) delivers 7,728 bomblets and the coverage achieved is considered sufficient to neutralise a 500m x 500m target. The weapon system is range dependent and therefore more rounds will be required to guarantee the effect as the range to the target increases. Ammunition for the MLRS is carried on the DROPS vehicle, a Medium Mobility Load Carrier. Each DROPS vehicle with a trailer can carry 8 x Rocket Pod Containers and there are 15 x DROPS vehicles supporting the 9 x M270 Launcher vehicles within each MLRS battery.

The handling of MLRS is almost a military "art form" and is an excellent example of the dependence of modern artillery on high technology. Getting the best out of the system is more than just parking the tubes and firing in the direction of the enemy. MLRS is the final link in a chain that includes almost everything available on the modern battlefield, from high speed communications, collation of intelligence, logistics and a multitude of high technology artillery skills and drills. Remotely piloted vehicles can be used to acquire targets, real time TV and data links are used to move information from target areas to formation commanders and onward to the firing positions. Helicopters can be used to dump ammunition and, in some cases to move firing platforms.

The British Army is currently looking at extremely long range terminally-guided submunitions (TGSMs) to be delivered by MLRS.

The US Army is currently operating 416 MLRS, the French have 82, the West Germans 206 and the Italians 21.

Starstreak HVM
(108 Fire Units In Service) Missile length 1.39m: Missile diameter 0.27m: Missile speed mach 3+: Maximum range 5.5 kms:

Short Missile Systems of Belfast is the prime contractors for the HVM (High Velocity Missile) which continues along the development path of both Blowpipe and Javelin. The system can be shoulder launched or by mounting on the LML (lightweight multiple launcher) or vehicle borne on the Alvis Stormer APC. The Stormer APC has an eight round launcher and 12 reload missiles can be carried inside the vehicle.

HVM has been optimised to counter threats from fast pop-up type strikes by attack helicopters. The missile employs a system of three dart type projectiles which can make multiple hits on the target. Each of these darts has an explosive warhead. It is believed that the HVM has an SSK (single shot to kill) probability of over 95%.

12 Regiment RA stationed at Sennelager in Germany is equipped with HVM and supports 1 (UK) Division. The Regiment has 108 launchers divided among the three missile batteries (36 per battery). An HVM detachment of 4 is carried in a Stormer armoured vehicle and in each vehicle there are 4 personnel. Inside the vehicle there are twelve ready to use missiles with a further 8 stored inside as reloads.

Rapier
(64 fire units in service) Guidance semi automatic to Line of Sight (SACLOS): Missile diameter 13.3 cm: Missile length 2.35 m: Rocket solid fuelled: Warhead high explosive: Launch weight 42 kg: Speed Mach 2+: Ceiling 3,000 m: Maximum range 6,800 m: Fire unit height 2.13 m: Fire unit weight 1,227 kg: Radar height (in action) 3.37 m: Radar weight 1,186 kg: Optical Tracker height 1.54 m: Optical tracker weight 119 kg: Generator weight 243 kg: Generator Height 0.91 m.

The Rapier system provides 24 hour coverage through cloud, and provides Low Level Air Defence

(LLAD) over the battlefield. The two forms of Rapier in service are as follows:-

Rapier Field Standard B2 consists of an Optical Tracker, a launcher, a Radar and a Generator. The into-action time of the system is thought to be about 15 minutes and the surveillance radar is believed to scan out to 15 km. Each fire unit can therefore cover an Air Defence Area (ADA) of about 100 square kms. Having discharged the 6 missiles on a Fire Unit, 2 men are thought to be able to carry out a reload in about 3 minutes.

Rapier Field standard C (FSC) incorporates a range of technological improvements including an advanced 3 dimensional radar tracker acquisition system designed by Plessey. The towed system launcher will mount eight missiles (able to fire two simultaneously) which will be manufactured in two warhead versions. One of these will be a proximity explosive round and the other a kinetic energy round. The total cost of the Rapier FS"C" programme is £1,886 million.

The Royal Artillery has two regiments equipped with Rapier and both are in the UK. In the Falklands campaign, Rapier was credited with 14 kills and 6 probables from a total of 24 missiles fired.

Rapier has now been sold to the armed forces of at least 14 nations. We believe that sales have amounted to over 25,000 missiles, 600 launchers and 350 Blindfire radars.

Lynx AH - Mark 7/9
(111 in service). Length fuselage 12.06 m: Height 3.4 m: Rotor diameter 12.8 m: Max speed 330 kph: Cruising speed 232 kph: Range 885 km: Engines 2 Rolls-Royce Gem 41: Power 2 x 850 bhp: Fuel capacity 918 litres(internal): Weight (max take off) 4,763 kg: Crew one pilot, one air-gunner/observer: Armament 8 x TOW Anti-tank missiles: 2-4 7.62 mm machine guns: Passengers-able to carry 10 PAX: Combat radius approximately 100kms with 2 hour loiter.

Lynx is the helicopter currently used by the British Army to counter the threat posed by enemy armoured formations. Armed with 8 x TOW missiles the Lynx is now the mainstay of the British armed helicopter fleet. However, in addition to its role as an anti-tank helicopter, Lynx can be used for fire support using machine guns, troop lifts, casualty evacuation and many more vital battlefield tasks.

During hostilities we would expect Lynx to operate on a section basis, with 2 or 3 Lynx aircraft armed with TOW directed by a Section Commander possibly flying in a Gazelle. The Section Commander would control what is in reality an airborne tank ambush and, following an attack on enemy armour decide when to break contact. Having broken contact, the aircraft would return to a forward base to refuel and rearm. Working from forward bases, some of which are within 10kms of the FEBA, it is suggested that a Lynx section could be "turned around" in less than 15 minutes. Lynx with TOW replaced SCOUT with SS11 as the British Army's anti-tank helicopter.

We believe the majority of Lynx in British service to be Lynx Mark 7 and that there are currently 24 Lynx Mark 9 (the latest version) in the inventory.

Lynx is known to be in service with France, Brazil, Argentina, The Netherlands, Qatar, Denmark, Norway, Germany and Nigeria. The naval version carries anti-ship missiles.

Longbow Apache (WAH-64)

(67 On order) Gross Mission weight 7,746 kgs (17,077 lb; Cruise speed at 500 meters 272 kph; Maximum Range (Internal Fuel with 20 minute reserve) 462 kms; General Service ceiling 3,505 meters (11,500 ft); Crew 2; Carries - 16 x Hellfire II missiles (range 6,000 meters approx); 76 x 2.75" rockets; 1,200 30mm cannon rounds; 4 x Air to Air Missiles; Engines 2 x Rolls Royce RTM-332.

The UK MoD ordered 67 Longbow Apache from Westland during mid 1995 with the first aircraft being delivered to the Army Air Corps during 2000. From this figure of 67 aircraft we believe that there will be 48 aircraft in two regiments (each of 24 aircraft). The remaining 19 aircraft will be used for trials, training and a war maintenance reserve (WMR).

In September 1999 the first production WAH-64 Apache made its maiden flight and was handed over to GKN Westland (the UK contractor) at the Boeing aircraft plant in Arizona. Boeing has built the first eight aircraft and will partially assemble the other 59. GKN Westland will undertake final assembly, flight testing and programme support at its Yeovil factory.

In March 2000, GKN Westland delivered to the British Army the first of its WAH-64 aircraft. The first nine WAH-64s were declared operational in December 2000 and deliveries are due to be completed in 2003.

BR90 Family of Bridges

In early 1994 the UK MoD announced that the production order had been placed for the BR90 family of bridges that should have entered service between January 1996 and June 1997 as follows:

January 1996	General Support Bridge
November 1996	Close Support Bridge
May 1997	Two Span Bridge
June 1997	Long Span Bridge

Reports during 2000 indicate that, due to engineering problems, the in service date for all four types have slipped and that only the General Support and Close Support Bridges are actually in service.

BR90 will be deployed with Royal Engineer units in both Germany and the UK. The production order, valued at approximately £140 million, was issued and accepted in October 1993.

The components of the system are:

Close Support Bridge - This consists of three tank-launched bridges capable of being carried on the in-service Chieftain bridgelayer and a TBT (Tank Bridge Transporter) truck.

	Weight	Length	Gap
No 10 Bridge	13 tons	26m	45m
No 11 Bridge	7.4 tons	16m	14.5m
No 12 Bridge	5.3 tons	13.5m	12m

The existing No 8 and No 9 bridges previously carried in the Chieftain AVLB will be retained in service.

The Unipower TBT 8 x 8 truck can carry 1 x No 10 Bridge, 1 x No 11 Bridge or 2 x No 12 Bridges. The TBT has an unladen weight of 21 tons and is also used to transport the General Support Bridge.

General Support Bridge - This system utilises the Automated Bridge Launching Equipment (ABLE) that is capable of launching bridges up to 44 metres in length. The ABLE vehicle is positioned with its rear pointing to the gap to be crossed and a lightweight launch rail extended across the gap. The bridge is then assembled and winched across the gap supported by the rail, with sections added until the gap is crossed. Once the bridge has crossed the gap the ABLE launch rail is recovered. A standard ABLE system set consists of an ABLE vehicle and 2 x TBT carrying a 32 metre bridge set. A 32m bridge can be built by 10 men in about 25 minutes.

Spanning Systems - There are two basic spanning systems. The long span systems allows for lengthening a 32 metre span to 44 metres using ABLE and the two span system allows 2 x 32 metre bridge sets to be constructed by ABLE and secured in the middle by piers or floating pontoons, crossing a gap of up to 60 metres.

CHAPTER 4 - THE ROYAL AIR FORCE

General - Royal Air Force Squadrons (as at 1 Jan 2001)

	2001	1980
Strike/Attack Squadrons	5	14
Offensive Support Squadrons	5	5
Air Defence Squadrons	5	16
Maritime Patrol Squadrons	3	4
Reconnaissance Squadrons	5	5
Airborne Early Warning Squadrons	2	1
Transport/Tanker Squadrons	8	9
Helicopter Squadrons	9	4
Surface to Air Missile Squadrons	4	8
Ground Defence Squadrons	5	5
	51	71

Note: 1980 figures are for comparison purposes. The total RAF manpower figures for 1 October 2000 are as follows:

	Trained	Untrained	Total
Officers	9,800	1,200	11,000
Other Ranks	41,200	2,500	43,700
Totals	51,000	3,700	54,700

Note: As of early 2001 there were about 1,860 qualified pilots included in the above totals.

Royal Air Force Squadron Listing (as at 1 Jan 2001)

We estimate that there were some 482 combat aircraft capable of delivering missiles or ordnance in front-line service on 1 January 2001.

1 Sqn	12 x Harrier GR7	RAF Wittering (JFH)
	1 x Harrier T10	
2 Sqn	12 x Tornado GR1A	RAF Marham
3 Sqn	12 x Harrier GR7	RAF Cottesmore (JFH)
	1 x Harrier T10	
4 Sqn	12 x Harrier GR7	RAF Cottesmore (JFH)
	1 x Harrier T10	
5 Sqn	13 x Tornado F3	RAF Coningsby
6 Sqn	12 x Jaguar GR1A/B (1)	RAF Coltishall
	1 x Jaguar T2A	
7 Sqn	11 x Chinook HC2	RAF Odiham (JHC)
8 Sqn	3 x Sentry AEW1	RAF Waddington
9 Sqn	12 x Tornado GR1	RAF Marham
10 Sqn	8 x VC10 C1K	RAF Brize Norton

11 Sqn	13 x Tornado F3	RAF Leeming
12 Sqn	12 x Tornado GR1B	RAF Lossiemouth
13 Sqn	12 x Tornado GR1A	RAF Marham
14 Sqn	14 x Tornado GR1	RAF Lossemouth
18 Sqn	10 x Chinook HC2	RAF Odiham (JHC)
22 Sqn	8 x Sea King HAR3	RMB Chivenor (Sqn HQ)*
23 Sqn	3 x Sentry AEW	RAF Waddington
24 Sqn	10 x Hercules C1/C3	RAF Lyneham
25 Sqn	13 x Tornado F3	RAF Leeming
27 Sqn	9 x Chinook HC2	RAF Odiham (JHC)
28 Sqn	12 x Merlin Mk3	RAF Benson (JHC)
30 Sqn	10 x Hercules C1/C3	RAF Lyneham
31 Sqn	12 x Tornado GR1	RAF Marham
32 (The Royal) Sqn	5 x BAe 125	RAF Northolt
	2 x BAe 146	
	2 x Twin Squirrel	
33 Sqn	15 x Puma HC1	RAF Benson (JHC)
39 Sqn	(1 PRU) 4 x Canberra PR9	RAF Marham
	1 x Canberra T4	
	2 x Jaguar T4	
41 Sqn	12 x Jaguar GR1A/B	RAF Coltishall
43 Sqn	13 x Tornado F3	RAF Leuchars
47 Sqn	10 x Hercules C1/C3	RAF Lyneham
51 Sqn	3 x Nimrod R1	RAF Waddington
54 Sqn	11 x Jaguar GR1A/B	RAF Coltishall
	1 x Jaguar T2A	
70 Sqn	10 x Hercules C1/C3	RAF Lyneham
72 Sqn	8 x Wessex HC2	RAF Aldergrove (JHC)
	5 x Puma HC1	
78 Sqn	1 x Chinook HC2	RAF Mount Pleasant (JHC)
	2 x Sea King HAR3	(Falklands)
84 Sqn	3 x Wessex HC2 RAF	Akrotiri
99 Sqn	4 x C-17	RAF Brize Norton (from May 2001)
100 Sqn	13 x Hawk T1/T1A	RAF Leeming
101 Sqn	12 x VC10 K2/K3/K4	RAF Brize Norton
111 Sqn	13 x Tornado F3	RAF Leuchars
120 Sqn	6 x Nimrod MR2	RAF Kinloss
201 Sqn	6 x Nimrod MR2	RAF Kinloss
202 Sqn	6 x Sea King HAR3	RAF Boulmer (Sqn HQ)*
206 Sqn	7 x Nimrod MR2	RAF Kinloss
216 Sqn	8 x Tristar K1/KC1/C2/C2A	RAF Brize Norton
230 Sqn	13 x Puma HC1	RAF Aldergrove (JHC)
617 Sqn	12 x Tornado GR1B	RAF Lossiemouth
1312 Flight	1 x Hercules C1K	RAF Mount Pleasant

	1 x VC10 K2	
1435 Flight	4 x Tornado F3	RAF Mount Pleasant

Notes:
(1) * 22 Sqn has detachments at RMB Chivenor, RAF Wattisham and RAF Valley. 202 Sqn has detachments at RAF Lossiemouth and RAF Leconfield.
(2) There are RAF flying units deployed in the Arabian Gulf (Op Jural) and Turkey (Op Warden) in support of United Nations operations in the Iraq no-fly zones. Other units are in Kuwait (Op Bolton) having been deployed there in late 1997.
(3) In addition, RAF units are supporting UN/NATO operations in the area of the former Yugoslavia and UK operations in Sierra Leone.
(4) JFH means that a squadron is assigned to the Joint Force Harrier and JHC means that a squadron is assigned to the Joint Helicopter Command.

Training Units

Unit	Aircraft	Location
15 (R) Sqn	26 x Tornado GR1	RAF Lossiemouth
16 (R) Sqn	8 x Jaguar GR1A/T2A	RAF Coltishall
19 (R) Sqn	12 x Hawk T Mk 1	RAF Valley*
20 (R) Sqn	9 x Harrier GR7	RAF Wittering
	5 x Harrier T10	
42 (R) Sqn	3 x Nimrod MR2	RAF Kinloss
45 (R) Sqn	10 x Jetstream T Mk 1	RAF Cranwell
55 (R) Sqn	8 x Dominie T Mk 1	RAF Cranwell
56 (R) Sqn	19 x Tornado F3	RAF Coningsby
57 (R) Sqn	5 x Hercules C1/C3	RAF Lyneham
60 (R) Sqn	Griffin HT Mk 1	RAF Shawbury
74 (R) Sqn	Hawk T Mk 1	RAF Valley
203 (R) Sqn	3 x Sea King HAR3	RAF St Mawgan
208 (R) Sqn	Hawk T Mk 1	RAF Valley

Note: The (R) in a squadron designation represents a training unit/reserve squadron. In the majority of cases this reserve squadron is the Operational Conversion Unit (OCU) for the particular aircraft type and the reserve squadron has a mobilisation role.

* There are 68 x Hawk at RAF Valley.

* CFS stands for Central Flying School.

Elementary Flying Training

Unit	Location	Aircraft
JEFTS*	RAF Barkston Heath	18 x Firefly
University Air Squadrons	Throughout UK	85 x Bulldog
Basic Flying Training		
1 Flying Training School	RAF Linton-on-Ouse	75 x Tucano
3 Flying Training School	RAF Cranwell	10 x Jetstream T1
		8 x Dominie
		11 x Bulldog

Advanced Flying Training

4 Flying Training School	RAF Valley	68 x Hawk T1/1A
DHFS*	RAF Shawbury	26 x Squirrel HT1
		6 x Griffin HT1
Search & Rescue Training Unit	RAF Valley	3 x Griffin HT1
Sea King Training Unit	RAF St Mawgan	Sea King
JFACTSU*	RAF Leeming	2 x Hawk T1/T1A

Note: * JEFTS - Joint Elementary Flying Training School; DHFS - Defence Helicopter Flying School; JFACTSU - Joint Forward Air Control Training and Standards Unit.

Royal Air Force Regiment

1 Sqn	RAF Regt	RAF St Mawgan	Ground Defence
2 Sqn	RAF Regt	RAF Honnington	Ground Defence
3 Sqn	RAF Regt	RAF Aldergrove	Ground Defence
15 Sqn	RAF Regt	RAF Honnington	6 x Rapier
16 Sqn	RAF Regt	RAF Honnington	6 x Rapier
26 Sqn	RAF Regt	RAF Waddington	6 x Rapier
34 Sqn	RAF Regt	RAF Leeming	Ground Defence (Reaction Force Air)
37 Sqn	RAF Regt	RAF Bruggen	Rapier (Bruggen closes in 2002)
63 (QCS) Sqn		RAF Uxbridge	Ground Defence & Ceremonial
RAF Regt Depot		RAF Honnington	Training & Administration
Rapier FSC OCU		RAF Honnington	2 x Rapier (Conversion Unit)

No 1 RAF STO HQ	RAF Wittering	(Tactical Survive to Operate HQ)
No 2 RAF STO HQ	RAF Leeming	(Tactical Survive to Operate HQ)
No 3 RAF STO HQ	RAF Marham	(Tactical Survive to Operate HQ)

Royal Auxiliary Air Force

No 1 Maritime HQ	RAF Northolt	Maritime HQ Unit
No 2 Maritime HQ	Edinburgh	Maritime HQ Unit
No 3 Maritime HQ	RAF St Mawgan	Maritime HQ Unit
2503 Sqn Regt	RAF Waddington	Ground Defence
2620 Sqn Regt	RAF Marham	Ground Defence
2622 Sqn Regt	RAF Lossiemouth	Ground Defence
2623 Sqn Regt	RAF Honnington	Training & Op Evaluation Unit
2624 Sqn Regt	RAF Brize Norton	Ground Defence
2625 Sqn Regt	RAF St Mawgan	Ground Defence
4626 Sqn	RAF Lyneham	Aeromedical Evacuation Unit
7006 Sqn	RAF Waddington	Intelligence
7010 Sqn	RAF Waddington	Photographic Interpretation
7630 Sqn	RAF Chicksands	Communications & Security
7644 Sqn	RAF Waddington	Public Relations
504 Sqn	RAF Cottesmore	Harrier Support Sqn
603 Sqn Edinburgh	General Support	
606 Sqn RAF Benson	Rotary Support	

609 Sqn	RAF Leeming	Air Defence Support Unit
Mobile Met Unit	RAF Benson	Meteorological Services
Surgical Unit (Airmobile)	RAF Leuchars	Casualty Treatment
Marham Support Flight	RAF Marham	Ground Crew
Reservist Aircrew Flight	RAF Lyneham	Aircrew personnel
TSS	RAF Halton	Training & Standardisation Sqn
TSS	RAF Shawbury	Training & Standardisation Sqn

British Airline Fleets

In an emergency, the Government has the power to enlist the assistance of the United Kingdom's civil airline fleets. In total there appear to be 36 registered airlines operating approximately 700 fixed-wing passenger and transport aircraft. The largest of these airlines is British Airways with some 50,000 employees operating about 250 aircraft, carrying on average about 30 million passengers and about half a million tons of freight per year.

Other major British airlines include Air UK with 28 aircraft, Britannia Airways the world's largest charter airline with 33 aircraft and carrying about 7 million passengers per year. British Midland Airways with 31 aircraft and Virgin Atlantic with 16 aircraft.

Air Force Board

The routine management of the Royal Air Force is the responsibility of the Air Force Board, the composition of which is shown in the next diagram:

Air Force Board
The Secretary of State for Defence

Minister of State (Armed Forces)
Minister of State (Defence Procurement)
Under-Secretary of State (Armed Forces)
Under-Secretary of State (Defence Procurement)
2nd Permanent Under Secretary of State

Chief of the Air Staff
Air Member for Personnel
Controller of Aircraft
Air Member for Logistics
AOC Strike Command
Assistant Chief of Air Staff

Decisions made by the Defence Council or the Air Force Board are implemented by the air staff at various headquarters worldwide. The Chief of the Air Staff is the officer ultimately responsible for the Royal Air Force's contribution to the national defence effort. He maintains control through the AOC (Air Officer Commanding), and the staff branches of each of these headquarters.

ACM Sir Peter Squire

Chief of The Air Staff (As at 1 Jan 2001)
Air Chief Marshal Sir Peter Squire

Air Chief Marshal (ACM) Sir Peter Squire was commissioned into the Royal Air Force in 1966, following a three year cadetship at the RAF College Cranwell. On completion of flying training he was posted to No 20 Squadron in Singapore where he flew Hunters in the day fighter/ground attack role and the single-engine Pioneer as an airborne forward air controller.

A further tour on Hunters followed, this time as a flying instructor at RAF Valley, during which he trained mainly foreign and commonwealth students. He was promoted to squadron leader in July 1973 and on completion of a conversion course to the Harrier in 1975, he took up a Flight Commander appointment on No 3(F) Squadron in Germany.

On his return to the UK in 1978, ACM Squire was posted to a staff appointment in Headquarters Strike Command and two years later he attended the Royal Naval Staff College at Greenwich. He was promoted to wing commander at the end of the course and took command of No 1(F) Squadron at RAF Wittering, again flying Harriers.

Following a second tour of duty at Headquarters Strike Command, firstly as leader of the newly formed Command Briefing and Presentation Team and then as the Personal Staff Officer to the Air Officer Commanding-in-Chief, Air Marshal Squire was promoted to Group Captain and was posted to command the Tri-National Tornado Training Establishment at RAF Cottesmore.

Subsequent senior appointments included Director Air Offensive, Senior Air Staff Officer Headquarters Strike Command, Deputy Chief of Staff Operations United Kingdom Air Force, Air Officer Commanding No 38 Group, Air Officer Commanding No 1 Group, Assistant Chief of the Air Staff and Deputy Chief of the Defence Staff (Programmes and Personnel). He assumed the post of Air Officer Commanding in Chief Strike Command and Commander Allied Air Forces Northwestern Europe in March 1999, when he was also made Air Aide de Camp to Her Majesty The Queen.

He was appointed Chief of the Air Staff on 19 April 2000. He is married and has three sons

Chain of Command
On the 1 April 2000, the Royal Air Force was reorganised with the resultant "Chain of Command" as follows:

Chief of the Air Staff
Commander - Air Chief Marshal
(Ministry of Defence)

HQSTC	HQPTC	Equipment Support (Air)
RAF Strike Command	RAF Personnel	(Wyton)
Air Chief Marshal	& Training Command	
(High Wycombe)	Air Chief Marshal	
	(Innsworth)	

Strike Command

From its headquarters at RAF High Wycombe, Strike Command now controls all of the United Kingdom's front-line aircraft world wide. Its assets include fighters, strike/attack, transport and maritime aircraft and helicopters.

As the commander of Strike Command the AOCinC is responsible for the day to day national peacetime operations of the Command. In war, Strike Command is an essential part of the NATO organisation and as such is a valuable component of SACEUR European Theatre air assets.

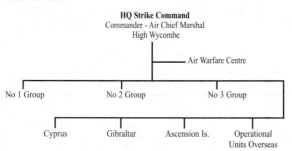

HQ Strike Command
Commander - Air Chief Marshal
High Wycombe

Air Warfare Centre

No 1 Group   No 2 Group   No 3 Group

Cyprus   Gibraltar   Ascension Is.   Operational Units Overseas

Notes:
Groups are normally commanded by Air Vice Marshals.
In general these 3 Groups are responsible for:

1 Group	All frontline fast jet aircraft (excluding Harrier)
2 Group	All aircraft and force elements that support frontline operations; including air transport, air-to-air refuelling, Nimrod R aircraft and E-3DSentry, RAF Regiment and ground-based air defence systems, ASTOR (airborne stand-off radar) and the RAF's information collection aircraft.
3 Group	Joint Force Harrier; Nimrod maritime patrol aircraft, search and rescue helicopters and mountain rescue teams.

During early 2001, Strike Command controlled about 5,700 civilians and 31,000 servicemen and women - well over half of the present strength of the Royal Air Force. The personnel and aircraft are spread through some 200 units of various sizes, the majority of which are in the United Kingdom.

No 1 Group

Strike Attack	Aircraft	Location
9 Squadron	12 x Tornado GR1	Marham
12 Squadron	12 x Tornado GR1 B	Lossiemouth
13 Squadron	12 x Tornado GR1 A	Marham
14 Squadron	12 x Tornado GR1	Lossiemouth
31 Squadron	12 x Tornado GR1	Marham
617 Squadron	12 x Tornado GR1 B	Lossiemouth
15 (Reserve) Squadron	26 x Tornado GR1	Lossiemouth

Air Defence	Aircraft	Location
5 Squadron	13 x Tornado F3	Coningsby
11 Squadron	13 x Tornado F3	Leeming
25 Squadron	13 x Tornado F3	Leeming
43 Squadron	13 x Tornado F3	Leuchars
111 Squadron	13 x Tornado F3	Leuchars
1435 Squadron	4 x Tornado F3	Mount Pleasant
56 (Reserve) Squadron	19 x Tornado F3	Coningsby

Offensive Support	Aircraft	Location
6 Squadron	12 x Jaguar GR1 A/B	Coltishall
	1 x Jaguar T2 A	
41 Squadron	12 x Jaguar GR1 /AB	Coltishall
	1 x Jaguar T2 A/B	
54 Squadron	12 x Jaguar GR1 A/B	Coltishall
	1 x Jaguar T2 A	
16 (Reserve) Squadron	8 x Jaguar GR1 A/T2A	Lossiemouth

Reconnaissance	Aircraft	Location
2 Squadron	12 x Tornado GR1 A	Marham
13 Squadron	12 x Tornado GR1 A	Marham

Miscellaneous	Aircraft	Location
100 Squadron	14 x Hawk T1/1A	Leeming (target towing)

Air Warfare Centre (AWC)

The Air Warfare Centre is responsible for formulating tactical doctrine and conducting operational trials. Formed from the old CTTO, DAW, EWOSE, ORB and OEUs the AWC also maintains liaison with MoD research establishments and industry, and close contact with RAF operational commands as well as with the Royal Navy, Army and Allied air forces.

The AWC is administered by HQ Strike Command, but is responsible jointly to the Assistant Chief of Air Staff, and to the Commander-in-Chief for the conduct of trials, and development of tactics for all Royal Air Force operational aircraft. Branches and locations of the AWC are as follows:

Operational Doctrine (OD&T)	Cranwell & High Wycombe
Tactics (TD&T)	Waddington
Electronic Warfare (EWOS)	Waddington
Operational Analysis (OA)	High Wycombe, Waddington & Cranwell
Operational Testing & Evaluation (OT&E)	Boscombe Down, Coningsby, Odiham & Ash

No 2 Group

Airborne Early Warning	Aircraft	Location
8 Squadron	3 x Sentry AEW1	Waddington
23 Squadron	3 x Sentry AEW1	Waddington

Intelligence, EW & Misc	Aircraft	Location
39 (1 PRU) Squadron	4 x Canberra PR9	Marham
	2 x Canberra T4	
51 Squadron	3 x Nimrod R1	Waddington

Air Transport	Aircraft	Location
24 Squadron	11 Hercules C1/C3	Lyneham
30 Squadron	11 Hercules C1/C3	Lyneham
47 Squadron	11 Hercules C1/C3	Lyneham
70 Squadron	12 x Hercules C1/C3	Lyneham
32 Squadron (The Royal)	5 x BAe 125	Northholt
	3 x BAe 146	
	2 x Twin Squirrel	
57 (Reserve Sqn)	5 x Hercules C1/C3	Lyneham

Air Movement/Tankers	Aircraft	Location
10 Squadron	8 x VC10 C1K	Brize Norton
101 Squadron	3 x VC10 K2	Brize Norton
	4 x VC10 K3	
	5 x VC10 K4	
216 Squadron	8 x Tristar K1/KC1/C2/A	Brize Norton
1312 Flight	1 x VC10 K2	Mount Pleasant
	1 x Hercules C1	Air transport only

No 3 Group

Joint Force Harrier	Aircraft	Location
1 Squadron	12 x Harrier GR7	Wittering
	1 x Harrier T10	
3 Squadron	12 x Harrier GR7	Cottesmore
	1 x Harrier T-10	
4 Squadron	12 x Harrier GR7	Cottesmore
	1 x Harrier T-10	
20 (Reserve) Squadron	9 x Harrier GR7	Wittering
	5 x Harrier T10	
800 Sqn (Fleet Air Arm)	7 x Sea Harrier FRS1, F/A2GR7	RNAS Yeovilton
801 Sqn (Fleet Air Arm)	7 x Sea Harrier FRS1, F/A2GR7	RNAS Yeovilton
899 Sqn (Fleet Air Arm)	10 x Sea Harrier FRS1, F/A2GR7	RNAS Yeovilton
	4 x Sea Harrier T4/T8	

Joint Force Harrier (JFH)

On 1 April 2000 the Sea Harrier FA.2 squadrons previously under a Naval Air Commander became part of the new JFH within No 3 Group, RAF Strike Command. Rear Adm Iain Henderson, previously Flag Officer Naval Aviation (FONA), became Air Officer Commanding No 3 Group (running JFH plus Nimrods and search and rescue (SAR) Sea King helicopters) marking the first time that a naval officer has been given charge of an RAF air group. This iniative was an outcomes of the 1998 Strategic Defence Review and JFH which combines RN Sea Harriers and RAF Harriers under one headquarters provides a significant contribution to Joint Operations.

In 2003 RAF and RN squadrons will be co-located at RAF Cottesmore and the Harrier training unit at RAF Wittering. The Royal Naval Squadrons will still be linked to specific aircraft carriers and the RAF's Harrier squadrons will be attached in rotation to form Joint Air Wings.

Maritime Patrol	Aircraft	Location
120 Squadron	3 x Nimrod MR2	Kinloss
201 Squadron	6 x Nimrod MR2	Kinloss
206 Squadron	6 x Nimrod MR2	Kinloss
42 (Reserve) Squadron	3 x Nimrod MR2	Kinloss

Search & Rescue	Aircraft	Location
22 Squadron	Headquarters	RMB Chivenor
A Flight	2 x Sea King HAR3	RMB Chivenor
B Flight	2 x Sea King HAR3	Wattisham
C Flight	2 x Sea King HAR3	Valley
202 Squadron	Headquarters	Boulmer
A Flight	2 x Sea King HAR3	Boulmer
D Flight	2 x Sea King HAR3	Lossiemouth
E Flight	2 x Sea King HAR3	Leconfield
203 (Reserve) Squadron	3 x Sea King HAR3	St Mawgan
78 Squadron	2 x Sea King HAR3	Mount Pleasant
78 Squadron total includes	1 x Chinook HC2	

Note: MoD figures show both 22 and 202 Squadrons as having 8 aircraft on strength.

No 3 Group's tasks include maritime surface and subsurface surveillance, Search And Rescue (SAR) and regular patrolling of the North Sea oil and gas installations, and fishery limits. Tasks are controlled from the Air Headquarters at Northwood, Middlesex. In war, the Nimrods would operate under the Supreme Allied Commander Atlantic (SACLANT), the AOC No 3 Group holding the NATO post of Commander Maritime Air Eastern Atlantic (COMMAIREASTLANT). As such, his main tasks would be to provide maritime strike/attack, maritime reconnaissance and anti-submarine support for naval operations and in protection of allied merchant shipping.

The major headquarters for co-ordinating this activity are:

    No 1 Maritime HQ   -   Northwood
    No 2 Maritime HQ   -   Pitrivie
    No 3 Maritime HQ   -   St Mawgan

In 1996, the UK MoD announced the opening of a Joint Maritime Communications Centre (JMCC) at St Mawgan in Cornwall. This headquarters has some 400 personnel of whom about 50% are from the US Navy. Of about 200 UK personnel, 50% are from the Royal Navy and 50% from the RAF. The UK MoD pays for the JMCC building and the US pays for the equipment. The JMCC comprises a buried, hardened communications building approximately 70 metres square within the perimeter of RAF St Mawgan. The centre is integrated within the existing RAF fixed communications system, and includes two additional satellite ground terminals, each approximately 3 metres in diameter, also sited within the station boundary.

No 3 Group also controls Search And Rescue (SAR) through the Rescue Co-ordination

Centres at Plymouth and Edinburgh. The Group's search and rescue Sea King helicopters with, where appropriate, the Nimrods and marine craft units, are frequently engaged in rescue work and mercy flights, saving several hundred lives each year. The Group is also responsible for photographic reconnaissance cover using Canberra PR9. The Canberra PR unit also undertakes photographic surveys for the Ministry of Defence and other government departments in many parts of the world.

UK Air Surveillance and Control System (ASACS)
One of Strike Command's main responsibilities is the UK ASACS. AOC Strike Command is tasked with providing early warning of air attack against the UK air defence region; to provide fighter and missile defences and the associated ground control system; fighter co-ordination with Royal Naval ships operating in adjacent waters and to maintain the integrity of UK air space in war.

United Kingdom Combined Air Operations Centre
The United Kingdom Combined Air Operations Centre (UKCAOC) is situated within Headquarters Strike Command at RAF High Wycombe. The UKCAOC is responsible for the overall coordination of the Air Defence, Ground Attack and Maritime Air elements of the RAF together with the air forces and navies of our NATO partners. It is from the UKCAOC that the Duty Controller orders any reaction in response to the UK ASACS's vigil over UK national and NATO airspace. The configuration of the UK ASACS is monitored and controlled 24 hours a day by a dedicated team working within the UKCAOC.

Within the UKCAOC control and reporting centres are linked with other elements of the NATO Air Defence Ground Environment (NADGE) and with the Ballistic Missile Early Warning Systems (BMEWS) station at Fylingdales, Yorkshire, which is networked with the US operated BMEWS at Thule (Greenland) and Clear (Alaska). By extending high-level radar cover some 3,000 miles across eastern Europe, Fylingdales would give advance warning of intermediate range ballistic missiles launched against the UK and western Europe, and of inter-continental ballistic missiles against the North American continent. Fylingdales also tracks satellites and space debris.

UK Air Surveillance and Control System (ASACS)

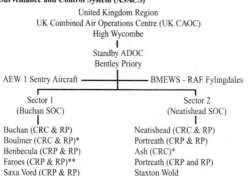

United Kingdom Region
UK Combined Air Operations Centre (UK CAOC)
High Wycombe

Standby ADOC
Bentley Priory

AEW 1 Sentry Aircraft ———————— BMEWS - RAF Fylingdales

Sector 1
(Buchan SOC)

Sector 2
(Neatishead SOC)

Buchan (CRC & RP)
Boulmer (CRC & RP)*
Benbecula (CRC & RP)
Faroes (CRP & RP)**
Saxa Vord (CRP & RP)

Neatishead (CRC & RP)
Portreath (CRP & RP)
Ash (CRC)*
Portreath (CRP and RP)
Staxton Wold

127

* Denotes Reserve SOC
** Operated by the Royal Danish Air Force
In Reserve - STC Mobile Radar Reserve (144 Signals Unit)

Key: SOC - Sector Operations Centre
        CRC - Control Reporting Centre
        CRP - Control Reporting Point
        RP   - Reporting Post

In the Falkland Islands there are Reporting Posts at Mount Kent, Mount Alice and Byron Heights. The majority of UK ASACS units are under the command of 2 Group.

I-UKADGE (Improved- UK Air Defence Ground Environment) is the communications system upon which the air defences depend for their operational effectiveness. The system is fully automated. Computerised data exchange and information from a number of sources such as radars, ships and aircraft is moved around the system on a number of routes to minimise the disruptive effects of enemy action. Generally speaking, if a command bunker or radar is rendered inoperable, the system will automatically switch to another node allowing a secure, free and uninterrupted flow of information. ICCS (Integrated Command and Control System) provides the commanders and air defence staff with the information gathered in the system and UNITER brings together all the nodes on a digital network.

JTIDS (Joint Tactical Information Distribution System) is a secure communications network. The MoD has ordered 60 terminals and the majority of these will equip two Tornado F3 squadrons and the AEW1 Sentry aircraft.

Joint Helicopter Command

The UK armed forces' Joint Helicopter Command (JHC) became operational on 1 April 2000. Its first commander is Air Vice Marshal David Niven, who has under his command about 12,000 service personnel and 350 helicopters.

These helicopters include those operated by the British Army's 16 Air Assault Brigade (currently using Lynx light utility and anti-tank helicopters, but soon to include the WAH-64D Apache Longbow attack helicopters).

In total, the JHC will include 33 Royal Navy helicopters (Sea King Mk4), 230 British Army helicopters (Gazelle, Lynx utility/TOW, Apache), and 80 RAF helicopters (Wessex, Puma, Chinook, Chinook Mk3, and Merlin Mk3).

The first major tests for the JHC were in Kosovo during 1999 when a detachment was sent to Pristina Airport and Sierra Leone in 2000 when JHC helicopters supported British troops engaged in operations in support of UN forces.

During peace the JHC comes under the command of HQ Land (see Army section) and for operations an appropriate force package will be assigned to PJHQ.

The following RAF aircraft are assigned to the JHC.

Support Helicopters	Aircraft	Location
7 Squadron	11 x Chinook HC2	Odiham
18 Squadron	10 x Chinook HC2	Odiham
27 Squadron	9 x Chinook HC2	Odiham
33 Squadron	15 x Puma HC1	Benson
72 Squadron	8 x Wessex HC2	Aldergrove
78 Squadron	5 x Puma HC1	
	1 x Chinook HC2	Mount Pleasant
	2 x Sea King HAR3	(SAR capable)
84 Squadron	3 x Wessex HC2	Akrotiri (SAR capable)
230 Squadron	13 x Puma HC1	Aldergrove

RAF Personnel & Training Command (RAF PTC)

HQ PTC controls all personnel aspects ranging from conditions of service, recruiting, training, education, manning, career management, resettlement and pensions. The headquarters also deals with all policy matters relating to medical, dental, legal and chaplaincy. The command employs more than 14,700 personnel including 3,700 civilians at 30 locations and has over 350 training aircraft. HQ PTC staff number 1,500, about 50% of whom are civilians.

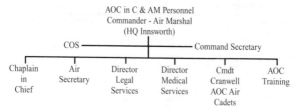

Chief of Staff's Branch (COS)

Air Secretary

Director Medical Services

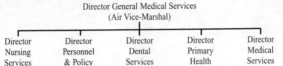

Director General Medical Services
(Air Vice-Marshal)

Director Nursing Services	Director Personnel & Policy	Director Dental Services	Director Primary Health	Director Medical Services

Air Officer Training

Air Officer Training
(Air Vice-Marshal)

Air Commodore Flying Training	Air Commodore Ground Training	RAF Sports Board	Air Commodore Training Support/ Director Education

Note: We believe that the Red Arrows (10 x Hawk T1/T1A - based at RAF Scampton) are under the control of AOC Flying Training.

PTC Flying Training Units

Elementary Flying Training	Aircraft	Location
Joint Elementary Flying Training School (JEFTS)	18 x Mk 1 Firefly	Barkstone Heath
University Air Squadrons (UAS)	47 x Bulldog T1 47 x Tutor	Various Locations
Volunteer Gliding School (VGS)	141 Gliders including Kestrel, Valiant, Viking & Vigilant	Various Locations
Basic Flying Training	**Aircraft**	**Location**
No 1 Flying Training School (1 FTS)	75 x Tucano T1	Linton (includes Central Flying School at Topcliffe)
No 3 Flying Training School (3 FTS)	10 x Jetstream T1 8 x Dominie T1 8 x Bulldog T1 8 x Tutor	Cranwell
Advanced Flying Training	**Aircraft**	**Location**
No 4 Flying Training School (4 FTS)	68 x Hawk T1/1A	Valley
SAR Training Unit	3 x Griffin HT1	Valley
Defence Helicopter Flying School (DHFS)	26 x Squirrel HT1 6 x Griffin HT1	Shawbury

RAF Logistics

The majority of RAF Logistic support is incorporated within the Defence Logistics Organisation. However many aspects of RAF logistic support have been retained within the organisation under arrangements co-ordinated by Equipment Support (Air). ES (Air), commanded by an Air Vice Marshal and located at the Brampton/Wyton complex has about 4,000 service and civilian personnel of whom over 70% are civilians. ES (Air) had a budget of over £2 billion in 2001.

The headquarters "core" staff numbers about 200 and the vast majority of the staff are involved in the direct management and control of maintenance activities such as provisioning, storage, distribution, logistic operations, information systems and communications. The command supports over 1,000 fixed-wing aircraft and some 4,000 aero engines plus various ground-based systems and equipment.

Maintenance

The maintenance functions at ES (Air) can be divided into aero systems engineering (those engineering functions concerned with aircraft) signals and movements. ES (Air) provides aircraft engineering support for the RAF, and for fixed-wing aircraft of the Royal Navy and Army Air Corps. Scheduled major maintenance, rectifications, reconditioning and modification for a wide variety of aircraft are undertaken for tasks beyond the normal capability of operational stations.

Maintenance Units (MUs) also hold reserve stocks of fixed-wing aircraft, which they prepare for storage and maintenance against deterioration. Continuous effort is devoted to the improvement of maintenance facilities, the introduction of improved tools and better working methods to increase efficiency and reduce costs.

Work on aircraft is carried out at RAF St Athan. The engineering unit at St Athan, the largest in the RAF, is manned jointly by service personnel and civilians, with an Aircraft Servicing Wing and a General Engineering Wing. The former has been engaged for many years on the maintenance of Harriers and Tornados, with the capacity to work on 58 aircraft at any one time.

In July 1992, the engineering facilities at RAF Abingdon were concentrated at St Athan. This move brought responsibility for the major maintenance and modification of Jaguar, Hawk and VC10 aircraft and the Repair and Salvage Squadron, which is responsible for salvaging crashed RAF, Army and Navy fixed-wing aircraft in most parts of the world and carries out aircraft recovery for the Department of Transport. In addition to crash recovery, the Repair and Salvage Squadron also sends teams of tradesmen to operational stations to undertake modifications and repairs that are beyond the capacity of unit personnel, but do not necessitate the aircraft being returned to a maintenance unit. In realistic scenarios, aircraft battle damage repair techniques are formulated and tested for all of the British Services, and some 18 other nations have benefited from such training.

No 30 Maintenance Unit (30 MU) at RAF Sealand near Chester, is the main engineering unit for airborne electronic and instrument equipment. Large workshops and test facilities are laid out on production lines to enable the unit to service more than 100,000 items of airborne radio, radar, electrical, instrument and missile engineering equipment per year. The unit also provides a test equipment calibration service and manufactures test equipment, aircraft cables and looms.

The RAF Armament Support Unit (RAFASUPU) at RAF Wittering houses the RAF Explosive Ordnance Disposal (EOD) Squadron which is responsible for all aspects of RAF EOD training and trials, as well as actual clearance operations. RAFASUPU also trains aircrew and groundcrew in all aspects of special weapons functions and moves weapons as required.

In addition to the major aircraft engineering tasks, ES (Air) repairs almost any kind of equipment when it is expedient and economical to do so. Parachutes, ground equipment, furniture and domestic equipment are typical examples. There are large workshops at each of the Equipment Supply Depots that undertake the modification, repair and servicing of almost any item of equipment that comes from units in an unserviceable condition. A considerable sum of money is saved by this repair facility, enabling requirements for scarce equipment to be met more quickly.

Signals

The units controlled by the RAF Signals Staff based at RAF Henlow, are responsible for the support aspects of telecommunications, ground radio repair and signals engineering. The Signal Staff is responsible for operating the RAF element of the Defence Communications Network (DCN) and acts as a consultant to MoD, other RAF Commands and to Allied Air Forces for all aspects of communications. The Signal Staff is also responsible for the Henlow based Communications-Electronic Multi Disciplinary Group, responsible to the MoD for support authority functions in respect of telegraphic automatic routeing equipment, telegraph, ground radio and ground radar equipments for the three services and other organisations.

Communications operating responsibilities fall into four categories. First, there is a large complex of HF transmitter and receiver facilities in the UK, including communications centres with automatic message routeing equipment. Operations include those on behalf of Strike Command, the Military Air Traffic Organisation, NATO and the Meteorological Office.

Second, the RAF Signals Staff operate message relay centres, both automatic and manual and also manages the RAF's General Purpose Telephone network. The RAF has also procured a fixed telecommunications network called Boxer which will save the increasing expense of renting lines from the private sector. Command operating procedures are monitored on all networks to ensure high standards are achieved and maintained. To reduce risk of compromise, all RAF communications facilities, designed to carry classified information are checked for communications electrical security by Command staff.

Thirdly, the main operation of the Skynet Satellite Communications System, which offers overseas formations telegraphed, data and speech communications, is controlled by the Command. In February 1994, a contract for £300 million was awarded for the development, production and delivery of 2 x Skynet 4 Stage 2 military communications satellites. These replaced the existing Skynet satellites when they reached the end of their operational life, and entered service late in 1998. In addition, a management service for the NATO 4 series of satellites is provided.

Fourth, the deep maintenance and repair of ground radio and radar equipments are carried out by the Ground Radio Servicing Centre (GRSC). This includes radars, radio navigation aids and point-to-point and ground-to-air communications. ES (Air) also provides an antenna systems maintenance service on a worldwide basis, embracing the fields of communications, radar and navigation aids. The men required for this highly specialised work are trained at the Aerial Erector School at RAF Digby.

ES (Air) responsibilities for electrical engineering range over the entire field of communications equipment, air traffic control and defence radar systems and ground-based navigational equipment. They include feasibility studies, project management, design, development, manufacture, refurbishment, installation and commissioning of the majority of communications equipment procured by the MoD (PE).

AOC Signals has a large engineering design staff of engineers, technicians and draughtsmen. Manufacturing resources include a general mechanical engineering and calibration capacity at RAF Henlow plus a facility for the systems design, development and installation of certain airborne signals role equipment.

Supply

The size and composition of the logistic supply units vary according to their respective functions, from equipment supply depots to comparatively small petroleum supply depots. The equipment supply depots hold nearly one and a half million different types of technical and domestic equipment. Quantities vary from a few months to several year's consumption, according to whether this item can be replenished quickly or can be bought in economic quantities only when the manufacturer is tooled-up to produce it. The number of different items held in stock is greater, and the variety wider, than would be found in any one civilian firm in the UK.

Over the years, the technique of stock recording and stock location and the speedy handling of stores items continually has improved. Today, the highest priority demands for equipment are fully processed within six hours of their receipt at the depot for delivery throughout the world. This service, which operates 24 hours a day every day has of the year, is supported by one of the UK's most powerful computers installed at the RAF Supply Control Centre. It is here that a central record of the location and quantity of nearly every item of equipment held throughout facilities of the RAF can be found.

The equipment supply depots and about 100 stations at home and overseas are linked to the Supply Control Centre. As a result, the computer is able to direct any urgently required item of equipment from the appropriate depot or, if quicker, to be transferred from another RAF station. It also provides accurate consumption information to ensure that the item is purchased in the most cost-effective quantities.

Operationally, ES (Air) also supports major force deployments through PJHQ via a rapid deployment unit based at RAF Stafford. This organisation is equipped to move at very short notice to provide a range of support facilities, including fuel and spares, anywhere in the world.

Overseas Bases

Strike Command has responsibility for all RAF bases overseas, including the units in Germany, the Mediterranean, Far East, and North America.

AHQ Cyprus has Group status within the Strike Command. In Cyprus, facilities exist at RAF Akrotiri to support aircraft detached from UK. In addition, a detachment of the RAF Regiment is stationed at Akrotiri to assist with airfield defence. RAF Gibraltar is operated by 116 RAF personnel although there is no resident squadron.

In North America there is a Strike Command detachment at Offutt Air Force Base, Nebraska, to support overseas training detachments, and a permanent unit is established at Goose Bay in Labrador for a similar purpose.

Strike Command also provides a Tornado Air Defence Unit, a flight of Hercules transports/tankers and Sea King and Chinook helicopters in the Falkland Islands. In early 2001, there were Strike Command units operating in Saudi Arabia, Bahrain, Kuwait, Sierra Leone, Turkey and the former Yugoslavia.

During operations and exercises, aircraft often visit overseas airfields where no regular RAF ground handling organisation exists. For this purpose, the Group has a Mobile Air Movement Squadron (MAMS) at RAF Lyneham, which provides teams who are expert in all aspects of loading and unloading aircraft. The MAMS teams log a large number of flying hours annually and are normally on the first aircraft in, and last aircraft out, in any major overseas operation, exercise or relief operation.

RAF Station Organisation

An indication of the manner in which an RAF Station might be organised is as follows. This example is an RAF Station with 3 x Tornado GR1 flying squadrons - each with 12 x aircraft. The 36 aircraft will have cost at least £780 million in total purchase costs, and the combined running costs for the operation of these three squadrons will be in the region of some £90 million per annum.

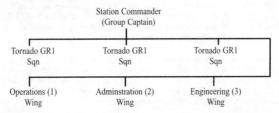

Notes: (1) Ops Wing; (2) Admin Wing; (3) Eng Wing; (4) Expect the commanders of the Tornado Sqns to be Wing Commanders aged between 34-40; Ops, Admin and Eng Wings will almost certainly be commanded by Wing Commanders from their respective branch specialities - these Wing Commanders will probably be a little older than the commanders of the flying squadrons.

Flying Squadron Organisation

Note: Generally 1 x Tornado GR1 will be held in reserve (IUR)

Note: (1) These departmental leaders have responsibility for weapons, airframes, propulsion, electronics, flight guidance and control systems, communications, automatic navigation and attack controls and report to the squadron commander.

Administration Wing Organisation

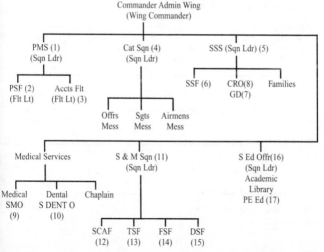

Notes: (1) Personnel Management Squadron; (2) Personal Services Flight; (3) Accounts Flight; (4) Catering Sqn; (5) Station Services Sqn; (6) Station Services Flight; (7) General Duties Flight; (8) Community Relations Officer (9) Senior Medical Officer; (10) Senior Dental Officer; (11) Supply & Movements Sqn; (12) Supply Control & Accounts Flight; (13) Technical Supply Flight; (14) Forward Supply Flight; (15) Domestic Supply Flight; (16) Senior Education Officer; (17) Physicial Education.

Operations Wing Organisation

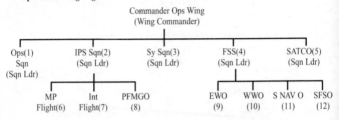

Notes: (1) Operations Sqn; (2) Intelligence & Planning Sqn; (3) Security Sqn - includes RAF Police & Station Defence Personnel; (4) Flying Support Sqn; (5) Senior Air Traffic Control Officer; (6) Mission Plans Flight; (7) Intelligence Flight; (8) Pre-flight Message Generation Officer; (9) Electronic Warfare Officer; (10) Wing Weapon Officer; (11) Senior Navigation Officer; (12) Station Safety Officer.

Engineering Wing

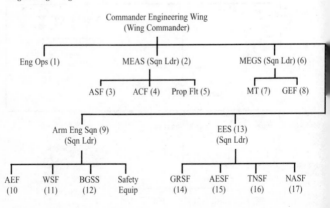

Notes: (1) Engineering Ops; (2) Mechanical Engineering Aircraft Sqn; (3) Aircraft Servicing Flight; (4) Aircraft Components Flight; (5) Propulsion Flight; (6) Mechanical Engineering Ground Squadron; (7) Mechanical Transport; (8) General Engineering Flight; (9) Armament Engineering Sqn; (10) Armament Engineering Flight; (11) Weapon Storage Flight; (12) Bomb Group Supply Section (13) Electrical Engineering Squadron; (14) Ground Radio Servicing Flight; (15) Avionics Electrical Systems Flight; (16) Tornado Navigation Systems Flight; (17) Navigation and Attack Systems Flight.

Operational Conversion Unit (OCU)

The RAF has a number of OCU's designed to train pilots for front-line squadron service as follows:

Tornado OCU	26 x Tornado GR1	RAF Lossiemouth	(15 Reserve Sqn)
Tornado F3 OCU	19 x Tornado F3	RAF Coningsby	(56 Reserve Sqn)
Jaguar OCU	8 x Jaguar	RAF Lossiemouth	(16 Reserve Sqn)
Harrier OCU	14 x Harrier	RAF Wittering	(20 Reserve Sqn)
Nimrod OCU	3 x Nimrod	MR2 RAF Kinloss	(42 Reserve Sqn)
Hercules OCU	5 x Hercules	RAF Lyneham	(57 Reserve Sqn)
Sea King OCU	3 x Sea King HAR3	RAF St Mawgan	(203 Reserve Sqn)

The organisation of an OCU is obviously tailored to fit the size of the aircraft fleet being supported. As an example No 56 Reserve Sqn (Tornado F3 OCU) is organised along the following lines:

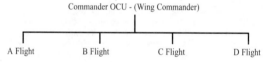

A and B Flights provide flying training with about 19 x staff crews and 12 x student crews. C Flight is a standards flight - training instructors, and D Flight provides simulators and a dome air combat trainer.

Tornado GR1/GR4

In service with:

9 Squadron	12 x Tornado GR1	Bruggen
12 Squadron	12 x Tornado GR1B	Lossiemouth
14 Squadron	12 x Tornado GR1	Lossiemouth
17 Squadron	12 x Tornado GR1	Bruggen
31 Squadron	12 x Tornado GR1/GR4	Marham
617 Squadron	12 x Tornado GR1B	Lossiemouth
15 (Reserve) Squadron	26 x Tornado GR1	Lossiemouth

Crew 2; Wingspan (open) 13.9m; Wingspan (swept) 8.6m; Height 5.9m; Length 16.7m; Max weapon load 7,250kg; Max take off weight 27,900kg; Max speed Mach 2.2 (1,452 mph); Max ferry range approx 3,900km; Armament 2 x 27mm Mauser Cannon, 3 x weapon points under fuselage, 4 x weapon points under wings; Engines 2 x Turbo-Union RB 199-34R Turbofans; Required runway length approx 900m.

The Tornado GR-1 is an aircraft jointly developed by the UK, Germany and Italy under a collaborative agreement and manufactured by a consortium of companies formed under the name of Panavia. The Tornado is the most numerous and important aircraft in the RAF inventory and the GR1 operates in the strike/attack and reconnaissance roles. The first prototype flew in 1974 and the first RAF Squadron equipped with the GR1 became operational in 1982.

The GR-1 is capable of carrying both nuclear and conventional weapons at tree-top height, in all weathers, by day or by night. It has a very advanced terrain-following radar and sophisticated electronic countermeasures which assist in penetrating hostile airspace. For self-defence a 27 mm cannon and Sidewinder missiles are carried. The Tornado GR1A is the reconnaissance version of the aircraft, and the GR-1B is an aircraft Modified to allow the Sea Eagle missile to be used to its full capability.

During the Gulf War, Tornado GR1s were amongst the first aircraft in action from 17 January 1991. Equipped with JP233 airfield denial weapons, 1,000 pound bombs and ALARM anti-radar missiles, GR1s attacked a number of the Iraqi Air Force's huge airfields. During the first week of operations, the majority of the GR1 sorties were flown at low level and at night, an environment in which few other aircraft could operate.

The deployment of a squadron of Buccaneer aircraft equipped with Pavespike laser designators enabled the Tornado GR1s to use Laser-Guided Bombs (LGBs) with great precision during daylight raids on interdiction and airfield targets. The GR1s capability was further enhanced with the deployment of a small number of aircraft fitted with the Thermal Imaging Airborne Laser Designator (TIALD) which gave the Tornado GR1s a precision night attack capability. The final three weeks of the air war saw the Tornado GR1 force concentrating almost exclusively on day and night precision attacks, dropping LGBs from medium altitude.

A total of six GR1s was lost in action, five of which were involved in low-or medium- level attacks with 1,000 pound bombs and one that was flying a low-level JP233 mission. During the war, the Tornado GR1 force flew 1,500 operational sorties divided almost equally between offensive counter air targets such as airfields and air defence sites, and interdiction targets such as bridges. Between them, Tornado GR1 and Jaguar GR1As dropped some 100 x JP233 airfield denial weapons, 5,000 x 1,000 pound bombs, 1,000 x LGBs, 100 x

ALARM missiles and 700 x Air to Ground Rockets onto Iraqi positions. The RAF deployed 48 x GR1 in the area during hostilities.

During the 1999 campaign in Kosovo, RAF Tornado GR1 were once again deployed. On 1 April, eight 14 Squadron Tornados flying from RAF Bruggen in Germany supported by three VC-10 tankers were deployed during the initial phase of the air campaign. On 28 May a further 12 Tornados from 9 and 31 Squadrons were deployed to Corsica supported by five VC-10 tankers and the 14 Squadron aircraft stood down. In the main these aircraft dropped either cluster bombs, gravity bombs or precision guided weapons. No aircraft were lost during the campaign.

The first aircraft of the Tornado GR4 MLU version (Mid-Life Update) took off from British Aerospace (Warton) during June 1993. The development contract for the MLU programme was signed with BAe in 1989 and includes introducing new equipment and updated avionics into the basic Tornado GR1 airframe. In addition, lessons from the Gulf War have been incorporated in the programme and it is believed that an improved thermal imaging laser designator pod and integrated global positioning system have been included. Funds of approximately £1 billion are believed to have been allocated for the MLU. In October 1997, the first two 'production' Tornado MLU aircraft were officially handed over to the RAF.

The arrival into RAF service of the Tornado MLU (designated GR4/4A) will improve its operational capability to 2018, after which it will be withdrawn from service. In total, 142 aircraft will be upgraded.

The MLU covers a number of planned extra 'packages' of work, principally involving software updates. Package 1, covers integration of the Paveway III laser-guided bomb; the TIALD 400-series pod; a six-channel VRS; and provision to operate with the Matra BAe Dynamics Sea Eagle anti-ship missile. At present, only the Tornado GR.1B can operate with Sea Eagle.

Package 2, will integrate a new generation of weapons: the Matra BAe Dynamics Storm Shadow Conventional Attack Stand-off Missile (CASOM) and GEC-Marconi Brimstone Advanced Anti-Armor Weapon (AAAW), procurement of which has been contracted; and the Hughes Aircraft RAPTOR reconnaissance pod, which is under final development.

The LINS 764GT ring-laser gyro inertial navigation system (INS), with an integrated GPS was selected in November 1997 and will be incorporated in Package 3. For the GR.4, this system will include a Ground Proximity Warning System (GPWS) using the BASE Terrain Profile Matching (TERPROM) digital terrain system embedded within the unit on a single electronic card.

Plans were for the last Tornado GR.4 to be handed over to the RAF in October 2002. However, there has been slippage in the programme and the ISD for Package 1 aircraft, featuring full integration of the Paveway III low-level LGB, should have occurred in December 2000, but a full Paveway III/GR4 capability is still some way from service, according to MoD sources. By early 2001 some 30 aircraft had been handed over to the RAF with the first aircraft going to 31 Squadron.

Package 2 aircraft, featuring the MBD Storm Shadow conventional air- launched cruise missile and the Alenia Marconi Systems Brimstone anti-tank missile (and latterly the Raytheon RAPTOR reconnaissance pod), was set to have entered service in December of 2000, but that date, too, was unachievable given both weapons are still in development.

The GR4 will remain in service until 2018, when it will be replaced by the Future Offensive Air System (FOAS). Studies to define the kind of weapon system FOAS will be - derivative aircraft, new-design stealth bomber, cruise missile or unmanned combat air vehicle are still underway.

Expect a Tornado GR1 (GR4) Squadron to have 15 established crews.

Future Offensive Air System (FOAS)

This programme was launched in December 1996 when £35 million was assigned for allocation to feasibility studies of the broadest possible range of options, including variants of Eurofighter Typhoon, Lockheed Martin F-22 and Joint Strike Fighter; new manned combat aircraft; uninhabited air vehicles, both combatant and non-combatant; and standoff missiles launched from transport aircraft. Development will be in close parallel with the Royal Navy's Future Carrier Borne Aircraft FCBA.

A complete range of technologies including fly-by-light, stealth, virtual reality cockpits and integrated modular avionics is being considered. Over 100 companies were working on FOAS feasibility during 2000. A firm requirement for the aircraft will be issued in 2008. Assessment phase and risk-reduction studies are due to begin in 2001. The current in service date is 2018 although this is expected to slip until 2020.

If a crewed aircraft is selected, the RAF requirement would be for approximately 200.

Tornado GR1A

In service with:

2 Squadron	12 x Tornado GR1A	Marham
13 Squadron	12 x Tornado GR1A	Marham

The Tornado GR1A is the Recce version of the Tornado and has what the RAF describes as "a unique day/night low-level reconnaissance capability". During the Gulf War, six Tornado GR1A aircraft, usually flying in pairs at night and at low level, flew some 140 operational sorties.

Tornado F3

In service with:

5 Squadron	13 x Tornado F3	Coningsby
11 Squadron	13 x Tornado F3	Leeming
25 Squadron	13 x Tornado F3	Leeming
43 Squadron	13 x Tornado F3	Leuchars
111 Squadron	13 x Tornado F3	Leuchars
1435 Flight	4 x Tornado F3	Mount Pleasant
56 (Reserve) Squadron	19 x Tornado F3	Coningsby

Crew 2; Wingspan (open) 13.9m; Wingspan (swept) 8.6m; Height 5.9m; Length 18.6m; Max weapon load 8,500kg; Max take off Weight 27,900kg; Max speed Mach 2.2 (1,452 mph); Armament 1 x 27mm Mauser Cannon, 4 x Sky Flash; 4 x AIL 9L Sidewinder; Engines 2 x Turbo-Union RB 199-34R-Mk104 Turbofans; Intercept radius 1,850 km (subsonic) or 550 km (supersonic).

The Tornado F3 is armed with 4 x semi-recessed Sky Flash, 4 x Sidewinder AIM 9L missiles and a single Mauser 27 mm cannon and has about 80% commonality with the Tornado GR1. The main difference is the extended fuselage, longer range air intercept Foxhunter Radar (replacing the terrain-following/ground mapping radar of the Tornado GR1) and the armament. Extension of the fuselage provides additional space for avionics and an extra 900 litres of fuel.

The F3 was designed to meet the RAF's commitment for the air defence of the extensive UK Air Defence Region (UKADR). The aircraft has a long-range autonomous capability that enables operations to be conducted some 350 nm away from bases in bad weather, in an ECM environment and operating against multiple targets at high or low level, which can be engaged at distances in excess of 20 nm. With tanker support the Tornado F3 Combat Air Patrol (CAP) time is increased from 2 hours and 30mins to a loiter time of several hours.

The Air Defence Variant (ADV) of the Tornado from which the F3 was developed flew for the first time in October 1979, and the F3 will almost certainly stay in service until it is replaced by the European Fighter Aircraft (EFA) during the early part of the next century. RAF Tornado F3s were sent to the Gulf in August 1990 and, by the end of hostilities on the 28 Feburary 1991, 18 x F3 aircraft had flown some 2,500 sorties during their deployment including 700 sorties during the period of hostilities. Between 1993 and 1997, the RAF has participated in NATO operations to enforce a No-Fly Zone over Bosnia as part of Operation Deny Flight and, during that time, an average of 8 x F-3 aircraft had been operating from airbases in Italy.

There were no reports of RAF Tornado F3s being deployed during the 1999 Kosovo Campaign.

Under a £140 million Tornado F3 Capability Sustainment Programme (CSP), being carried out by BAE Systems, 100 upgraded aircraft will enter service with only limited use of their primary air-to-air armament, the Raytheon AIM-120 Advanced Medium-Range Air-to-Air Missile (AMRAAM) and the Matra BAe Dynamics Advanced Short- Range Air-to-Air Missile (ASRAAM).

In March 2000 UK MoD officials said that the the decision not to add a datalink between the aircraft and its new AMRAAM weapon system was deliberate. The F3 is expected to engage most enemy fighters at the medium ranges. "Our conclusion, based on extensive simulations, was that you are better off not using mid-course guidance with AMRAAM", one official said.

In addition, limited resources have also hit the F3 and its ASRAAM capability,however. Under CSP, F3s will emerge without the digital interfaces needed by the weapon to achieve its full dogfighting agility, nor will pilots have helmet-mounted sights. Under difficult trade-off, forced on the RAF by limited resources, F3 CSP was procured as a stop-gap measure pending the arrival of the Eurofighter Typhoon. Unmodified F3s will be withdrawn from 2007, with CSP aircraft removed by 2010.

Expect a Tornado F3 Squadron to have between 16 and 20 established crews. In early 1994 Italy leased 24 x Tornado F3s from the UK to bridge the gap until the Eurofighter enters service.

Tornado in World Service
(Original Procurement Figures)

	GR1/IDS	F2/F3/ADV	ECR/GR1A/Recce
UK	199	170	26
Germany	302	-	36
Italy	70	24 (leased from UK)	-
Saudi Arabia	48	24	-

Jaguar GR Mark 1A and T Mk 2A

In service with:

6 Squadron	11 x Jaguar GR1 A/B	Coltishall
	1 x Jaguar T2A	
54 Squadron	11 x Jaguar GR1 A/B	Coltishall
41 Squadron	12 x Jaguar GR1 A/B	Coltishall
	1 x Jaguar T2A	
16 (Reserve Squadron)	8 x Jaguar GR1 A/T2A	Lossiemouth

Crew (GR 1A) 1 (T Mark 2A) 2; Length (GR 1A) 15.52m (T Mark 2A) 16.42m; Wingspan 8.69m; Height 4.89m; All up operational weight approx 11,000kg; Max speed 1,350 k/ph (1,056mph); Armament (GR 1A) 2 x 30mm Aden Cannon (T Mark 2A) 1 x 30mm Aden Cannon, Martel, Sea Eagle, BL 755, bombs and rockets; Engines 2 x Rolls-Royce Turbomeca Adour Mk 104s.

The Anglo-French Jaguar entered RAF service in 1973, the first aircraft being delivered to the Operational Conversion Unit at RAF Lossiemouth. Powered by two Rolls Royce/Turbomeca Adour turbofan engines, the Jaguar was built by the BAC/Breguet consortium Sepecat. Two RAF versions remain in service the GR1A and the T2A.

The Jaguar carries an impressive weapons load beneath four wing pylons and a centreline pylon. Weapons include cluster bombs, 1,000 pound retarded and free fall bombs and other bombs, rockets and missiles. The aircraft carries 30 mm cannon internally and for self-defence the GR1A has a comprehensive suite of electronic countermeasures, a radar warning receiver and overwing Sidewinder missiles.

The most impressive feature of the Jaguar is the highly advanced and automated navigation and attack system. The "chisel" nose contains the Laser Ranging and Marked Target Seeker and, in addition to the on-board computer, there is a moving map display and a head-up display. The pilot can feed the data for his mission into the computer and all the relevant information required for pin-point attack is supplied on the head-up display, showing him where the target is located and where to release the particular weapons being carried. During the Gulf War, the RAF deployed a Squadron of 12 x Jaguar GR1A to the region. This squadron was employed on a variety of battlefield interdiction (BAI) and close air support (CAS) missions. Although only operating during daylight, the Jaguars displayed great versatility and flew over 600 operational sorties without loss. In addition to their operations over land, the Jaguars were also successful in destroying Iraqi patrol boats and landing craft in the Gulf. Jaguars also flew tactical reconnaissance sorties. Tornado GR1 and Jaguar GR1As dropped some 100 x JP233 airfield denial weapons, 5,000 x 1,000 pound bombs, 1,000 x LGBs, 100 x ALARM missiles and 700 x Air-to-Ground rockets onto Iraqi positions.

According to UK MoD sources it does not appear that RAF Jaguars were used in the 1999 campaign in Kosovo.

In June 2000 the first RAF Jaguar to be equipped with the upgraded Rolls-Royce Turbomeca (RTM) Adour Mk 106 turbofan engine made its first flight from BAE Systems' Warton Aerodrome. The trials aircraft, equipped with one Mk 106 engine in combination with a baseline Adour Mk 104, conducted a 55-minute flight which included a simulated single-engine approach using the Mk 106 engine. The first flight with two Mk 106 engines took place in August 2000. The first of 61 RAF Jaguars to receive the more powerful engines is scheduled to undergo modification from February 2001 under a £61 million contract, which is expected to keep the GR1A operational until at least 2008.

Expect a Jaguar GR1A Squadron to have 16 established crews.

Harrier

In Service With:

1 Squadron	12 x Harrier GR7	Wittering
	1 x Harrier T10	
3 Squadron	12 x Harrier GR7	Cottesmore
	1 x Harrier T-10	
4 Squadron	12 x Harrier GR7	Cottesmore
	1 x Harrier T10	
20 Reserve (Reserve Squadron)	9 x Harrier GR7	Wittering
	5 x Harrier T10	

Note: All of these aircraft are now part of the Joint Force Harrier (JFH) organisation.

Crew (GR7) 1; (T Mark 10) 2; Length (GR7) 14m; Length (T10) 17m; Wingspan (normal) 9.3m; Height (GR7) 3.45m; Height (T10) 4.17m; Max Speed 1,083 k/ph (673mph) at sea level; All Up operational weight approx 13,494 kg; Armament 2 x 30mm Aden guns, 4 x wing weapon pylons and 1 x underfuselage weapon pylon, conventional or cluster bombs; Engine 1 x Rolls-Royce Pegasus 11-21; Ferry range 5,382 kms (3,310 miles) with 4 x drop tanks.

Capable of taking off and landing vertically, the Harrier is not tied to airfields with long concrete runways but can be dispersed to sites in the field close to the forward edge of the battle area. The normal method of operation calls for a short take-off and vertical landing (STOVL), as a short ground roll on take-off enables a greater weapon load to be carried. The Harrier GR3 was the mark of the aircraft that was taken into service in large numbers, starting in 1969.

The Harrier GR5 entered service in 1988 with the intention of replacing all of the RAF's GR3s on a one for one basis. However, the GR5 has been upgraded to the GR7 which, in turn, entered service in June 1990. All three of the operational Harrier squadrons have been equipped with the GR7 and all of the GR3s and GR5s have either been upgraded or withdrawn from service.

The differences in the GR5 and the GR7 are mainly in the avionics. The GR7 is equipped with the Forward Looking Infra-Red (FLIR) equipment which, when combined with the night vision goggles (NVGs) that the pilot will wear, gives the GR7 a night, low-level, poor-weather capability. There are small differences in the cockpits of the two aircraft including layout and internal lighting standards. In most other respects, the GR7 is similar to the GR5.

The GR7 offers many advantages over the older GR3. It possesses the capability to carry approximately twice the weapon load over the same radius of action, or the same weapon load over a much increased radius. In addition, it carries a comprehensive ECM (Electronic Counter Measures) suite which can operate in the passive or active Mode and will greatly enhance the GR5/7s chances of survival in today's high threat environment. The GR7 also has an inertial navigation system that is significantly more effective than that of the GR3.

The cockpit of the GR7 has been completely revised. The raising of the cockpit in relation to the aircraft has vastly improved the pilot's outlook. Furthermore, the design has incorporated the principle of Hands-On-Throttle and Stick (HOTAS). To aid systems management Cathode Ray Tube (CRT) displays are much in evidence for the display of the FLIR image, moving map, systems status and flying instruments displays. Each CRT has numerous multifunction reprogrammable keys for each function selection, again aiding systems management.

The LRMTS of the GR3 has been replaced with the Angle Rate Bombing System (ARBS) as the primary weapon aiming system. The ARBS incorporates a dual mode tracker, either TV colour contrasts or laser spot tracker. The GR7 has an increased wing area, improved aerodynamic qualities and the incorporation of Leading Edge Root Extensions which all combine to give the GR7 much improved manoeuvrability over that of the GR3. However, the GR7 maintains its ability to vector the engine's thrust in forward flight (VIFF), again increasing manoeuvrability.

The GR7 was derived from the McDonnell Douglas/British Aerospace AV-8B. Noteworthy changes include the addition of a moving map display, Martin Baker ejection seat, increased bird strike protection, a new Aden 25 mm cannon and additional electronic countermeasures equipment.

During the 1999 campaign in Kosovo, RAF Harrier GR7 were deployed. At the beginning of 1999 eight Harriers were deployed to a base in Italy together with two Tristar tankers to support the Kosovo Verification Mission. This force was increased to 12 Harriers in late March. In the main these aircraft dropped either cluster bombs, gravity bombs or precision guided weapons. No aircraft were lost during the campaign.

The T10 is an advanced trainer version of the aircraft. A total of 13 x Harrier T10 are available.

Expect a Harrier GR7 Squadron to have 17 established crews.

Nimrod

In Service With:

120 Squadron	6 x Nimrod MR2	Kinloss
201 Squadron	6 x Nimrod MR2	Kinloss
206 Squadron	6 x Nimrod MR2	Kinloss
42 (Reserve) Squadron	3 x Nimrod MR2	Kinloss

Note: This group of units is known as the Kinloss Air Wing. We are reasonably certain that there are approximately 21 aircraft in this group at any one time. Aircraft are shown as being allocated to squadrons for ease of accounting - real numbers may change almost daily.

51 Squadron	3 x Nimrod R1	Waddington

Characteristics MR2P:

Crew 12; Length 38.60m; Span 35m; Height 9.08m; Max speed 926km ((575mph); Max All up weight 87,090 kg; Endurance 12 hrs; Ferry range 9,265 kms; Armament Harpoon, Sidewinder, Sea Eagle, 9 x Mark 46 or Stingray Torpedoes, bombs; Engines 4 x Rolls Royce Spey RB 168-20 Mark 250 turbofans.

There are currently two variants of the Nimrod in RAF service. The first is the MR Mark 2P, which has been developed for long-range maritime patrol. Its long ferry range enables the crew to monitor seaspace far to the north of Iceland and up to 4,000 kms out into the Western Atlantic. With AAR (Air-to-Air Refueling), its range and endurance is greatly extended. The MR Mark 2 is a very lethal submarine killer carrying the most up to date sensors and data processing equipment linked to the weapon systems. In addition to weapons and sonar-buoys, a searchlight mounted in the starboard wing pod can be used for search and rescue (SAR) operations.

The second version is the R Mark 1, an aircraft specially fitted out for the gathering of electronic intelligence and only three are known to be in service. This is a highly secret aircraft that has been in RAF service since 1971 and about which little is known except that it has been spotted on patrol over the Baltic Sea.

Nimrod is a development of the basic Comet No 4C airframe that dates from the late 1940's. Both the current variants are descended from the original Nimrod MR Mark 1 version (first flight May 1967) that is no longer in service.

The first phase of the refurbishment and rebuild of 21 Nimrod MR2 began February 1997 when the first of three fuselages was air-lifted from RAF Kinloss to FR Aviation at Bournemouth (Hurn).

Over the next three years 21 aircraft were refurbished with new wings, four new BMW/Rolls-Royce BR 710 turbofan engines, new undercarriage and internal systems. Upon completion of basic airworthiness flights, the Nimrod 2000 (as the project is known) were flown to British Aerospace at Warton where they were equipped with new mission systems avionics.

Sentry AEW1

Crew; 5 x Flight crew and 13 x mission Crew; Length 46.61m; Wingspan 44.42m; Height 12.73m; All up operational weight 147,400kg; Max speed 853 k/ph (530 mph); Patrol Endurance 6 hrs (can be enhanced by AAR); (Ferry Range 3,200 km; Engines 4 x CFM-56-2A-3 ; Armament provision for self-defence air-to-air missiles.
In service with:

| 8 Squadron | 3 x Sentry AEW1 | Waddington |
| 23 Squadron | 3 x Sentry AEW1 | Waddington |

Deliveries of the Sentry AEW1 commenced in March 1991 and delivery of all seven airframes was complete in early 1992. These seven aircraft are of the same type as the 18 delivered to the multi national NATO early warning force between 1982/1985. All are equipped with the Joint Tactical Information Distribution System (JTIDS) and a 665,360 word memory secure communication system.

Powered by four CFM 56-2A-3 engines, the Sentry is designed to cruise at 29,000 feet whilst detecting air and surface contacts with its AN/APY-2 surveillance radar. Information is then transmitted back to interceptor aircraft and, ground air-and-ship-based units using a wide variety of digital datalinks.

Almost certainly the most complex airborne system yet to enter RAF service, the Sentry carries a full crew of 17 which includes 5 x flight deck crew, 9 x mission crew and 3 x airborne technicians.

Three AEW1 aircraft were used by the RAF during operations over Yugoslavia during 1999.

Hawk

In service with:

100 Squadron	13 x Hawk T1/1A	Leeming (target towing)
No 4 Flying Training School (4 FTS)	68 x Hawk T1/1A	Valley
Red Arrows	10 x Hawk T1/1A	Scampton

Crew 2; Span 9.39m; Length 11.17m; Height 3.99m; Weight Empty 3,647kg; Max Take Off Weight 8,569kg; Max Speed 1,038 kph (645 mph) at 3,355m; Combat Radius 556 km (345 miles); Engine 1 x 2,359 kg thrust Rolls Royce/Turbomecca Adour Mk 151 turbofan; Armament 30 mm Aden cannon, 2 x AIM-9L Sidewinder plus assorted bombs and rockets.

The Hawk first flew in 1974, and entered RAF service two years later both as an advanced flying trainer and a weapons training aircraft. It has an economical Adour engine - an unreheated version of the same turbofan powering the Jaguar.

Hawks are used to teach operational tactics such as air-to-air and air-to-ground firing, air combat and low-level operating procedures to pilots destined for the "fast-jet" squadrons. As a weapons trainer the Hawk is armed with an Aden cannon carried beneath the fuselage, and rocket pods or practice bombs can be fitted to underwing pylons. To fulfil its mobilisation role as a fighter aircraft, the Hawk carries a 30 mm Aden cannon and two Sidewinder air-to-air missiles and is designated T1A. About 50 Hawks are believed to be equipped for the air defence mobilisation role.

The Hawk is a strong and rugged aircraft designed to cut training and maintenance costs. The aircraft has a long fatigue life to ensure a service career throughout the 1990s and beyond.

During January 1998, the MoD announced plans to extend the fatigue life of the Hawk T1/1A in RAF service. Up to 80 Hawks will be involved in a 'return-to-works' (RTW) programme that will see their centre and rear fuselage sections being replaced with new production units from the Hawk Series 60 production line. RAF Hawks have already received re-lifed wings and tailplanes. The programme is began in September 1999 and 2 aircraft per month will be completed until the end of 2003. The first refurbished aircraft was delivered back to the RAF in May 2000.

Eurofighter 2000

The Eurofighter 2000 (formerly EFA) is a highly agile, single seat, STOL capable aircraft optimised for air superiority/air defence and ground attack roles. The aircraft is part of a European co-production programme with the major manufacturing firms involved being British Aerospace, DASA, CASA and Alenia. British Aerospace (BAe) is responsible for the front fuselage, foreplanes, starboard leading edge flaps and flaperons; BAe/CASA the starboard wing; Alenia the port wing; DASA the centre fuselage, fin and rudder; Alenia/CASA the rear fuselage.

Eurofighter is designed to carry 6 x medium-range and 2 x close-range air-to-air missiles. The aircraft has 13 x store stations and an internal gun fitted on the starboard side. No modifications will be necessary to carry "smart" weapons and 3 stations can carry external fuel pods. The Defensive Aids Sub-System (DASS) equipment is carried in 2 x wing pods that are an integral part of the wing. The aircraft will weigh about 37,000 lbs (approx 16,800 kgs) and be able to operate from a 500 metre strip. In May 2000 the Matra BAe Dynamics Meteor was selected as the beyond-visual-range air-to-air missile (BVRAAM) for Eurofighter.

In May 2000 the UK MoD also confirmed that the Eurofighter will not use its 27mm Mauser gun while in RAF service. While the UK's first batch of 55 Eurofighters will be supplied with and will carry the internally-housed gun, the MoD has decided against procuring support equipment and ammunition for the weapon, and will procure future examples of the aircraft without it. As a result the MoD expects an initial saving of £19 million, with annual operational savings of £3.5 million.

The aircraft is designed to operate with a minimum of ground support requiring only four fitters to change an engine in 45 minutes, and a standard of nine man/servicing hours per flying hour as opposed to from 20 to 60 hours for other modern combat aircraft. The first flight of the Eurofighter 2000 was made on 15 April 1994 from Manching Air base near Munich in Germany.

The UK MoDs latest estimate is that some 300 British companies are in the Eurofighter supply chain, and that the project is currently supporting about 9,000 jobs. This figure is expected to rise to about 28,000 UK jobs during the peak production years.

In February 1998, Germany, Italy, Spain and the UK signed nine contracts, worth approximately £32 billion covering production and support of 620 Eurofighters. The four air forces will receive:

Germany	-	180
Italy	-	121
Spain	-	87
UK	-	232

A further 90 aircraft will be on option. Most analysts believe that each aircraft could cost about £40 million (US$64 million) and, if development and maintenance costs are taken into account the cost per aircraft could be as high as £65 million (US$104 million) per aircraft. The launch customers will sign a contract for 236 Tranche 2 aircraft in 2003, with Greece also expected to order between 60 and 90 Eurofighter Typhoons.

The first production aircraft are due to fly in August 2001, and delivery should start in 2002. Export versions of the Eurofighter will be called Typhoon. The original Typhoon that flew during WWII cost £5,100 per aircraft (£150,000 at 2000 prices).

C-130 Hercules

In service with:

24 Squadron	10 x Hercules C1/C3	Lyneham
30 Squadron	10 x Hercules C1/C3	Lyneham
47 Squadron	10 x Hercules C1/C3	Lyneham
70 Squadron	10 x Hercules C1/C3	Lyneham
57 Squadron (Reserve Sqn)	65 x Hercules C1/C3	Lyneham

The LTW (Lyneham Transport Wing) appears to have a total of 50 aircraft (including 5 in reserve). The squadron totals are given as a guide to what we believe are the average aircraft figures per squadron and the OCU at any one time.

Crew 5; Capacity 92 troops or 62 paratroops or 74 medical litters or 19,686kg of freight; Length 29.78m; Span 40.41m; Height 11.66m; Weight empty 34,287kg; Max load 45,093kg; Max speed 618 k/ph (384mph); Service ceiling 13,075m; Engines 4 x Allison T-56A-15 turboprops.

The C-130 Hercules C1 is the workhorse of the RAF transport fleet. Over the years it has proved to be a versatile and rugged aircraft, primarily intended for tactical operations including troop carrying, paratrooping, supply dropping and aeromedical duties. The Hercules can operate from short unprepared airstrips, but also possesses the endurance to mount long range strategic lifts if required. The aircraft is a derivative of the C-130E used by the United States Air Force, but is fitted with British avionic equipment, a roller-conveyor system for heavy air-drops and with more powerful engines. The crew of five includes, pilot, co-pilot, navigator, air engineer and air loadmaster.

As a troop carrier, the Hercules can carry 92 fully armed men, while for airborne operations 62 paratroops can be dispatched in two simultaneous "sticks" through the fuselage side doors. Alternatively, 40 paratroops can jump from the rear loading ramp. As an air ambulance the aircraft can accommodate 74 stretchers.

Freight loads that can be parachuted from the aircraft include: 16 x 1 ton containers or 4 x 8,000 pound platforms or 2 x 16,000 pound platforms or 1 x platform of 30,000 pounds plus. Amongst the many combinations of military loads that can be carried in an air-landed operation are: 3 x Ferret scout cars plus 30 passengers or 2 x Land Rovers and 30 passengers or 2 x Gazelle helicopters.

Of the original 66 C1 aircraft, some 31 have been given a fuselage stretch producing the Mark C3. The C3 "stretched version" provides an additional 37% more cargo space. Refuelling probes have been fitted above the cockpit of both variants and some have received radar warning pods under the wing tips. One aircraft, designated Mark W2, is a special weather version and is located at the DERA Farnborough.

RAF Hercules are often involved in humanitarian tasks in support of UN operations in many areas of the world. For example, working from a forward airhead at Ancona on the eastern coast of Italy, a detachment of 38 officers and men with a single Hercules from 47 Sqn, averaged almost three flights a day for the year 3 July 1992 - 3 July 1993. Over 900 sorties lifted more than 19 million pounds of freight into Sarajevo. The aircraft were flown by six crews on a two-week rotation from RAF Lyneham.

Current plans appear to be for the replacement of the RAF's ageing 1960s Hercules fleet during the next ten years and, in 1995, the UK MoD announced the purchase of 25 x C-130J from the US company Lockheed. This aircraft has improved engines, a new glass cockpit with flat screen displays and a two-man crew. After some delay with Lockheed admitting problems in getting demonstrator and production aircraft to the correct configuration by the end of 2000, seven aircraft had been delivered to the RAF.
The MoD has been considering ordering a second batch of transport aircraft and in mid 2000 announced the intention to procure 25 x A400M (FLA) The A400M which will be built by the Rome based Euroflag Consortium, will probably be ready for service from about 2007 and could be capable of carrying a maximum payload of 30 tons as opposed to the 20 tons of the C-130J. British Aerospace is a member of the Euroflag consortium.

The most commonly quoted argument in favour of the A400M is that this aircraft could carry a 25 ton payload over a distance of 4,000 km. Thus it is argued that a fleet of 40 x

FLA could carry a UK Brigade to the Gulf within 11.5 days, as opposed to the 28.5 days required to make a similar deployment with 40 x C-130s.

Over 1,000 x C-130 have been manufactured and 467 are in service with the US Armed Forces.

C-17 Globemaster

In service with:

99 Squadron	4 x C-17A	Brize Norton

Wingspan 51.74 m; Length overall 53.04 m; Height overall 16.79 m; Loadable width 5.49m; Max payload 78,655 kg (77 tons); Cruising speed 648 kph (403 mph); Range (max payload) 4,444 km (2,400 miles)

The UK will also acquire four Boeing C-17s in a seven-year lease starting in 2001, that will provide the RAF with a strategic lift capability before initial deliveries of the tactical and strategic A400M around 2007. No 99 Sqn will be reformed at RAF Brize Norton in May 2001 and four aircraft will be in place by late August.

The aircraft will be able to carry one Challenger 2 MBT or a range of smaller armoured vehicles and if, necessary could carry up to three WAH-64 Apache aircraft at one time. If necessary over 150 passengers can be carried. Inflight refuelling will greatly increase the aircraft range.

No 99 Sqn will have 158 flight crew and ground staff.

Tucano
In service with:

No 1 Flying Training School (1 FTS)	75 x Tucano T1	Linton (includes Central Flying School at Topcliffe)

Crew 2; Length 9.86m; Height 3.40m; Span 11.14m; Max Speed 458 k/ph (254mph); Service Ceiling 8,750m; Range 1,916kms; Engine 1,100shp Garrett 8TPE-331 turboprop.

Originally designed by the Brazilian aerospace company Embraer, the Tucano was selected in 1985 to replace the Jet Provost as the RAF's basic trainer. The development and production contract was awarded to Shorts of Belfast, who have incorporated a number of MoDifications to meet the RAF's specifications.

The first aircraft was delivered in June 1988, although two aircraft had been at Boscombe Down undergoing flight trials since late 1987. Student training on the aircraft started at RAF Church Fenton in December 1989.

The RAF version of the Tucano, designated the Tucano T1, has been modified in many ways from the basic Embraer 312. A Garrett TOE 331 engine which develops 1,100 shp, is fitted in place of the original PT6 and represents a 50% power increase. Fatigue life has been extended from 8,000 to 12,000 hours by fitting strengthened wings and landing gear, a ventral air brake has been added, plus a new canopy which is bird strike resistant up to 270 knots.

The Tucano heralds a new concept of flying training within the RAF. The tandem seating, in Martin Baker ejector seats, allows a smaller aerodynamic frontal area than the Jet Provost, leading to lower power requirements and greater fuel efficiency. Visibility from the cockpit is also improved and the student is better prepared to progress to the Hawk advanced trainer. The turbo-engine is both flexible and economic, helping the Tucano to out-perform the Jet Provost in every area except maximum straight-and-level speed. For example, the Tucano time to 15,000 feet is half that required by the Jet Provost.

The Tucano has been manufactured around the concept of reliability and maintainability to provide a cost-effective trainer and fulfil the requirements of the RAF through the 1990s and beyond. The original RAF purchase was for 126 x Tucano.

Chinook
In service with:

7 Squadron	11 x Chinook HC2	Odiham
18 Squadron	10 x Chinook HC2	Odiham
27 Squadron	9 x Chinook HC2	Odiham
78 Squadron	1 x Chinook HC2	Mount Pleasant

All the above aircraft are under the control of the Joint Helicopter Command (JHC).

Crew 3; Fuselage length 15.54m; Width 3.78m; Height 5.68m; Weight (empty) 10,814kg; Internal payload 8,164kg; Rotor diameter 18.29m; Cruising speed 270 k/ph (158mph);

Service ceiling 4,270m; Mission radius(with internal and external load of 20,000kgs including fuel and crew) 55kms; Rear loading Ramp Heigth 1.98m; Rear loading ramp Width 2.31m; Engines 2 x Avco Lycoming T55-L11E turboshafts.

The Chinook is a tandem-rotored, twin-engined medium-lift helicopter. It has a crew of four (pilot, navigator and 2 x crewmen) and is capable of carrying 45 fully equipped troops or a variety of heavy loads up to approximately 10 tons. The first Chinooks entered service with the RAF in 1982.

The triple hook system allows greater flexibility in load carrying and enables some loads to be carried faster and with greater stability. In the ferry configuration with internally mounted fuel tanks, the Chinook's range is over 1,600 km (1,000 miles). In the medical evacuation role the aircraft can carry 24 stretchers.

RAF Chinook aircraft have recently been upgraded to the HC2 standard. The first of the 32 aircraft being upgraded was delivered to the RAF in the Spring of 1993, with the remaining aircraft delivered during 1996. The HC2 upgrade, for which a total of £145 million was allocated, allows for the aircraft to be modified to the US CH-47D standard with some extra enhancements. These enhancements include fitting infra-red jammers, missile approach warning indicators, chaff and flare dispensers, a long-range fuel system and machine gun mountings.

This is a rugged and reliable aircraft. During the Falklands War reports suggest that, at one stage, 80 fully equipped troops were carried in one lift and, during a Gulf War mission a single Chinook carried 110 Iraqi POWs. The Chinook mid-life update will significantly enhance the RAF's ability to support the land forces during the next 25 years.
Analysts suggest that since 1 April 1990 the RAF Chinook fleet has flown some 60,000 hours during which time the operating costs (personnel, fuel and maintenance) have been £310 million, a figure that results in a cost of about £5,200 per flying hour. On average, 27 of 32 aircraft have been available for front-line service at any one time, a figure reflecting the need for planned maintenance and servicing. On 9 March 1995, the UK MoD announced a purchase of a further 14 x Chinooks and a separate buy of 22 x EH 101 (Merlin) . The contract for the 14 x Chinooks was signed in early September 1995 at a price of £240 million (US $365 million), resulting in a possible unit cost of £17 million per aircraft.

In mid 2000 RAF Chinook helicopters were in operational service with UK forces in Sierra Leone. Getting the aircraft on station included the staggered dispatch of two pairs of Chinook HC2 helicopters plus 85 air crew and ground support staff from RAF Odiham on 5 May. Over the next four days the Chinooks were flown to Sierra Leone via Portugal, Gibraltar, Tenerife and Senegal. Internal long-range tanks were used for the journey, with one stretch being more than 1,200km over water.

In June 2000 the UK MoD formally refused to accept delivery of the first of eight special operations configured Boeing Chinook Mk3 helicopters. Although the first helicopter flew in October 1998 and initial delivery was due in February 2000, current estimates suggest that the first HC3 aircraft may not enter service until February 2003. The UK MoD states that the delay has been caused by 'minor software' problems.

The JHC is keen for these aircraft to be in service as soon as possible because they have in-flight refuelling, forward looking infrared and extra fuel because they are capable of self-deployment. When these aircraft enter service we believe that they will be based at RAF Odiham.

Puma
In service with:

All the above aircraft are under the control of the Joint Helicopter Command (JHC).

33 Squadron	15 x Puma HC1	Benson
72 Squadron	5 x Puma HC1	Aldergrove
	Plus 8 x Wessex HC2	
230 Squadron	13 x Puma HC1	Aldergrove

Crew 2 or 3; Fuselage length 14.06m; Width 3.50m; Height 4.38m; Weight (empty) 3,615kg; Maximum take off weight 7,400kg; Cruising speed 258 k/ph (192mph); Service ceiling 4,800m; Range 550kms; 2 x Turbomecca Turmo 111C4 turbines.

The "package deal" between the UK and France on helicopter collaboration dates back to February 1967 when Ministers of the two countries signed a Memorandum of Understanding (MoU). The programme covered the development of three helicopter types - the Puma, Gazelle and Lynx. The main contractors engaged on the programme were Westland and SNIAS for the airframe, and Rolls Royce and Turbomeca for the engines.

Development of the Puma was already well advanced in France when collaboration began. However, the flight control system has been developed jointly by the two countries, and a great deal of work done by Westland to adapt the helicopter for the particular operational requirements of the RAF. Production of the aircraft was shared between the two countries, the UK making about 20% by value of the airframe, slightly less for the engine, as well as assembling the aircraft procured for the RAF. Deliveries of the RAF Pumas started in 1971.

The Puma is powered by 2 x Turbomeca Turmo 111C4 engines mounted side by side above the main cabin. Capable of many operational roles, Puma can carry 16 fully equipped troops, or 20 at light scales. In the casualty evacuation role (CASEVAC), 6 stretchers and 6 sitting cases can be carried. Underslung loads of up to 3,200 kg can be transported over short distances and an infantry battalion can be moved using 34 Puma lifts.
In September 1994 a contract was announced for a navigation upgrade for 41 x RAF Puma helicopters with Racal Avionics acting as the prime contractor. The programme was completed in 1998.

In total we believe that there are currently (early 2001) 39 x Pumas available for operational service.

Sea King HAR3
In service with:

22 Squadron	Squadron	RMB Chivenor
A Flight	Headquarters	RMB Chivenor
B Flight	3 x Sea King HAR3	Wattisham
C Flight	3 x Sea King HAR3	Valley
202 Squadron	2 x Sea King HR3	Boulmer
A Flight	Headquarters	Boulmer
D Flight	3 x Sea King HAR3	Lossiemouth
E Flight	3 x Sea King HAR 3	Leconfield
203 (Reserve) Squadron	2 x Sea King HAR 3	St Mawgan
78 Squadron	2 x Sea King HAR 3	Mount Pleasant
Squadron total includes	2 x Chinook HC2	

Note: Both 22 and 202 Squadrons have 8 x Sea King HAR3. Numbers of aircraft have been allocated to flights for rounding purposes.

Crew 1-3; Length 17.01m; Height 4.72m; Rotor diameter 18.9m; Weight (empty) 6,201kg; Cruising Speed 208 k/ph (129mph); Range 1,230kms; Engine 2 x Rolls Royce Gnome H1400.1 turboshafts.

The Westland Sea King HAR3 Search and Rescue helicopter entered RAF service in 1978. The aircraft is powered by two Rolls Royce Gnome gas-turbine engines, each rated at 1,660 shp and is fitted with advanced all-weather search and navigation equipment, as well as autopilot and onboard computer to assist positioning and hovering at night or in bad weather. In addition to four crew members the HAR3 can carry up to six stretchers, or 18 survivors. Under normal conditions expect the HAR3 to have an operational radius of approximately 448 kms (280 miles).

The Sea King HAR3 replaced the Wessex HC2 in the SAR role in 1996. An early 1990s MoD report concluded that a total of 25 Sea Kings was required to ensure that SAR duties were carried out effectively and an announcement was made in 1992 of an order for 6 more HAR3, to bring the total up to the required 25. Of these 25 aircraft, 16 are allocated for SAR duties in the UK, 2 in the Falkland Islands, 3 for conversion training and the remaining 3 form an engineering and operational pool.

EH101 Merlin Mk3
In service with:

| 28 Squadron | 12 x Merlin Mk3 | Benson (from 2001) |

All the above aircraft will be under the control of the Joint Helicopter Command (JHC).

Crew 2; Length 22.81m; Rotor diameter 18.59m; Max speed 309k/ph (192mph); Engine 3 x Rolls Royce/Turbomeca RTM 322 three-shaft turbines of 2,312 shp each; Up to 35 fully equipped troops can be carried or 16 stretchers and a medical team.

The RAF ordered 22 EH101 (Merlin) support helicopters in March 1995. Merlin is a direct replacement for the Westland Wessex and it will operate alongside the Puma and Chinook in the medium lift role. Its ability to carry troops, artillery pieces, light vehicles and bulk loads, means that the aircraft will be ideal for use with the UK Army's 16 Air Assault Brigade.

The aircraft can carry a maximum load of 35 troops with support weapons. The maximum payload is 4,000 kg and Merlin has a maximum range of 1,000km, which can be extended by external tanks or by air-to-air refuelling. The Merlin Mk 3 has sophisticated defensive aids and the aircraft is designed to operate in extreme conditions and is corrosion-proofed for maritime operations. All weather, day/night precision delivery is possible because of

GPS navigation, a forward-looking infra-red sensor and night vision goggle compatibility.

The first production model was 'rolled out' by GKN Westland in November 1998 and by late 2000 it would appear that the RAF had taken delivery of 12 aircraft. The first operational squadron will be 28 Squadron based at Benson in Oxfordshire. We would expect 28 Squadron to be operational by mid 2001.

In the longer term the aircraft could be fitted with a nose turret mounting a .50 calibre machine gun. It is claimed that the noise level inside the aircraft will be no higher than that of a commercial turboprop aircraft.

RAF Weapons

ALARM
Length 4.24m: Diameter 0.22m: Span 0.72m: Total weight 175kg: Propellant 1 x Royal Ordnance Nuthatch solid fuel two-stage rocket: Range and speed not yet revealed, however these figures are probably comparable with those of HARM which has a speed of Mach 3+ and a range of 75kms+.

ALARM stands for Air-Launched Anti-Radiation Missile and this type was introduced into RAF Service in the early 1990s. The missile is launched at low level near the suspected site of an enemy radar and, after launch, rapidly climbs to about 12,000 m. At this height, a small parachute opens and the missile descends earthwards while the on-board radar searches the broadband for emissions from enemy radar. Once a target has been identified, the motor is re-ignited and the missile makes a supersonic dive on to the target.

The total RAF buy in the first manufacturing run was believed to be some 750 missiles.

AMRAAM
Length 3.6 metres; Weight 340 lbs; Cruising speed Mach 4; Range approx 30 miles.

AMRAAM (Advanced medium-range air-to-air missile) is an air fighting weapon that matches the fire-and-forget capability of the ASRAAM, but with greater range. There is increased immunity over electronic countermeasures and a low-smoke, high-impulse rocket motor to reduce the probability of an enemy sighting the missile. This system is in use by Tornado F3 and will be used by the Eurofighter. In addition, trials were underway during late 2000 with AMRAAM fitted to Jaguar GR1B. AMRAAM has been in service with the Fleet Air Arm since 1995 and the initial purchase was believed to be about 210 missiles.

ASRAAM
The ASRAAM (Advanced Short-Range Air-to-Air Missile) fire-and-forget missile, is an air combat weapon that is highly manoeuvrable and requires minimal pilot input. The missile has an advanced high-sensitivity infra-red seeker, which can lock onto the target before launch or in flight, and results in an extremely high kill probability. ASRAAM is also highly resistant to electronic countermeasures. ASRAAM will be used by UK Eurofighters

when the aircraft enters service from 2002 onward.

BL 755 Cluster Bomb

Length 2.45 m; Diameter .41 m; Weight 277 kg; Payload 147 bomblets.

The BL 755 is a system that was designed to cope with some of the very large area targets that might have been encountered on the Central Front, especially large armoured formations of Regimental strength (90+ tanks) or more. The weapon can be carried by Tornado GR1, Harrier, Jaguar, Buccaneer and Phantom and consists of a large container which is divided into seven compartments. Each of these compartments contains 21 bomblets making a total of 147 bomblets in all.

After the bomb has been released from the aircraft, the 147 bomblets are ejected and fall to the ground covering a wide area. As each individual bomblet hits a target, a HEAT charge is detonated which can fire a large slug of molten metal through up to 250 mm of armour. In addition, the casing of the bomblet disintegrates and hundreds of fragments of shrapnel are dispersed over a wide area, with resultant damage to personnel and soft- skinned vehicles.

The BL 755 can be released at very low altitude and this is essential if pilots are to survive in the high-density SAM conditions that will apply over the Central Front. Aircraft will only have the chance to make one pass over the target before the defences are alerted, and for a pilot to make a second pass to ensure accuracy would be suicidal

Bombs

Paveway II is the standard 1,000 lb (454 kg) general purpose bomb for used against Moderately well-protected targets. Paveway II can be fitted with a laser guidance kit and the bomb can be used in the freefall or retarded mode.

Paveway III is a 2,000 lb (908 kg) laser guided bomb for use against well-protected targets. The bomb is guided to its target by a TIALD (Thermal Imaging and Laser Designation) pod that is carried on the aircraft or by a ground based observer using a target designator. The weapon can be carried on the Tornado GR4, Jaguar GR1A/B or the Harrier GR7.

Conventional 1,000 lb (454 kg) bombs are still in service as are Mark 1 and Mark 2 bombs weighing 570 lb (260 kg). By adding the Hunting 118 retarding tail the weight of the latter is increased to 670 lb (304 kg).

Brimstone

Length 1.63 m; Diameter 178 mm; Weight 50 kg; Range 8 km.

In the near future the BL 755 (previous entry) will be replaced by the Brimstone anti armour missile that is a development of the US Hellfire missile. Brimstone has a standoff capability allowing targets to be attacked from a good distance and each weapon pylon will have three missiles on a triple launcher. Brimstone is planned for deployment with the Tornado GR4 and the Harrier GR7.

CVR-7

This is an air-to-air and air-to-surface rocket system. Each rocket pod, weighing 240 kg carries 19 rockets. The HE warhead is designed for use against light armour, vehicles, small vessels and helicopters.

Harpoon

Length 3.84 m; Diameter 0.343 m; Total Weight 526 kg; Warhead Weight 225 kg; Range 110 km.

Harpoon, manufactured by McDonnell Douglas of the USA, is an extremely powerful anti-shipping missile that is carried in the bomb bay of the Nimrod MR2. The air to sea version of the missile has extremely sophisticated Electronic Counter Measures (ECM), and the ability to fly a sea-skimming course on a dog-leg path through three pre-programmed way-points. The warhead is extremely powerful and a hit from Harpoon is almost certain to result in the destruction or disablement of a major surface vessel.

Meteor (BVRAAM)

During June 2000 the UK MoD announced that the ramjet-powered Matra BAe Dynamics Meteor had been selected as the beyond-visual-range air-to-air missile (BVRAAM) for Eurofighter.

European companies on the Meteor team include Alenia Marconi Systems (a 50:50 joint venture between BAE SYSTEMS and Finmeccanica of Italy); CASA, LFK (the missiles division of DaimlerChrysler Aerospace), and Saab Dynamics. It is believed that initially, the Meteor programme will create about 2,500 jobs across Europe as a whole with about 1,200 of them in the UK.

The US member of the Meteor team is Boeing, which will assist the European companies in aircraft-weapon systems integration, risk management and marketing activities. However, Meteor will not be in service until 2008 and to bridge the gap, the UK has placed a further contract with Raytheon for the AIM-120 AMRAAM.

Sea Eagle

Length 4.14 m: Diameter 0.40 m: Span 1.20 m: Total weight 590 kg: Warhead weight (not yet revealed) believed to be 200 kg+: Speed Mach 0.9+: Range 50-100km depending on launch altitude: Propulsion 1 x Microturbo TRI -l-60-1 turbojet delivering 367 kg of thrust.

The Sea Eagle, a long-range anti-ship guided missile, is used by the Tornado GR1 and Nimrod in the maritime attack role. Developed from the Martel, Sea Eagle can attack targets over the horizon at very low level using radar guidance and an on-board microprocessor which stores the target's last known position and speed. Powered by a small air-breathing-turbojet, the missile skims the waves at just under the speed of sound and picks up the target with its very advanced active radar seeker.

Sidewinder AIM-9L

Diameter 0.127m: Span 0.63m: Length 2.85m: Total Weight 85.3 kg: Warhead weight 10.2

kg: Propulsion Solid fuel rocket: Speed Mach 2.5: Range 17.7 km.

The Sidewinder missile, which is carried by all of the RAF's air defence aircraft, is an infra-red weapon which homes on to the heat emitted by a hostile aircraft's engines. Sidewinder can operate independently of the aircraft's radar, and provides the air defence aircraft with an alternative method of attacking targets at shorter ranges. Sidewinder has an excellent dogfight capability.

Sky Flash
Length 3.66 m; Diameter 0.203 m; Span 1.02 m; Weight 192 kg; Warhead weight 30 kg; Marconi monopulse semi-active radar homing system; Range 50kms.

Sky Flash is an advanced radar-guided air-to-air missile based on the Sparrow which was taken into service in 1977, but with improved guidance and fusing systems. Designed to operate in severe electronic counter-measure conditions, it has an all-weather high/low altitude attack capability. Sky Flash is in service on F3 air defence variant of the Tornado. It is currently the RAF's major air defence weapon but could be replaced by AMRAAM.

Stingray
Length 2.6 m; Diameter 324 mm; Weight 265 kg; Warhead 40 kg of HE in a shaped charge; Speed 45 knots; Range in excess of 10 km.

Stingray is a lightweight homing torpedo that is carried in the bomb bay of the Nimrod MR2. The torpedo is fully programmable, with a number of search options and has been designed to destroy submarines. The torpedo seeker can either home in on the sound of the submarine or detect and track the target using its own sonar.

Storm Shadow
Length 5.10 m; Diameter 480 mm; Weight 1,100 kg; Range estimate 350 km.

Storm Shadow is a long-range, stand-off attack missile that will allow the RAF to attack high-priority targets deep inside enemy territory without exposing the launch aircraft to high-intensity enemy air defences. The missile is the BAe version (with some UK enhancements) of the French Matra APACHE missile and has an in service date of 2002. It will be fitted to Tornado GR4, Harrier GR7 and the Eurofighter. The RAF is believed to have purchased an initial batch of 500 missiles.

THAAD
Recent fears of nuclear proliferation, and the problems of nuclear-capable delivery systems such as the former Soviet Scud missile being used by nations who hitherto have not been able to mount a credible threat to the UK, have forced the MoD to look at the options offered by adopting a high-level missile defence.

We believe that the UK MoD is now looking at a Theatre High-Altitude Area Defence (THAAD) system to defend the UK against incoming missiles. The MoD appears to be interested in creating a layered anti-missile defence, capable of multiple attempts at hitting targets at ranges of over 100 miles at heights of over 100,000 feet, to shorter-range systems such as the US Patriot that could hit targets at much closer range.

During late 1993, officials from the US Lockheed Corporation briefed UK MoD staff on the capabilities of THAAD and, in November 1993, more than 60 companies attended a presentation regarding work on such a system. However, we believe that the UK can only proceed with such an expensive programme as a partner in a European collaborative project, and there are some reports that preliminary talks have taken place to explore options.

A layered system based upon low-medium and high-level missiles, employing satellite and early warning aircraft detectors would have a very high percentage chance of success against everything except a saturation attack by large numbers of missiles. However, the defence budgets of the nations that really count in the European procurement scene (France, Germany and the UK) appear to be fully committed until at least 2005. An expensive THAAD system costing many billions of pounds is almost certainly not going to appear in the short term and it is likely that any future European system will be based around current US THAAD technology.

NATO is to award a two-year contract worth approximately £10 million each to two multinational teams in early 2001 for initial feasibility studies of an alliance-wide upper-tier TMD (Theatre Missile Defence) system that could defend Europe from ballistic missiles with a range of up to 3,000km. The Active Layered Theatre Ballistic Missile Defence system would complement lower-tier weapons, and advanced versions of the US Patriot, that are already in development or on order by European countries. This upper-tier system could be land-based or at least partially deployed aboard ships.
There are plans for a system in service date of 2010.

RAF Regiment
The need to raise a dedicated specialist force to protect air installations became apparent during WWII when unprotected aircraft on the ground were vulnerable to enemy air and ground attack. Consequently, the RAF Regiment was raised on 1 February 1942 by a Royal Warrant of King George VI. At the end of WWII, there were over 85,000 personnel serving in the RAF Regiment manning 240 operational squadrons. During late 1993, the strength of the RAF Regiment was approximately 3,000 (including 264 officers). During early 2001 the strength of the RAF Regiment is believed to be about 2,400.

Currently the RAF Regiment exists to provide ground and short- range air defence for RAF installations, and to train all the RAF's combatant personnel to enable them to contribute to the defence of their units. RAF Regiment units are under the operational command of No 2 Group. As of 1 January 2001 RAF Regiment units are as follows:

Field Squadrons
No 1 Squadron	St Mawgan	Field Squadron
No 2 Squadron	Honnington	Field /Para Sqn

No 3 Squadron	Aldergrove	Field Squadron
No 34 Squadron	Leeming	Field Squadron
No 63 (QCS)	Uxbridge	Ceremonial /Field Sqn

Air Defence

No 15 Squadron	Honnington	6 x Rapier
No 16 Squadron	Honnington	6 x Rapier
No 26 Squadron	Waddington	6 x Rapier
No 37 Squadron	Honnington	6 x Rapier
Joint Rapier Training Unit	Honnington	2 x Rapier

RAF Regiment Depot	Honnington
No 1 RAF STO HQ*	RAF Wittering
No 2 RAF STO HQ	RAF Leming
No 3 RAF STO HQ	RAF Marham

* STO - Tactical Survive to Operate HQ

The RAF Regiment also provides some of the 244 personnel of the Joint NBC Regiment alongside two squadrons of the Royal Tank Regiment all of whom are stationed at Honnington.

Specialist RAF Regiment training for gunners is given at the RAF Regiment Depot at Honnington. On completion of training at the RAF College Cranwell officers also undergo further specialist training at RAF Honnington and, in some cases, the School of Infantry at Warminster in Wiltshire or the Royal School of Artillery at Larkhill.

The RAF Regiment also mans the Queen's Colour Squadron (QCS) which undertakes all major ceremonial duties for the Royal Air Force. These duties involve mounting the Guard at Buckingham Palace on an occasional basis, and providing Guards of Honour for visiting Heads of State. The Queen's Colour Squadron also has a war role as a field squadron.

The regiment is not alone in defending any RAF station. Every airman based at a station has a ground defence role and is trained to defend his place of work against ground attack and attack by NBC weapons. Training for this is given by RAF Regiment instructors who provide courses at station level, for all personnel on various aspects of ground defence.

There are now two basic RAF Regiment squadron organisations - the field squadron organised for ground defence against possible enemy ground action and the Rapier squadron organised for defence against low-flying enemy aircraft.

Rapier Squadron-Possible Organisation

Rapier Characteristics - Guidance Semi-Automatic to Command Line of Sight (SACLOS); Missile diameter 13.3 cm; Missile length 2.35m; Rocket solid fuelled; Warhead high Explosive; Launch weight 42kg; Speed Mach 2+; Ceiling 3,000m; Maximum Range 6,800m; Fire unit height 2.13m; Fire unit weight 1,227kg; Radar height (in action) 3.37m;

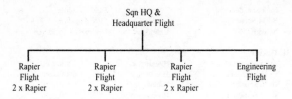

```
                        Sqn HQ &
                    Headquarter Flight
                            |
      ┌─────────────┬─────────────┬──────────────┐
   Rapier        Rapier        Rapier       Engineering
   Flight        Flight        Flight         Flight
  2 x Rapier    2 x Rapier    2 x Rapier
```

Radar weight 1,186kg; Optical tracker height 1.54m; Optical tracker weight 119kg;
Generator weight 243kg; Generator height 0.91m.

The Rapier system provides area, Low Level Air Defence (LLAD) over the area around the
airbase to be defended. It consists of an optical tracker, a fire unit, a radar and a Generator.
The into-action time of the system is thought to be about 15 minutes and the radar is
believed to scan out to 12 km. Each fire unit can therefore cover an Air Defence Area
(ADA) of about 100 km. Having discharged the 4 missiles on a Fire Unit, 2 men are
thought to be able to carry out a reload in about 3 minutes. During the Falklands
Campaign, Rapier was credited with 14 kills and 6 probables from a total of 24 missiles
fired.

Rapier in service with the RAF Regiment has been upgraded from Field Standard B1(M) to
Field Standard C (Rapier 2000). Rapier FSC offers significant enhancements to
performance. The towed system launcher mounts eight missiles (able to fire two
simultaneously at 2 separate targets) and is manufactured in two warhead versions. One of
these warheads is armour piercing and able to deal with fixed-wing targets, while the other
is a fragmentation warhead for the engagement of cruise missiles and RPVs. Rapier 2000
has the Darkfire tracker and a tailor-made 3-dimensional radar system for target
acquisition, developed by Plessey.

A Joint Service Rapier FSC OCU was formed at RAF Honnington to oversee both the
RAF's and Army's conversion to the new system.

Rapier has now been sold to the armed forces of at least 14 nations. We believe that sales
have amounted to over 25,000 missiles, 600 launchers and 350 Blindfire radars.

Royal Auxiliary Air Force Regiment (RAuxAF Regt)

Airfield defence is further enhanced by squadrons of the RAuxAF Regt who are recruited
locally and whose role is the ground defence of the airfield and its associated outlying
installations. A RAuxAF Regiment Squadron has an all-up strength of about 120 personnel
and costs approximately £500,000 a year to keep in service. As a general rule, a squadron
has a headquarters flight, two mobile flights mounted in Land Rovers and two flights for
static guard duties. RAuxAF Regt squadrons are as follows:

1310 Wing RAuxAF Regt	RAF Honnington	HQ Unit
2503 Sqn RAuxAF Regt	RAF Waddington	Ground Defence

2622 Sqn RAuxAF Regt	RAF Lossiemouth	Ground Defence
2623 Sqn RauxAF Regt	RAF Honnington	Training Squadron
2624 Sqn RAuxAF Regt	RAF Brize Norton	Ground Defence
2625 Sqn RAuxAF Regt	RAF St Mawgan	Ground Defence

RAF Reserves

The reserve component of the Royal Air Force on 1 April 2000 was as follows:

RAuxAF & RAFVR Reserves	-	1,800
Reserve officers	-	610*
Royal Air Force Reserve	-	14,300
Individuals liable to recall	-	27,600
Total	-	44,310

* Aircrew who have served on Short Service Commissions have a mandatory reserve liability of four years.

The Controller Reserve Forces (RAF) is located at RAF Innsworth as part of RAF PTC. He is responsible for all non-operational aspects of reserve forces policy and co-ordination, ranging from recruitment, through training, promotions and welfare to future planning. The following are the formed Reserve Units (RAuxAF Regt Squadrons are listed in the preceding RAF Regiment section).

Royal Auxiliary Air Force

No 1 Maritime HQ	Northwood (London)	
No 2 Maritime HQ	Pitrivie (Scotland)	
No 3 Maritime HQ	RAF St Mawgan	
4626 Sqn	RAF Lyneham	Aeromedical Evacuation Unit
7006 Sqn	RAF Waddington	Intelligence
7010 Sqn	RAF Waddington	Photographic Interpretation
7630 Sqn	RAF Chicksands	Communications & Security
7644 Sqn	RAF Waddington	Public Relations
504 Sqn	RAF Cottesmore	Harrier Support Sqn
603 Sqn	Edinburgh	General Support
606 Sqn	RAF Benson	Rotary Support
609 Sqn	RAF Leeming	Air Defence Support Unit
Mobile Met Unit	RAF Benson	Meteorological Services
Surgical Unit (Airmobile)	RAF Leuchars	Casualty Treatment
Marham Support Flight	RAF Marham	Ground Crew
Reservist Aircrew Flight	RAF Lyneham	Flight personnel
TSS Sqn	RAF Halton	Training & Standardisation
TSS Sqn	RAF Shawbury	Training & Standardisation

Royal Auxiliary Air Force Defence Force Flights

RAuxAF Defence Force Flight	RAF Brampton
RAuxAF Defence Force Flight	RAF High Wycombe
RAuxAF Defence Force Flight	RAF Lyneham
RAuxAF Defence Force Flight	RAF St Athan

In war, these four flights would provide specialist assistance in public relations, foreign language interrogation, photographic interpretation and intelligence support.

Note: The RauxAF and the RAFVR were amalgamated on 5 April 1997.

CHAPTER 5 - MISCELLANEOUS

The Mod's Civilian Staff

The three uniformed services are supported by the civilian staff of the MoD. On the 1st
April 2000 some 107,644 civilian personnel (92,900 in the UK and 14,744 overseas
(locally engaged) were employed by the MoD. This figure has fallen from 316,700 civilian
personnel in 1980. UK based civilians are employed in the following areas:

Navy Operational Areas	-	4,400
Army Operational Areas	-	10,100
Air Forces Operational Areas	-	5,700
Service Personnel Commands	-	13,400
Logistics, Support & Maintenance	-	30,300
MOD Head Office, HQ Procurement	-	14,900
Defence Evaluation & Research Agency	-	11,100
UK Hydrographic Office	-	800
Meteorological Office	-	2,200

In a recent clear and unambiguous statement the UK MoD stated that " The Department
remains committed to a process of civilianisation. Increasingly, it makes no sense to
employ expensively trained and highly professional military personnel in jobs which
civilians could do equally well. Civilians are generally cheaper than their military
counterparts and as they often remain longer in post, can provide greater continuity. For
these reasons, it is our long-standing policy to civilianise posts and so release valuable
military resources to the front line whenever it makes operational and economic sense to do
so".

In addition to the permanent UK based civilians there were approximately 14,744 locally
entered civilian personnel distributed around the following locations:

Continental Europe *	-	10,132
Gibraltar	-	982
Malta	-	5
Cyprus	-	2,523
Brunei	-	255
Nepal	-	314
Elsewhere	-	22

Note * - The overwhelming majority of this figure are locally entered civilians supporting
BFG (British Forces Germany).

In general MoD Civil Servants work in a parallel stream with their respective uniformed
counterparts. There are some "stand alone" civilian agencies of which the DERA is
probably the largest.

The Defence Evaluation & Research Agency (DERA)

From 1st April 1995, the Defence Evaluation & Research Agency (DERA) assumed the responsibilities of its predecessor the Defence Research Agency (DRA). This new organisation combined the activities of a number of research and evaluation agencies under the umbrella of a top level budget holder. Agencies such as the Directorate General of Test and Evaluation, the Chemical and Biological Defence Establishment and the Defence Operational Analysis Centre were grouped together in the new agency with a staff strength of some 11,100 people and an operational budget of just over £697 million (2000 figure).

DERA is organised into four major operational divisions:

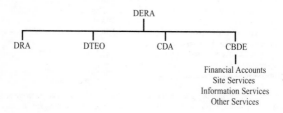

DRA Division - Includes all except two of the old DRA's scientific business operations.

DTEO - The Defence Test and Evaluation Organisation consists of the Director General of Tests and Evaluation plus some other smaller elements operating in the DTEO sector from the from the old DRA.

CBDE - This division combines the activities of the old Chemical and Biological Defence Establishment at Porton Down in Wiltshire with the old DRA's Chemical and Electronics department.

CDA - Centre for Defence Analysis combines the activities of the old Defence Operational Analysis Centre and the DRA's Operational Studies Department.

The current priorities of the DERA as described by the UK MoD are:

a. To keep the armed forces well equipped with modern capable equipment.
b. To support mobile and flexible response forces.
c. Support the procurement of military equipment which is sustainable, has high reliability and availability, and gives good value for money.
d. Ensure that the research programme reflects the changing international situation and defence objectives.
e. Maintain the longer-term research programme to sustain the science and technology base.

168

f. Place greater emphasis on research programmes aimed at reducing 'through life' costs.

g. Encourage the greatest possible industrial participation in maintaining the technological base; and exploit academic expertise.

The United Kingdom Defence Industry

Despite the demise of the Warsaw Pact, uncertainties over our future defence strategy and substantial cuts in defence spending, the United Kingdom's Defence Industry has proved to be a remarkably resilient and successful element of our national manufacturing base.

In the early 1990's defence related production accounted for some 11% of manufactured output in the United Kingdom. Coincidentally, defence work also provided employment for just under 10% of our manufacturing workforce employing 410,000 individuals in 1991. Despite the rationalisation which is still taking place within the defence sector, it is generally accepted that defence employment still puts around £6 billion annually into the broader UK economy via salaries paid throughout the supply chain.

Historically, the UK defence industry has possessed the capability and competence to provide a wide range of advanced systems and equipment to support our own armed forces. This capability, matched with their competitiveness, has enabled UK companies to command a sizeable share of those overseas markets for which export licence approvals are available. At home, UK industry has consistently provided some 75% by value of the equipment requirements of the Ministry of Defence. In simple terms, in recent years our industry has supplied £9 - £10 billion worth of goods and services for our Armed Forces annually while a further £3 -5 billion worth of business has accrued to the UK defence industry from sales to approved overseas customers. The spread of overheads resulting from export sales has also benefited The Ministry of Defence to the extent of approximately £350 million per annum.

The United Kingdom's defence companies are justifiably proud of their record in recent years in the face of fierce overseas competition. Reductions in the UK's armed forces and the heavy demands on our remaining Service personnel, who face an unpredictable international security environment, make it inevitable that considerable reliance will be placed upon the support and surge capacity offered by our comprehensive indigenous defence industrial base. Without this effective industrial base, the ability of the UK to exert independence of action or influence over collective security arrangements would be constrained. It is essential that government policies ensure that industry retains the necessary capabilities to support our forces in a changing world.

Up until now the United Kingdom's defence industry has been highly successful in supporting the United Kingdom's armed forces with high quality equipment and it has also made a significant contribution to our balance of payments. As a strategic resource it is vitally important that it should attract the appropriate levels of research and development funding to maintain the necessary technical excellence and production facilities to meet the needs of the future.

As importantly, the defence industry is not only a major employer but it is also the generator of high technology that is readily adaptable to civilian use in fields such as avionics and engine technology. The future of the UK's defence industry will almost certainly have to be properly planned if it is to remain an efficient and essential national support organisation in times of crisis. A look at MoD payments to contractors during 1999-2000 identifies some of the larger manufacturers.

Major Contractors Listing

Contractors paid more than £250 million by the UK MoD during 1999-2000
British Aerospace PLC
BAe Systems Electronics Ltd
BAe Systems Marine Ltd
Matra BAe Dynamics (UK) Ltd
Devonport Royal Dockyard
DERA
GKN PLC
Hunting PLC
Lockheed Martin Group
Rolls Royce PLC
NETMA
Contractors paid between £100 million and £250 million during 1999-2000
Annington Receivables Ltd
Babcock International Group PLC
British Telecommunications PLC
John Mowlem & Company Ltd
Other UK Government Departments
Racal Defence Electronics Ltd
Serco Group PLC
EDS Defence Ltd
Vickers Engineering Ltd
ICI Ltd
Alenia Marconi Systems Ltd
Contractors paid between £50 million and £100 million during 1999-2000
BAe Systems Avionics Ltd
Vosper Thornycroft Holdings Ltd
Price Waterhouse Coopers
The British Petroleum Company PLC
General Electric Company Ltd
Fleet Support Ltd
Amey Holdings Ltd
Cobham PLC
Meteorological Office
WS Atkins PLC
IBM UK Holdings Ltd

The Services Hierarchy

Officer Ranks

Army	Navy	Air Force
Field Marshal	Admiral of the Fleet	Marshal of the Royal Air Force
General	Admiral	Air Chief Marshal
Lieutenant-General	Vice-Admiral	Air Marshal
Major-General	Rear-Admiral	Air Vice Marshal
Brigadier	Commodore	Air Commodore
Colonel	Captain	Group Captain
Lieutenant-Colonel	Commander	Wing Commander
Major	Lieutenant-Commander	Squadron Leader
Captain	Lieutenant	Flight-Lieutenant
Lieutenant	Sub-Lieutenant	Flying Officer
Second Lieutenant	Midshipman	Pilot Officer

Non Commissioned Ranks

Army	Navy	Air Force
Warrant Officer 1/2	Warrant Officer	Warrant Officer
Staff/Colour Sergeant	Chief Petty Officer	Flight Sergeant
Sergeant	Petty Officer	Sergeant
Corporal	Leading Rate	Corporal
Lance Corporal	Able Rate	Senior Aircraftsman
Private	Ordinary Rate	Leading Aircraftsman
		Aircraftsman

Note: In general terms the rank shown in each column equates to the other service ranks in the columns alongside.

Pay Scales (From 1 April 2000)

The following are a selection from the Army pay scales relevant from 1 April 2000. Approximate scales for the other two services can be identified by using the previous table of of commissioned and non-commissioned ranks. Pay scales apply to both males and females.

Officers	On Appointment (£ per day)	Rising To (£ per day)
University Cadet	26.67	36.11
Officer Cadets	31.41	-
Second Lieutenant	49.66	-
Lieutenant	59.70	65.98
Captain	76.12	88.48
Major	95.89	114.85
Lieutenant Colonel	135.26	149.50
Colonel	156.63	173.11
Brigadier	191.31	-

Adult Soldiers	Band	(£ per day)
Private (over 17½ on entry)	1	28.34
Private Class 3	1	32.64
Private Class 2	1	37.76
Private Class 1	1	39.51
Lance Corporal Class 1	1	45.31
Corporal Class 1	1	51.41
Sergeant	4	56.46
Staff Sergeant	5	65.17
Warrant Officer Class 2	6	76.72
Warrant Officer Class I (RSM)	7	88.43

Notes:

(1) Pay scales apply to both males and females. (2) These rates only show the most common basic pay rates. (3) From 1991 all recruits have been enlisted on an Open Engagement. The Open Engagement is for a period of 22 years service from the age of 18 or the date of enlistment, whichever is the later. Subject to giving 12 months notice, and any time bar that may be in force, all soldiers have the right to leave on the completion of 3 years reckonable service from the age of 18.

Daily Rates - After 9 years service, personnel are eligible for extra daily long service increments of pay. These vary according to rank and for example a Corporal with 12 years service will get an extra £1.32 per day.

Accommodation - All corporals and below living in barracks are charged £11.34 for their accommodation and £22.61 for food per week. Single sergeants and officers are charged at a higher rate.

Additional Pay - There is additional pay for certain tasks For example personnel stationed in Northern Ireland receive an extra £4.77 per day. Flying pay is paid at the following rates:

Initial Rate	£10.49 per day
Middle Rate	£17.61 per day
Top Rate	£26.61 per day

The Middle Rate is usually paid after 4 years on the Initial Rate. The Top Rate is paid after another 4 years on the Middle Rate.

Codewords and Nicknames

A Codeword is a single word used to provide security cover for reference to a particular classified matter, eg "Corporate" was the Codeword for the recovery of the Falklands in 1982. In 1997 "Bolton" was used to refer to operations during the reinforcement of Kuwait and Op Grapple was used for operations in support of the UN in the former Yugoslavia. A for Nickname consists of two words and may be used for reference to an unclassified matter, eg "Lean Look" referred to an investigation into various military organisations in order to identify savings in manpower.

Dates and Timings

When referring to timings the Armed Forces use the 24 hour clock. This means that 2015 hours, pronounced twenty fifteen hours, is in fact 8.15pm. Soldiers usually avoid midnight and refer to 2359 or 0001 hours. Time zones present plenty of scope for confusion! Exercise and Operational times are expressed in Greenwich Mean Time (GMT) which may differ from the local time. The suffix Z (Zulu) denotes GMT and A (Alpha) GMT + 1 hour. B (Bravo) means GMT + 2 hours and so on.

The Date Time Group or DTG can be seen on military documents and is a point of further confusion for many. Using the military DTG 1030 GMT on 20th April 2001 is written as 201030Z APR 01. When the Armed Forces relate days and hours to operations a simple system is used:

a. D Day is the day an operation begins.
b. H Hour is the hour a specific operation begins.
c. Days and hours can be represented by numbers plus or minus of D Day

Therefore if D Day is the 20th April 2001, D-2 is the 18th April and D + 2 is the 22nd April. If H Hour is 0600hrs then H+2 is 0800 hours.

ARRC Groupings

Composition of the Multinational Division (Central) - MND(C)

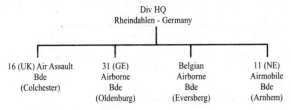

Composition of the Multinational Division (South) - MND(S)

Composition of the 1st (UK) Armoured Division

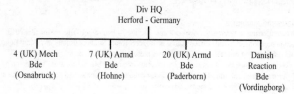

Div HQ
Herford - Germany

| 4 (UK) Mech Bde (Osnabruck) | 7 (UK) Armd Bde (Hohne) | 20 (UK) Armd Bde (Paderborn) | Danish Reaction Bde (Vordingborg) |

Composition of the 3rd (UK) Mechanised Division

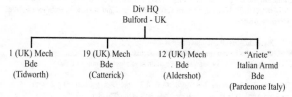

Div HQ
Bulford - UK

| 1 (UK) Mech Bde (Tidworth) | 19 (UK) Mech Bde (Catterick) | 12 (UK) Mech Bde (Aldershot) | "Ariete" Italian Armd Bde (Pardenone Italy) |

Composition of the 3rd Italian Mechanised Division

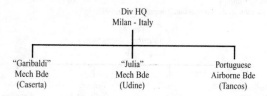

Div HQ
Milan - Italy

| "Garibaldi" Mech Bde (Caserta) | "Julia" Mech Bde (Udine) | Portuguese Airborne Bde (Tancos) |

Composition of the 7th German Panzer Division

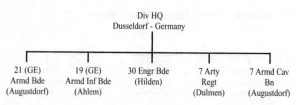

Div HQ
Dusseldorf - Germany

| 21 (GE) Armd Bde (Augustdorf) | 19 (GE) Armd Inf Bde (Ahlem) | 30 Engr Bde (Hilden) | 7 Arty Regt (Dulmen) | 7 Armd Cav Bn (Augustdorf) |

Composition of the 2nd Greek Mechanised Division

Div HQ
Edessa - Northern Greece

33 (GR)
Mech Bde
(Polikastru)

34 (GR)
Mech Bde
(Thessaloniki)

Mech Bde
(To be allocated)

Note: Other NATO nations could be invited to contribute a similar brigade to act as the third brigade within this divisional framework structure.

Composition of the 1st United States Armoured Division

Div HQ
Bad Kreuznach - Germany

1 (US)
Armd Bde
(Friedberg)

2 (US)
Mech Inf Bde
(Baumholder)

Aviation Bde
(Hanau)

Composition of the 1st Turkish Mechanised Division

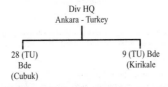

Div HQ
Ankara - Turkey

28 (TU)
Bde
(Cubuk)

9 (TU) Bde
(Kirikale)

Composition of the Spanish FAR Contingent

(Fuerza De Accion Rapida)
HQ
Madrid - Spain

Airborne
Bde
(Alcala De Henares)

Spanish Legion
Inf Bde
(Madrid)

Airportable
Brigade
(Almeria)

Note: The Spanish FAR equates roughly to the size of a conventional division.

Phonetic Alphabet

To ensure minimum confusion during radio or telephone conversations difficult words or names are spelt out letter by letter using the following NATO standard phonetic alphabet.

ALPHA - BRAVO - CHARLIE - DELTA - ECHO - FOXTROT - GOLF - HOTEL - INDIA - JULIET - KILO - LIMA - MIKE - NOVEMBER - OSCAR - PAPA - QUEBEC - ROMEO - SIERRA - TANGO - UNIFORM - VICTOR - WHISKEY - X RAY - YANKEE - ZULU.

Useful Quotations

There are two groups - Military and General.

Military

"The military value of a partisan's work is not measured by the amount of property destroyed, or the number of men killed or captured, but the number he keeps watching."
John Singleton Mosby 1833-1916
Confederate Cavalry Leader

"Peace - In international affairs, a period of cheating between two periods of fighting."
The Devils Dictionary 1911

"A few honest men are better than numbers."
Oliver Cromwell

" Mr Smith Sir! - As an obvious outsider what is your opinion of the human race?"
Drill Sergeant to a cadet at the Royal Military Academy 1998.

"The beatings will continue until morale improves."
Attributed to the Commander of the Japanese Submarine Force.

"When other Generals make mistakes their armies are beaten; when I get into a hole, my men pull me out of it".
The Duke of Wellington - after Waterloo

"One might as well try to charge through a wall".
Napoleon - On St Helena - Regarding the British Infantry

"Take short views, hope for the best and trust in God."
Sir Sydney Smith

"There is no beating these troops in spite of their generals. I always thought them bad soldiers, now I am sure of it. I turned their right, pierced their centre, broke them everywhere; the day was mine, and yet they did not know it and would not run.
Marshal Soult - Albuhera 1811

"Confusion in battle is what pain is in childbirth - the natural order of things".
General Maurice Tugwell

"This is right way to waste money"
PJ O'Rourke - Rolling Stone Magazine
(Watching missiles firing during an exercise)

" This is just something to be got round - like a bit of flak on the way to the target".
Group Captain Leonard Cheshire VC - Speaking of his incurable illness in the week before he died.

"Pale Ebenezer thought it wrong to fight,
But roaring Bill, who killed him, thought it right".
Hillare Belloc

"Everyone wants peace - and they will fight the most terrible war to get it".
Miles Kington - BBC Radio 4th February 1995

"The easiest and quickest path into the esteem of traditional military authorities is by the appeal to the eye rather than to the mind. The `polish and pipeclay' school is not yet extinct, and it is easier for the mediocre intelligence to become an authority on buttons than on tactics".
Captain Sir Basil Liddel Hart
Thoughts on War 1944

"Having lost sight of our objectives we need to redouble our efforts".
Anon.

"The purpose of war is not to die for your country. The purpose of war is to ensure that the other guy dies for his country".

General Patton.

"War is a competition of incompetence - the least incompetent usually win".

Pakistani General Tiger - after losing Bangladesh.

"The number of medals on an officer breast varies in inverse proportion to the square of the distance of his duty from the front line."

Charles Montague 1867-1928

"Nothing is so good for the morale of the troops as occasionally to see a dead general".

Field Marshal Slim

"It makes no difference which side the general is on".

Unknown British Soldier

General

"Success is generally 90% persistence".

Anon.

"You Liberals think that goats are just sheep from broken homes."

Anon

"Anyone sitting on a bus after the age of 30 should consider themself a failure".

Lady Westminster

"A statesman is a politician who's been dead for ten to fifteen years."

US President Harry S Trueman

"It is only worthless men who seek to excuse the deterioration of their character by pleading neglect in their early years".

Plutarch - Life of Coriolanus - Approx AD 80

" They say hard work never hurt anybody, but I figured why take the chance".

Ronald Regan

"To applaud as loudly as that for so stupid a proposal means that you are just trying to fill that gap between your ears".
David Starkey - BBC Radio (4 Feb 95)

"Its always best on these occasions to do what the mob do".
"But suppose that there are two mobs?" suggested Mr Snodgrass.
"Shout with the largest" replied Mr Pickwick.
Pickwick Papers Chapter 13

"Ah, these diplomats! What chatterboxes! There's only one way to shut them up - cut them down with machine guns. Bulganin, go and get me one!"
Joseph Stalin - As reported by De Gaulle during a long meeting.

"The primary function of management is to create the chaos that only management can sort out. A secondary function is the expensive redecoration and refurbishment of offices, especially in times of the utmost financial stringency".
Theodore Dalrymple "The Spectator" 6 November 1993.

"He knows nothing and thinks that he knows everything. That points to a political career."
George Bernard Shaw

"The men who really believe in themselves are all in lunatic asylums."
GK Chesterton

"The best sound is always the sound of your best friend falling off a 40 storey building."
Chairman Mao

"I consider myself to be the most important figure in the world."
His Royal Highness - Field Marshal Idi Amin Dada VC

"There are five Great National Delusions. The first is that there are solutions to all the problems. The second is that only a strong centre can solve the problems. The third is that the strong centre must embody one's own views exclusively. The fourth Great Delusion is that heroic surgery is required, and the fifth, that the heroic surgeons must be oneself and once's cronies armed with scalpels as big as machettes."
Louis de Bernieres - The Troublesome Offspring of Cardinal Guzman.

"What all the wise men promised has not happened and what all the dammed fools said would happen has come to pass".

Lord Melbourne

Abbreviations

The following is a selection from the list of standard military abbreviations and should assist users of this handbook.

AAC	Army Air Corps
AAR	Air to Air Refuelling
AAAW	Advanced Anti-Armour Weapon
AAW	Anti-Air Warfare
AB	Airborne
ABLE	Automotive Bridge Launching Equipment
ac	Aircraft
accn	Accommodation
ACE	Allied Command Europe
ACLANT	Allied Command North Atlantic
ACOS	Assistant Chief of Staff
ACV	Armoured Command Vehicle
AD	Air Defence/Air Dispatch/Army Department
ADA	Air Defended Area
ADAD	Air Defence Alerting Device
Adjt	Adjutant
admin	Administration
admin O	Administrative Order
ADP	Automatic Data Processing
ADR	Airfield Damage Repair
AEW	Airborne Early Warning
AFCENT	Allied Forces Central European Theatre
AFNORTHWEST	Allied Forces Northwestern Europe
AFSOUTH	Allied Forces Southern Europe
AFV	Armoured Fighting Vehicle
AGC	Adjutant General's Corps
AGLS	Autonomous Navigation And Gun Laying System

AHQ	Air Headquarters
AIFV	Armoured Infantry Fighting Vehicle
AIRCENT	Allied Air Forces Central Europe
Airmob	Airmobile
ALARM	Air Launched Anti Radiation Missile
AMF(L)	Allied Mobile Force (Land Element)
AMRAAM	Advanced Medium Range Air-to-Air Missile
AOC	Air Officer Commanding
AP	Armour Piercing/Ammunition Point/Air Publication
APC	Armoured Personnel Carrier
APDS	Armour Piercing Discarding Sabot
APO	Army Post Office
ARBS	Angle Rate Bombing System
armd	Armoured
armr	Armour
ARRC	Allied Rapid Reaction Corps
ARRF	Allied Rapid Reaction Forces
arty	Artillery
ARV	Armoured Recover Vehicle
ASRAAM	Advanced Short-Range Air-to-Air Missile
ASTOVL	Advanced Short Take Off and Vertical Landing
ASW	Anti Submarine Warning
ATAF	Allied Tactical Air Force
ATGW	Anti-Tank Guided Weapon
att	Attached
ATWM	Army Transition to War Measure
AVLB	Armoured Vehicle Launched Bridge
AWC	Air Warfare Centre
AWOL	Absent without leave
BALTAP	Baltic Approaches
BAOR	British Army of the Rhine
BC	Battery Commander
Bde	Brigade
BE	Belgium (Belgian)
BFG	British Forces Germany

BFPO	British Forces Post Office
BG	Battle Group
BGHQ	Battlegroup Headquarters
BK	Battery Captain
BMA	Battery Manoeuvre Area
BMEWS	Ballistic Missile Early Warning System
BMH	British Military Hospital
Bn	Battalion
Bty	Battery
c sups	Combat Supplies
C3I	Command, Control, Communications & Intelligence
CAD	Central Ammunition Depot
cam	Camouflaged
CAP	Combat Air Patrol
cas	Casualty
CASEVAC	Casualty Evacuation
CASOM	Conventional Attack Stand-Off Missile
CASTOR	Corps Airborne Stand Off-Radar
cat	Catering
CATO	Civilian Air Traffic Operation
CCM	Counter Counter Measure
CCP	Casualty Collecting Point
CCS	Casualty Clearing Station
Cdo	Commando
CDS	Chief of the Defence Staff
CEP	Circular Error Probable/Central Engineer Park
CEPS	Central European Pipeline System
CET	Combat Engineer Tractor
CGRM	Commander General Royal Marines
CGS	Chief of the General Staff
CinC	Commander in Chief
CINCENT	Commander in Chief Central European Theatre
CINCUKAIR	Commander in Chief UK Air
civ	Civilian
CJO	Chief of Joint Operations

CJRDFO	Chief of the Joint Rapid Deployment Force Operations
Cmdt	Commandant
CO	Commanding Officer
COBRA	Counter Battery Radar
Col GS	Colonel General Staff
comd	Command/Commander
comp rat	Composite Ration (Compo)
COMRFA	Commander Royal Fleet Auxiliary
COMSEN	Communications Centre
coord	Co-ordinate
COS	Chief of Staff
coy	Company
CP	Close Protection/Command Post
CPO	Command Pay Office/Chief Petty Officer
CQMS	Company Quartermaster Sergeant
CRC	Control Reporting Centre
CRP	Control Reporting Point
CTOL	Conventional Take Off and Landing
CTTO	Central Trials and Tactics Organisation
CUP	Capability Upgrade Period
CV	Combat Vehicle
CVD	Central Vehicle Depot
CVR(T)	Combat Vehicle Reconnaissance Tracked
CVR (W)	Combat Vehicle Reconnaissance Wheeled
CW	Chemical warfare
DAA	Divisional Administrative Area
DAG	Divisional Artillery Group
DASS	Defensive Aids Sub-System
DAW	Department of Air Warfare
def	Defence
DERA	Defence Evaluation & Research Agency
det	Detached/Detachment
DF	Defensive Fire
DHFS	Defence Helicopter Flying School
DISTAFF	Directing Staff (DS)

Div	Division
DK	Denmark
DMA	Divisional Maintenance Area
dml	Demolition
DMR	Daily Messing Rate
DRA	Defence Research Agency
DROPS	Demountable Rack Off Loading & Pick Up System
DS	Direct Support/Dressing Station
DTG	Date Time Group
ech	Echelon
ECM	Electronic Counter Measure
EDP	Emergency Defence Plan
emb	Embarkation
EME	Electrical and Mechanical Engineers
EMP	Electro Magnetic Pulse
en	Enemy
engr	Engineer
EOD	Explosive Ordnance Disposal
eqpt	Equipment
ETA	Estimated Time of Arrival
EW	Early warning/Electronic Warfare
EWOSE	Electronic Warfare Operational Support Establishment
ex	Exercise
FAC	Forward Air Controller
Fd Amb	Field Ambulance
Fd	Field
FEBA	Forward Edge of the Battle Area
FFR	Fitted for Radio
FGA	Fighter Ground Attack
FLA	Future Large Aircraft
FLET	Forward Location Enemy Troops
FLIR	Forward Looking Infra Red
FLOT	Forward Location Own Troops
fmm	Formation
FOC	First of Class

FONA	Flag Officer Naval Aviation
FOO	Forward Observation Officer
FOSF	Flag Officer Surface Fleet
FOSM	Flag Officer Submarines
FOST	Flag Officer Sea Training
FR	France (French)
FRG	Federal Republic of Germany/Forward Repair Group
FRT	Forward Repair Team
FTS	Flying Training School
FUP	Forming Up Place/Forming Up Point
FWAM	Full Width Attack Mine
FY	Financial Year
GDP	General Defence Plan/Gross Domestic Product
GE	German (Germany)
GOC	General Officer Commanding
GPMG	General Purpose Machine Gun
GPWS	Ground Proximity Warning System
GR	Greece (Greek)
GRSC	Ground Radio Servicing Centre
HAS	Hardened Aircraft Shelter
HE	High Explosive
HEAT	High Explosive Anti-Tank
hel	Helicopter
Hesh	High Explosive Squash Head
HOTAS	Hands on Throttle and Stick
HV	Hyper Velocity
HVM	Hyper Velocity Missile
Hy	Heavy
ICCS	Integrated Command & Control System
IFF	Indentification Friend or Foe
IFOR	Implementation Force
II	Image Intensifier
illum	Illuminating
Inf	Infantry
INTSUM	Intelligence Summary

IO	Intelligence Officer
IRF	Immediate Reaction Forces
IRG	Immediate Replenishment Group
IS	Internal Security
ISD	In Service Data
IT	Italy (Italian)
ITS	Inshore Training Squadron
IUR	Immediate Use Reserve
IW	Individual Weapon
JFHQ	Joint Force Headquarters
JHQ	Joint Headquarters
JRC	Joint Regional Command
JRDF	Joint Rapid Deployment Force
JSRC	Joint Sub-Regional Command
JSSU	Joint Services Signals Unit
KFOR	Kosovo Force
L of C	Lines of Communication
LAD	Light Aid Detachment (REME)
LANDCENT	Commander Allied Land Forces Central Europe
LGB	Laser Guided Bomb
LLAD	Low-Level Air Defence
LML	Lightweight Multiple Launcher
LO	Liaison Officer
Loc	Locating
Log	Logistic
LPH	Landing Platform Helicopter
LRATGW	Long-Range Anti-Tank Guided Weapons
LSL	Landing Ships Logistic
LSW	Light Support Weapon
LTW	Lyneham Training Wing
maint	Maintain
MAMBA	Mobile Artillery Monitoring Battlefield Radar
MAMS	Mobile Air Movement Squadron
MAOT	Mobile Air Operations Team
MATO	Military Air Traffic Operations

mat	Material
MBT	Main Battle Tank
MCM	Mine Countermeasures
MCMV	Mine Countermeasures Vessels
mech	Mechanised
med	Medical
MFC	Mortar Fire Controller
MG	Machine Gun
MIRV	Multiple Independently Targeted Re-entry Vehicle
MLRS	Multi-Launched Rocket System
MLU	Mid-life update
MNAD	Multi-National Airmobile Division
MND	Multi-National Division
MO	Medical Officer
mob	Mobilisation
MoD	Ministry of Defence
MoU	Memorandum of Understanding
MP	Military Police
MRG	Medium Repair Group
MRV	Multiple Re-entry Vehicle
msl	missile
MU	Maintenance Unit
NAAFI	Navy, Army and Air Force Institutes
NADGE	NATO Air Defence Ground Environment
NAEW-F	NATO Airborne Early Warning Forces
NATO	North Atlantic Treaty Organisation
NATS	National Air Traffic Services
NBC	Nuclear, Biological and Chemical Warfare
NCO	Non-Commissioned Officer
nec	Necessary
NGFSO	Naval Gunfire Support Officer
ni	Night
NL	Netherlands
NO	Norway (Norwegian)
NOK	Next of Kin

NORTHAG	Northern Army Group
NTR	Nothing to Report
NYK	Not Yet Known
OC	Officer Commanding
OCU	Operational Conversion Unit (RAF)
OEU	Operational Evaluation Unit
OIC	Officer in Charge
OOTW	Operations other than war
OP	Observation Post
opO	Operation Order
ORB	Omni-Radio Beacon
ORBAT	Order of Battle
P info	Public Information
pax	Passengers
PJHQ	Permanent Joint Headquarters
Pl	Platoon
PO	Portugal (Portuguese)
POL	Petrol, Oil and Lubrication
Pro	Provost
PTC	Personnel and Training Command
QCS	Queen's Colour Squadron
QM	Quartermaster
R & D	Research and Development
RA	Royal Artillery
RAC	Royal Armoured Corps
RAFASUPU	RAF Armament Support Unit
RAMC	Royal Army Medical Corps
RAP	Rocket-Assisted Projectile/Regiment Aid Post
RCMDS	Remote-Control Mine Disposal System
RCZ	Rear Control Zone
RE	Royal Engineers
rebro	Rebroadcast
rec	Recovery
recce	reconnaissance
Regt	Regiment

REME	Royal Electrical and Mechanical Engineers
RFA	Royal Fleet Auxiliary
rft	Reinforcement
RGJ	Royal Green Jackets
RHA	Royal Horse Artillery
RHQ	Regimental Headquarters
RLC	Royal Logistic Corps
RM	Royal Marines
RMA	Rear Maintenance Area/Royal Military Academy
RMAS	Royal Military Academy Sandhurst
RMP	Royal Military Police
RN	Royal Navy
RNMC	Royal Netherlands Marine Corps
RO	Retired Officer
Ro-Ro	Roll On-Roll Off
RP	Reporting Point
RPV	Remotely Piloted Vehicle
RRF	Royal Regiment of Fusiliers/Rapid Reaction Forces
RSA	Royal School of Artillery
RSME	Royal School of Mechanical Engineering
RSS	Royal School of Signals
RTM	Ready to Move
RTU	Return to Unit
SACLOS	Semi Automatic to Command Line of Sight
SACEUR	Supreme Allied Commander Europe
SAM	Surface-to-Air Missile
SAR	Search and Rescue
SAS	Special Air Service
SBS	Special Boar Service
SDR	Strategic Defence Review
Sect	Section
SH	Support Helicopters
SHAPE	Supreme Headquarters Allied Powers Europe
SIB	Special Investigation Branch
Sig	Signals

sit	Situation
SITREP	Situation Report
SLBM	Submarine-Launched Ballistic Missile
SMG	Sub-Machine Gun
smk	Smoke
SNCO	Senior Non-Commissioned Officer
SOC	Sector Operations Centre
SP	Self Propelled/Start Point
SPS	Staff and Personnel Support
Sqn	Squadron
SSBN	Nuclear Powered Ballistic Missile Submarine
SSK	Single shot to kill
SSM	Surface-to-Surface Missile
SSN	Nuclear-Powered Attack Submarine
SSVC	Services Sound and Cinema Corporation
STC	Strike Command
STOBAR	Short Take-Off and Arrested Recovery
STOL	Short Take-Off and Landing
STOVL	Short Take-Off and Vertical Landing
TA	Territorial Army
tac	Tactical
TBT	Tank Bridge Transporter
TCC	Turret Control Computer
TCP	Traffic Control Post
TCV	Troop Carrying Vehicle
tgt	Target
THAAD	Theatre High-Altitude Area Defence
TIALD	Thermal Imaging Airborne Laser Designator
tk	Tank
TLAM	Tactical Land Attack Missile
TLAM-C	Tactical Land Attack Missile - Conventional
TLB	Top Level Budget
TMA	Troop Manoeuvre Area
TOT	Time on Target
tp	Troop